Bones
Incandescent
The Pajarito Journals
of Peggy Pond Church

Bones
Incandescent

The Pajarito Journals
of Peggy Pond Church

Edited with Essays by
Shelley Armitage

Texas Tech University Press

This book was set in Adobe Garamond. The paper used in this book meets the minimum requirements of ANSI/NISO Z39.48-1992 (R1997). ∞

Design by Bryce Burton

Library of Congress Cataloging-in-Publication Data
Church, Peggy Pond, 1903-1986
    Bones incandescent : the Pajarito journals of Peggy Pond Church / edited with essays by Shelley Armitage.
        p. cm.
    Includes bibliographical references (p.) and index.
    ISBN 0-89672-438-7 (alk. paper)
    1. Church, Peggy Pond, 1903---Diaries. 2. Poets, American—20th century—Diaries. 3. Pajarito Plateau (N.M.) I. Armitage, Shelley, 1947- II. Title.
    PS3505.H946 Z464 2001
    818'.5203--dc21
                                    2001000941

01 02 03 04 05 06 07 08 09 / 9 8 7 6 5 4 3 2 1

Texas Tech University Press
Box 41037
Lubbock, Texas 79409-1037 USA

1-800-832-4042
ttup@ttu.edu
www.ttup.ttu.edu

For Kathleen and Hugh Church, for sharing, and
my mother, Dorothy Armitage, always

Noon in the desert is a vast blaze overhead and a hard glow below. You're shut in by vast distances of light. You walk in the focus of the sun's rays. You are clothed in sun; sun glows in your blood, until even your bones feel incandescent.

Nancy Newhall
The Desert is No Lady: Southwestern Landscapes
in Women's Writing and Art

I'm an instinctive trail-follower. There's nothing I've loved better to do since I was "going-on-eleven" and went to live on the Pajarito Plateau. It was full of Indian trails and game trails and horseback trails and the kind of trails your imagination gets you into when you pick up pottery shards and arrowheads, to find your way around by blazes on trees, or if there aren't any, just by the lay of the land. If you got lost, you depended more on a feeling in your bones, a sort of inner compass, than on anything in your mind to get you out again. . . . I write to keep from getting lost.

Peggy Pond Church
"Trails Over the Pajarito"

Contents

Preface
Two Plateaus

When I first met Peggy Pond Church in 1980 in her home on Camino Rancheros in Santa Fe, I knew her only by reputation. Although she was the author of the best-selling memoir, *The House at Otowi Bridge: The Story of Edith Warner and Los Alamos* (1959), she chiefly was recognized, especially in Southwest letters, as a poet. "The First Lady of New Mexico poetry, who should be in all poetry collections," W. David Laid wrote in *Books of the Southwest,* in his review of *A Rustle of Angels* (1981). In 1984, with the publication of her eighth volume of poetry, Church won the Governor's Award for Literature in New Mexico, a state that historically has been home to notable writers. Fifty years before, poet and critic Elizabeth Shepley Sergeant exulted in *The Saturday Review of Literature* that here was "a pristine young poetess . . . probably the first real New Mexican to produce a book of undeniable poetic promise out of her region and life." During this same period Church was published in that periodical and in *Poetry* magazine. The Longmont Award, granted to her for the outstanding quality of *The House at Otowi Bridge,* and the Julia Ellsword Ford Foundation prize for the humorous children's tale *The Burro for Angelitos* (1936), indicated that the grace of an accomplished poet was at work in her nonfiction and fiction as well. First among the Southwest writers published by the exclusive Rydal Press in its Writer's Editions in the 1920s and 1930s, Church's maturation as a poet paralleled the flowering of New Mexico arts and letters. Not surprisingly, then, New York playwright Lansford Wilson, when asked to note his choice of best books of 1982 for the *New York Times Book Review,* instead lauded *The House at Otowi Bridge,* which he had just discovered. "One of the most wonderful and surprising books," he said he'd read in years.

What I didn't realize that summer day at Peggy's house in 1980, as a representative from the University of New Mexico and I

arranged for the gift of Church's papers to the university, was how
much I actually knew of the poet through her poetry. Years later, in
1986, at her memorial service, my early impressions were confirmed
by the number and variety of people honoring her at St. John's College in Santa Fe after her death. Her long-time Taos friend, Corina
Santistevan, noted of the turnout: "Her friends cut across borders of
age, race, religion, culture, and profession. Young people were at the
services, as well as old men and some friends from childhood, including an archaeologist, teachers, and librarians. It was a roomful of a
great variety of people who spoke lovingly about Peggy." In accordance with the Society of Friends service, the group of almost two
hundred people sat in four quadrants of the squarish room, all seats
facing the modest table in the center, a simple altar where stones
gathered by Peggy and her husband, Fermor, on their hikes and
walks rested. Most people spoke about her through her poems or
some memory associated with them. One young woman recounted
the circumstantial meeting of Peggy when, as employee of a tree service, she had come to cut down an ailing willow tree and later learned
Peggy deeply regretted the act and had written a poem about it. In
her sadness for the forlorn tree, Peggy hung an old hat on its few remaining branches. In a final statement, left by the poet with the
Church family, Peggy's coda for "Elegy for the Willow Tree" read:

> Now I, old willow tree from which the birds have fled,
> through whose branches the sap no longer rises
> leave my own vacancy on the waiting air.

I found my own voice joined the chorus of speakers that day,
though I had firmly planned to keep my seat and silence. The willow
poem prompted a memory of the effect Peggy's work had on one of
my students, and somehow I stood and recited the entire poem he
wrote when he learned of her death. "And have you danced/with
flowing hands," it began, in a lyrical fashion not unlike Peggy's. I
added that the poet's work seemed her real body. The corpus of the
work was a bodying out of the departed person.

Sifting through the afternoon, then, were memories of her
playful personality, her special gift of irony, a consistent reiteration
of New Mexico people and land, most often cited through lines from

her poems, committed by and to the heart. Somehow the range of her poetry—seventy years of work since she published her first poem in 1915—and the complexity of her life were reflected by this diverse audience united in verse. Yet, when encouraged to write her autobiography, Peggy admitted to the difficulty of assessing either herself or her work. In a letter to May Sarton—one of several in a correspondence which lasted from 1948 to 1986—she remarked that a young woman had come that day asking to look through her files and expressed an interest in writing her biography. "But who?" Peggy recounted her response to the visitor in the Sarton letter, "Which poet? Which Peggy?"

Ironically, I have been the one attempting to answer Peggy's question, for in 1983 a letter came from her asking me to come to Santa Fe to discuss her unpublished works. She needed someone to help her organize her files, unpublished manuscripts, and poetry— in short, a literary editor. Initially, I was shocked because I had met Peggy only once. I had just moved from Albuquerque, following the completion of my doctorate, to Vega, Texas, where I had inherited the farmhouse of my great aunt and uncle, fifty miles from a small, liberal arts university. Rather than "go on the market" aggressively, I had taken a job close to the house and farm with plans for a garden, orchard, and writing, and interest in helping my father on the family farm and pastureland. My own return to landscape included fifty acres fronting the 1920 prairie-bungalow house, with a three-acre pasture and a large barn I later discovered had been ordered from Sears, Roebuck and Company in 1926. As I read Peggy's letter, I surveyed the old implements, unopened Burpee seed packets left over from my uncle's gardening, the bed of iris, wild roses, still-sprouting asparagus beds, a fifty-year-old cling peach tree—all hidden in weeds, but once lovingly tended by my Aunt Alice. Across town my grandparents' house, bought by a young couple who had recently divorced, fell into disrepair. Broken windows marred my granddad's workshop where he had made furniture when I was a girl; the roof was pocked and blighted after seasonal hailstorms; my grandmother's gardens lay forgotten under the kitchen window. I clung more tenaciously to my house, which daily revealed forgotten treasures: in a rusted trunk in the root cellar, I discovered three quilts made by my great-grandmother, who at age 101 was still sewing. What did it mean to take in hand rakes, hoes, and scythes whose wood had lost its grain, smoothed by a generation of use?

My great uncle had come from Chicago where he worked for a printing company. Long standing area farmers often smirked at his farming practices, but he had made a living, leaving behind this house and a small farm. Like the man who built the house—Jess Giles—many of the early generation of farmers to break out the plains in the Panhandle had come from Illinois when word of flat, potentially bountiful wheat country reached them through word of mouth or promotional brochures often sponsored by the new railroad companies. Jess Giles had come with his family, but moved out at age sixteen, building his own dugout south of town. When he earned enough money working on the threshing crews, he bought a small acreage and built this house. Like so many men of his background and generation, he was, by necessity, a jack-of-all-trades. The house and barn were full of his wood-working projects: the fine five-inch baseboards, the cold-frame for plants built on the south side of the house, the windows situated for ventilation, the careful selection of beveled glass for the front door—all reflected an ingenuity and also a taste. When the first telephone lines were strung in the Panhandle on existing barbed wire fences, utilizing the already standing cedar posts, Jess Giles tried out the first connection in Vega by playing his fiddle into the wall phone. My uncle Vern bought the house and barn lot; he added land and outbuildings according to his own sensibilities. I thought of these things as I read Peggy's letter and listened to the drone of truck tires on Interstate 40, only a pasture away. For if the town had grown up around the railroad in 1905, the highway later skirted south, the highway department paying my uncle Vern a mere thousand dollars in 1966 to go through the middle of his farm.

So on the first trip to Santa Fe to answer Peggy's request, I realized that what I really knew of her was through our shared landscapes and our feelings about them. Dropping off what the Spaniards had called the *ceja* (eyebrow), I drove down the caprock, actually one of the largest plateaus in North America. On the western edge, leading to the escarpment (which Coronado disappointedly crossed in 1541 and later described), the highway parallels not only old Route 66 but also the original dirt road used in the 1920s, earlier routes followed by government expedition leaders Albert, Marcy, and Whipple, and much earlier Indian trails and trade routes—including those from prehistoric and *Comanchero* periods. Each of these original routes was near springs or water sources and chosen mainly for the easier passage on the flat caprock country before it becomes breaks as the land cleaves toward the Canadian River north.

Peggy's plateau was physically quite different. The Pajarito Plateau is located in the heart of the Rio Grande Valley. West of the river, nestled at the base of the Jemez Mountains, the southern third caught the imagination of early travelers. Rugged, with angular trails, narrow canyon bottoms, sharp canyon walls, the plateau was described by one observer as "stupendous . . . the wildest scenery . . . the grandest panoramas in New Mexico." The middle area, called the Ramon Vigil grant (after the eighteenth-century Spanish land grant)—where Peggy spent part of her childhood and most of her young adulthood until 1943—extended from the north rim of Frijoles Canyon to the seasonal creek of Guaje Canyon. Neither markedly rugged nor inaccessible, it afforded settlement to prehistoric Anasazi in thousands of sites in the fifty-six-thousand-acre area. Though Bandelier National Monument in the southern section of the plateau attracts interest and visitors, the largest prehistoric pueblo, Tshirege, and another very important pueblo of game traps, Navawi'i, are located in the Vigil section. The remaining section, beginning at the northern border of the Vigil grant and extending to the thirty-sixth degree longitude line that bisected nearby Española, has even softer, rolling contours. Sloping towards the Rio Grande, near the pueblo of Santa Clara, the ascent to the mountains in this section is gradual. Canyons open to meadows, and though it has no more water than the other two sections, the lower elevations and seasonal creeks create more abundant, if fragile, grass cover.

Whereas Coronado had dismissed the *llano estacado* as uninhabitable (by which he really meant lacking in mineral riches) and subsequent Anglo explorers echoed his judgment (an intimidating "sea of grass" eventually mapped as part of the Great American Desert), the Pajarito area, with mountain landscape and a multitude of uses, was coveted. And thus it was increasingly contested.

Throughout the three-year period I worked with Peggy on her "files," I often sat in her retirement apartment one block off the Santa Fe plaza underneath the watchful eye of Atilano Montoya, past governor of San Ildefonso and companion of Edith Warner, whose photograph hung on a wall near the kitchen table where Peggy and I worked. Peggy had written a poem about "Tilano," but when I asked her poet's credo, she replied: "It's the land that wants to be said." She had used the same refrain when assessing Mary Austin's life in the Owens Valley of California, in Lone Pine, and later in Santa Fe where she was the doyenne of activist and artistic groups in the 1920s and 1930s. Peggy had said Mary attempted to be "a tongue for the wilderness," capturing "beauty in the wild yearning to be made human." This description could be read as a trope common among women nature writers, except that there was no such group or school during either Austin's or Church's time. As we worked on her materials, I sensed this continuous impulse, a desire to find a language suitable for what Church called the wordless world.

In her regard for the Anasazi and contemporary pueblo culture and her attachment to landscape, Peggy also described a feeling shared among women. Often she sought to express her feeling of correspondence and admiration in her attempts to analyze women's relationships to their environments. No academic critic or feminist, she nevertheless understood that Mary Austin, for example, attempted to redefine women's nature, typically inscribed in western conventions, institutions, and perceptions, by altering the traditional perceptions of the Southwest desert as negative and subordinate. Through acute observation of the natural and human worlds, in *The Land of Little Rain* and *Land of Journey's Ending,* in particular, Austin rewrote certain tropes of landscapes worthy of attention and imagination. She challenged the assumptions about women's inherent weakness and incapacity to cope with the outdoors, their identification with culture rather than nature, and the stereotypes of women of color, who, when identified with raw nature, were exoticized.

As women "writing nature"—that is, rewriting the assumptions about female nature by inscribing Nature as positively feminine—both Austin and Church ultimately had to confront point-of-view. Though not exempt from the predominately individual or lone voice in the male model of the "I" in the wilderness, both women

experimented with multiple points-of-view in their nonfiction, poetry, and private writings. For Austin, being able to experience "the
friend in the wood" in her Carlinville, Illinois, girlhood, led to her
formulation of a strong identity, what she called the I-Mary, which
later, Church suggested, became "the noticing eye" in the very different and challenging California desert. Likewise, Church created an
alter ego, Quince, experimenting with telling her own story by
objectifying herself in the experiences and attitudes of the child-
hero. Thus, the way in which each woman described and reinscribed
herself through nature altered attitudes about women from objecti-
fication to writing Nature/one's nature as subject.

For Quince was not a well-behaved little girl, the product of the
early twentieth-century, somewhat-Victorian household. As Peggy
and I sat under the steady gaze of Tilano in his cornfield, a postcard
with the image of coyote was taped on one of the filing cabinets
nearby. The trickster, the renegade, the chameleon, and the survi-
vor—coyote was invoked when anything amiss happened. Missing
files were blamed on coyote and usually reappeared later.

Peggy's playfulness and sense of humor sometimes shaped even
the handling of the serious or sacred. On the kitchen table-turned-
desk, a photograph of Peggy waiting to get into a canoe on the Rio
Grande was propped on our reading lamp. "My fairy boat," she
called it. The reference, I learned years after her death, was to a passage from Rabindranath Tagore's *Gitanjali,* song offerings by the
Bengali poet translated with an introduction by W. B. Yeats.
Three days after Peggy took her life on October 23, 1986, I received
a letter with a reference to several sections in Tagore's book. Later,
after the estate was settled, I discovered she had left me the book with
notes of sections to read. One section included the boat reference:

> Early in the day it was whispered that we should sail in
>   a boat, only thou and I,
> and never a soul in the world would know of this our
>   pilgrimage to no country and to no end.
> In that shoreless ocean, in a silently listening smile my
>   songs would swell in melodies, free as waves, free
>   from all bondage of words.
> Is the time not come yet? Are there works still to do?

Lo, the evening has come down upon the shore and in
   the fading light
The seabirds come flying to their nests.
Who knows when the chains will be off, and the boat,
   like the last glimmer
of sunset,
vanish in the night?

I read the passage, at last understanding Peggy's canoe as the
fairy boat—but, of course, on the Rio Grande at the foot of the
Pajarito Plateau. Peggy had an inoperable eye condition; she was going blind. In a decision made in the 1930s, Peggy and her husband
had planned to take their own lives when they felt they no longer
could function meaningfully, though only Peggy would act on this
decision. Peggy's need of a literary assistant had much to do with her
inability to see well enough to do her work and her feeling pressed for
time. Fittingly, folded in with the notecard with this and other references to Tagore in the letter was a list. Would I attend to this and
that unfinished chore connected to her papers, files, manuscripts,
and poetry? Surely a voice from the other side, I thought, as I, in my
great sadness and yet earnestness, got back to work.

"Which Peggy? Which poet?"

My first meeting with Peggy, I came to the door to find a yellow
sticky note with her roundish handwriting, hinting at cartoonlike
communication, on the unlocked door. "Napping—10:30–11:30.
Come on in." Peggy was an early riser. She got up at least by 5 A.M.,
gathered up her lap table, and wrote, mainly poetry, in bed. Sometimes she napped (by midmorning and again in the afternoon) on a
daybed, which also served as a writing place. This was the Peggy who
gave me a book early on, one she had just finished as a labor of love
for her mentor and friend, Haniel Long. A prominent poet from
Pittsburgh who chose to work in New Mexico, Long had written a
long prose poem on Cabeza de Vaca, which had been published but
was out of print. Peggy had reedited the poem, found a fine-book
publisher in Tucson who enlisted an artist to make exquisite wood-
block print illustrations, and written an afterword. But when she inscribed the book for me, she wrote: "For Shelley Armitage to share
Haniel Long and Cabeza de Vaca and to propitiate the ghost of
Mary Austin!"

Indeed, Peggy's ghosts became my own during and after the period we worked together. I edited and researched the Church biography of Austin's first twenty years, published by the press of the Museum of New Mexico in 1992, wrote a monograph of her life and work for the Boise Writers Series and gathered with Kathleen Church a collection of her unpublished and out-of-print poems, *This Dancing Ground of Sky* (Red Crane Press), in 1993. But what began as possible publishing ventures for the Austin manuscript and the poetry, and included the reorganization of her files and placement of her papers at appropriate repositories, always had to do with the Pajarito Plateau and the Pajarito Journals. We might begin related projects, talking, looking at files, but always ended up in our work referring to the journals, notes, and files related to the Pajarito. Letters between Roy Chapin and her father, Ashley Pond; records of the Ramon Vigil land grant; reflections on hikes near Anasazi ruins; deconstructions of dreams about Mary Austin during the research and first writing of the Austin biography; explications of self, family, and friends; related readings; dream logs; meditations; notes for poems; references to correspondence with other poets such as May Sarton and Denise Levertov—these and much more composed the Pajarito Journals.

The answer to "Which poet? Which Peggy?" necessarily begins with the journals, which I like to think of as the closest she came to her own autobiography, or as she called it, a personal ecology. The "roads to utterness"—a phrase she used to describe the exquisite freedom she felt living on the Pajarito Plateau—were physical; they were also the writer's attempts, by turns, to write western history, prehistory, geography, family history, and psychology. They contain a women's history, or perhaps more accurately, the implication of the continuity of creative women's friendships, as they share their passion for the land. For in their efforts to write the environment, Edith Warner, Mary Austin, May Sarton, and Peggy Church constituted a lineage of sorts. As Alice Walker has so memorably described in *In Search of Our Mothers' Gardens,* literary friendships, notably women's friendships, exist through time and in various languages, forms, and cultural expressions. The lasting impression on Peggy Church when she discovered the potter's fingerprint on a piece of Anasazi pottery is akin to the tribute Walker pays, not only to the forgotten writer, Zora Neale Hurston, but to women whose creations were primarily domestic— handiwork, gardens, and various expressions of beauty in their daily lives. Peggy's journals thus explore what some historians have called doing the rest, or history from the ground up. The arid Southwest, said by one writer to be hell on horses and women, ironically implying conventional assessments of women's western experiences, Peggy treats in deeply spiritual ways —a place, rather, for "the provings of the heart."

My plateau is not Peggy's; perhaps neither is yours. Yet in the crossings and recrossings I made between the two during this project, I came to appreciate the physical reality of plateau as metaphor. There is first the experienced connection between our two places— the Pajarito and the Llano. Native American and other migratory and trade routes connect them, as do watersheds, riverbeds, and geologic features. But more: the view from each, different, yet connected, suggest a shared desire for perspective. From my plateau I am drawn to what exists below the horizon-line: a network of arroyos and canyons. From Peggy's she could see the Rio Grande Valley and the surrounding mountains, even eastward toward my plains. Each plateau is a centering place—one whose perspectives connect recall to response, one's personal allusions to the creation of a general, larger symbolic significance. For two women writers, the plateau, as representative and symbolic, embues a continuity in women's creative experiences, ultimately engaged in by the reader as the epitome of the human effort toward conciousness and meaning.

My last meeting with Peggy, we were sitting at right angles to each other in chairs, with our feet propped up. I knew it would be the last physical meeting, somehow, for she was giving me things. Not Tilano's impenetrable eyes, not even coyote on the card. Instead, she touched her socked foot to mine (it was cold, early October), handed me a brochure by the Hemlock Society, and talked about listening to T. S. Eliot's *Four Quartets* on Books-on-Tape for the blind. Despite her developing chemical sensitivity and her ever-worsening eyesight, we had taken a brisk hike in Hondo Canyon that day with Peggy loping ahead.

Among the things Peggy gave me that last evening were the Pajarito Journals, for possible publication as nature journals, or as part of a larger biographical project. The journals, dated sequentially, had been kept thematically in several folders, but in Peggy's penchant for reassessment and reorganization, they came to me as two large loose-leaf binders, the entries typed, one entitled "Pajarito—Subjective" and the other, "Littlebird." The Pajarito included the entries from the 1930s to the 1950s and sections from the 1970s and 1980s. Littlebird contained the 1960s' period and the section, "Quince," named for the child-narrator Peggy created. Peggy told me she destroyed the earlier journals. Only these and several specialized journals—one on her dog, Poli; a "Terminal Journal" on the events of her husband's brain tumor and death; a dream journal; and those on Mary Austin—remained.

On the basis of my discussions with Peggy about her work, I decided to combine the two journals into one manuscript, creating a sequential book. I corrected or standardized spelling, lightly edited for clarity, and took out some of the repetitive passages. The subsequent preface, introduction, and afterword I wrote to help ensure the integrity and intentionality of the journals, while suggesting contextual and critical materials. The introduction provides basic background for the reading of the journals, but I reserved interpretation and criticism for the afterword to allow the journals to speak first for themselves. The section introductions likewise are designed to create a context for the period of the journal entries and to relate the journals to creative writing of that time and Peggy's preoccupations as a writer. I thus have avoided the temptation to recast or reshape Peggy's work, choosing the titles for each section from her entries as a kind of evolving marker of her emerging ideas and feelings. The four sections, I believe, allow the reader to appreciate the odyssey of Peggy's life and work, since each section is distinguished by its emphasis and style.

Unlike a standard autobiography, these journals may be read in sections or by picking them up, sifting through them, and taking one's time to digest philosophical and aesthetic observations and poetic musings. Rather than footnote the journals themselves and thus distract from the spontaneity of their readings, I have tried to confine necessary explanatory information to the front matter and introductory sections, leaving the work open-ended for the shared imaginings of writer and reader.

The book is intended for students and scholars of women's writing, gender and landscape studies, and regional writing, as well as for the general audience, so I have chosen an organic and suggestive style as editor and writer. For, in the spirit of the poet, Peggy, whose inspiration and reciprocity with other creative women prompted her to interpret their lives and works primarily as a writer, this is a creative and multivocal text, seeking in its organization, style, and spirit to facilitate the voice of another but most to join in a collaborative work of shared and beloved places.

Shelley Armitage
Vega, Texas

The first trails over Pajarito were made by water shaping the canyons begun in the moist cooling ash. Grass spread over the mesa, and probably following the trails of animals to hunt them, ancient man and later the ancestors of the Keres and Tewa Indians. The mesas were dotted, the canyon walls honeycombed with dwelling places abandoned before the Spanish came into the Rio Grande Valley in the 1500s.

One of the largest and longest occupied villages was called Tshirege by the Tewa who lived at San Ildefonso and claimed to be descendants of the ancient ones. Tshirege is a word that means "bird" or "place of the bird."

When the Spanish came they translated the Tewa "bird" into *pajarito,* meaning "little bird," giving the name to the canyon which spreads wide and fairly shallow just below Tshirege. In their matter-of-fact way, the Tewa had called it simply "bird place canyon." Tshirege is situated on a low mesa that overlooks the present town of White Rock. When I used to steal off with my tattered poetry notebook to a secret ledge I had among the caves below the ruin, all I could see were miles of sky and a wide spread of sage brush and willow where the canyon walls swindled away toward the Plateau rim.

The archaeologist, Dr. Edgar Hewett, came along at the turn of the century to explore the ruins, giving the name "Pajarito" to the whole plateau which extends from Santa Clara canyon on the north to Cochiti canyon on the south; from the base of Jemez mountains on the west to the Rio Grande winding far below the steep edge to the east.

Peggy Pond Church
"Trails Over the Pajarito"

Acknowledgments

The essentially collaborative nature of a book makes me thankful for the support and encouragement of a number of people during this project which began so many years ago. First there is Peggy Church, who not only entrusted her unpublished work to me as her literary editor, but encouraged a kind of collaboration in this work, two women writers in creative conversation across time.

Portions of my introduction and afterword appeared initially in the introduction to *This Dancing Ground of Sky* and *Peggy Pond Church* (The Boise State Writers Series) and were inspired by thinking about the essays I wrote for *Winds Trail* and articles on Austin, Church, and Sarton in *Women Writing Culture*. Like Peggy, I have had my own conversations with myself.

I am very grateful to the following people for supporting Peggy's and my work through many stages and cycles: Hedy Dunn, director, Marianne Mortenson, curator, Rebecca Collinsworth, and other staff of the Los Alamos Historical Society; my colleagues at the Liberal Arts computer and technology lab at the University of Texas at El Paso; the Zimmerman Library staff, the University of New Mexico; research librarians at the Huntington Library; Cynthia Garcia, secretary of the Women's Studies Program, the University of Texas at El Paso, and staff. Listeners and critics, Larry Cook, Tom Inge, and Leslie Ullman, and the entire National Endowment for the Humanities fellows in the seminar "Nature and Society" at the University of Illinois, summer 1999—I thank you. The Ted, Allen, and Hugh Church families, I appreciate so very much for making me feel a part of your lives. In memory for discussions about Peggy and poetry, May Sarton. And kindest regards to Denise Levertov, who encouraged. Warmest thanks to those artistic women friends—Gail Hovey, Pat Hickman, and Deborah Moore—who across geographies and years always had time for eyes to be ears.

Introduction
Landscape of a Life:
Place of the Bird People

Peggy Pond Church was born in 1903 near Watrous, the territory of New Mexico, in a settlement known as Valmora, east of the Rocky Mountains and the Rio Grande Valley. She was the eldest of three siblings born to Ashley Pond and Hazel Hadley. Her mother's grandfather, A. Hadley, one-time acting governor of Arkansas during Reconstruction, came to New Mexico in 1879 on the first train through the Raton tunnel. He settled first on the Eagle Tail Ranch in Colfax County and then managed the Palo Blanco Ranch for Arkansas Senator Dorsey, a somewhat notorious land and cattle speculator. Later, he ran a ranch for Dorsey's ex-partner, John B. Alley. In 1888, Hadley moved to Mora County and bought the W. B. Tipton ranch and house in Tiptonville, raising Clydesdale horses as a hobby and for use in the mining and lumber industries.

In 1898, Ashley Pond arrived in the New Mexico Territory after an almost fatal bout with typhoid fever near the end of the Spanish-American War. Reared in Detroit and Yale-educated, he was attracted to the spacious Southwest because of his adventuresome spirit and love of the outdoors. After a small cattle venture near Raton, New Mexico, he married Governor Hadley's seventeen-year-old granddaughter, Hazel, in 1903. Planning to start a ranch school for boys, he had his initial hopes dashed by a flood on September 29, 1904. The flood, one of the worst in New Mexico history, destroyed all of his property except for a two-story brick house built by one of the Tipton family members in 1883.

Returning to Detroit with his family until the death of his father in 1910, Pond worked his college and business connections there as his family grew. A second daughter, Dorothy ("Dotty"), was born May 20, 1906; a son, Ashley Pond III ("Laddie"), was born August 4, 1908. After his father died, he moved the family to Roswell, to a farm irrigated by an artesian well. Here he hoped to prosper in the new state of New Mexico. The rigors of that venture (after a summer there, only a garage had been built to house the family of five) resulted in a near breakup of his marriage as Hazel took the children to California for schooling and to be near some of her friends. Pond found a more salubrious place for his family in the Pajarito Canyon, northwest of Santa Fe, in the area of the Pajarito Plateau, on the Ramon Vigil land grant of 32,000 acres. With four absentee industrialist partners, he formed the Pajarito Club, supposedly a recreational organization for his wealthy business friends, which he would manage. In 1917, on the Plateau's high mesa—leased originally by the partnership—far from floods, he began the Los Alamos Ranch School, the boys' school he had dreamed of.

Like other visitors to the plateau, Pond was drawn by its beauty and rich human history. A considerable network of Anasazi ruins dotted the mesa and canyon areas, as well as more recent evidence of Spanish, Mexican, Anglo, and, of course, Native American residence. The grant originally was made to Pedro Sanchez by the Viceroy Don Gaspar Domingo de Mendoza in 1742. It remained in the Sanchez family more than a hundred years. In 1851—the same year American soldiers built an early road across the plateau to reach their hay camp—Antonio Sanchez sold the thirty-two thousand acres to Ramon Vigil for the price of a yoke of oxen, thirty-six ewes, and twenty dollars in cash.

Even though Ramon Vigil had owned the land for only eight years, when it came time to establish Spanish land grant titles before the American court of private land claims, the grant was given his name. He and the Sanchez family, who lived in the Rio Grande Valley, used it mostly for grazing their small flocks of goats, sheep, and a few cattle. Ramon Vigil may have tried to farm, for there are references around 1900 to the ruins of a house that once belonged to him at the lower end of the Los Alamos Canyon.

In 1879, the Denver and Rio Grande Western Railroad made its way into the Rio Grande Valley, and land speculators arrived. A priest serving under Archbishop Lamy, Thomas Aquinas Hayes, persuaded Ramon Vigil to sell him the grant for four thousand dollars. The priest had served at Santa Clara Indian Pueblo where he probably learned of the grant. He sold it in 1884 to speculative *gringos* for one hundred thousand dollars. When Pond purchased the land for the Pajarito Club in 1914, for eighty thousand dollars, he idealized the plateau as his own, well suited for his outdoor-education school for boys and for raising cattle.

With the outbreak of World War I, the differences between the desires of the landowners and Pond's plans for the land were apparent, especially when he asked for money for development. In an effort to keep his dream going, Pond worked out an arrangement with Harold Brook, who operated a farm on the nearby mesa. Los Alamos, as Brook called his farm, seemed an even better location for the boys' school than the Pajarito Canyon. Finally, in 1917, the school opened at Los Alamos and flourished for twenty-five years, although not under Pond's management. He withdrew from any active participation after the initial year so that he could go to France with the Red Cross in the spring of 1918 for the war effort. Subsequently, the owners of the Ramon Vigil grant sold it to Frank Bond, an Española sheep and cattleman, for about what they paid for it. It seemed ironic that Ashley Pond's original plan that had included generating income through cattle ranching had been ignored previously by the partnership as a development strategy.

By the 1930s, when a severe drought affected New Mexico, the grant had been badly overgrazed. Subsequently, the United States government acquired the land from the Bonds for $34,330.47—around a dollar an acre. The grant was administered by the Soil Conservation Service until 1939 when it was transferred to the United States Forest Service. The fact that so much land contiguous to the Los Alamos Ranch School was already government-owned no doubt influenced its choice as the location for the Manhattan Project, eventually responsible for the development of the atomic bomb. In her notes, part of the personal papers collected by the University of New Mexico, Peggy Church reflected on this period of the plateau's history and its consequences for her:

> Before my father left Pajarito, New Mexico had already entered another of its inevitable series of dry years. The stream that had been like a playfellow for us children slowed to a trickle. The spring from which water was piped to the ranch began to dry up. My mother asked firmly to be counted out of future ranch ventures, reminding my father that Los Alamos was always known as

a "ranch school." He gave in and bought a house in Santa
Fe, which became our permanent home. He did persist in
pasturing a jersey cow on his front yard there, however. I
remember how we children sat in the back seat of the car,
as we were driven down Pajarito Canyon the last time,
singing over and over, "When we come to the end of a
perfect day," while we looked back as long as we could see.
Many years afterward, we were again displaced from Los
Alamos—which had become what I thought was my permanent home in 1924. My husband and I came back to
the plateau later and camped for a night at Pajarito Canyon, just below the guarded fence that shut us out of my
old playground and from the ruins of Tshirege. Later I
wrote a poem about it, called "Morning on Tshirege":

When I was a child I climbed here
at sunrise, barefooted among the grasses.
I searched for arrowheads among the ruins
and stood wondering on the rims of the broken kivas.
I had no language to say what it was that moved me,
the voiceless communication that thundered all about
     me,
the wisdom of rocks and old trees, of buried rivers,
of the great arcs and tangents of sky and mountain,
and always the grass that whispered upon the ruins
where a people had lived and fought, had died and had
     been forgotten.

They had left drawn on the rocks their suns, their
     serpents,
and scattered among the dust, the broken potsherds
with their symbols of cloud, of rain, of the eagle flying.
And so without words I knew that man is mortal
and doomed both to live and to die, but what he
     worships lives on forever.

Today with my own world crumbling toward ruin
I know this still, and I greet the child who will stand
   here
upon Tshirege and watch the morning blossom
and feel under her questioning hand, the living grasses
weaving substance of sunlight and the dust of a fallen
   city.[1]

Throughout the time of modern human occupation of the plateau, many scientists, historians, and writers like Peggy have felt
compelled to celebrate the remarkable place and its first people.
Adolphe Bandelier, adventurer and archaeological hobbyist, for whom
the national monument containing some major Anasazi ruins in
Frijoles Canyon would be named, first visited the area in 1880–81.
He wrote:

> The Rito is a beautiful spot. . . . In a direct line not
> over twenty miles from Santa Fe, it can still be reached
> only after a long day's tedious travel. It is a narrow valley,
> nowhere broader than half a mile; and from where it be-
> gins in the west to where it closes in a dark and gloomy en-
> trance, scarcely wide enough for two men to pass abreast,
> in the east its length does not exceed six miles. Its south-
> ern rim is formed by the slope of a timbered mesa, and
> that slope is partly overgrown with shrubbery. The north-
> ern pumice, projecting and re-entering like the decora-
> tion of a stage, now perpendicular and smooth for some
> distance, now sweeping back in the shape of an arched
> segment. The cliffs vary in height, although nowhere are
> they less than 200 feet. Their tops rise in huge pillars, in
> crags and fantastic projections . . . [creating] a shaggy bor-
> der.[2]

Like Bandelier, artists and writers such as Erna Fergusson, who
lived in Albuquerque, attempted to describe the attraction they felt
for northern New Mexico. In *New Mexico*, Fergusson idealized the
plateau in poetic language:

In sublime quietude the peaks lift their deeper blue against the sky's clarity. The patches of bright green, like lawns, are aspen groves, and those rough rocky knuckles thrusting toward the Rio Grande divide leafy canyons wherein tiny streams live as long as they can before they are buried in sand. . . . All around the Jemez rough perimeter are such cliffs, stratified in terracotta red, sulphur yellow and dusty while often topped by dark basalt. The mesa itself is crossed by miles of trails, worn by padding moccasins.[3]

In Peggy Church's time, writers like Fergusson, largely because of the such captivation, moved to Santa Fe, Taos, and Albuquerque, forming what has been called The Santa Fe Artists Colony, during the 1920s and 1930s.[4] In these early decades, artists and writers looked to the region for their roots in an America seeking to define itself. "Why go to Greece or China?" asked Harriet Monroe, editor of the Chicago magazine, *Poetry*. "This Southwest, which is but one chapter of our rich tradition, is our own authentic wonderland—a treasure-trove of romantic myth—profoundly beautiful and significant, guarded by ancient races practicing their ancient rites, in a region of incredible color and startling natural grandeur."[5] The artistic discovery of the Southwest, along with anthropological and archaeological discoveries of Bandelier, Sylvanus Morley, Edgar Hewett, and others, led to a new consideration of Native American prehistoric and historic life and culture, as well as the rich history of Mexican and Spanish influences. Friends or acquaintances of the Churches—Haniel Long, Witter Bynner, Alice Corbin Henderson, Mary Austin, Gustave Baumann, Laura Gilpin, and others—published poetry, folklore collections, novels, and plays, becoming activists for historic preservation and for the rights of native people.[6]

As late as 1977, social scientist Robert Coles wrote of the mystery and power of the Pajarito region by linking the approach of scientists with the language of the poets. In *Eskimos, Chicanos, and Indians*, Coles states that at the altitudes of northern New Mexico, the air loses one-fourth of its weight; it is thus low in carbon dioxide and oxygen and therefore also loses its capacity to refract or diffuse light. He connects this scientific reality with a new way of seeing:

The hazy, somewhat softened, even blurred vision
of the coastal plains or the prairie gives way to a clear,
bright, almost harsh, sometimes blinding field of view.
Air that an outsider has come to regard as transparent suddenly becomes translucent—so sharp, so clean, so light
that one feels in a new world or possessed of new eyes.[7]

Whereas Coles and others echo Peggy's awe of the Pajarito's
beauty as an avenue for renewed perception and personal rebirth, recent research by environmental historians further explains the reasons for her feeling that the Pajarito's people and environment were
extremely fragile and even more precious. Historian Hal K. Rothman, in *On Rims & Ridges,* relates the fragile and changing ecosytems
to human settlement and use of the plateau. In what Rothman calls
environmental gridlock, native cultures and Euro-American commercial interests ultimately competed in this remote area for its limited resources.

As Rothman explains, before the coming of the railroad in
1880, the Pajarito Plateau was open, capable of supporting the
small-scale agriculture of the Pueblo Indians and seasonal Hispanic
pobladores (settlers). But in the half-century after the arrival of the
Denver, Texas, and Fort Worth Railroad, the area was gradually
claimed by competing special interests: the original inhabitants, archaeologists and anthropologists, homesteaders, ranchers, the United
States Forest Service, the National Park Service, and ultimately the
Los Alamos National Laboratory.[8]

Like Peggy Church, at least half of these groups were attracted
to the area because of the Anasazi ruins. To imagine how profoundly
affected Peggy was by these ruins and manifestations of culture, we
must remember that the Pajarito's quarter of a million acres may
hold as many as seven thousand archaeological sites. These sites—
the abandoned dwellings, caved-in kivas, and half-buried pottery
shards that Church repeatedly refers to in her poetry and journals—
recall a rich culture expressive of the Pajarito environment. Until
A.D. 1100, the high, forested mesa country was empty with the exception of occasional hunting parties and expeditions to quarry the
Jemez caldera's glassy obsidian, prized for arrowheads. A succession
of climatic and human events probably led to the Anasazi people's
taking refuge in the plateau canyons. By 1175, a number of small

masonry pueblos were founded, mostly of blocks, two rows deep with ten to twenty rooms in areas where there were ponderosa or mixed ponderosa and piñon forests. About 1200, cliff houses appeared in mountain areas, including the Pajarito Plateau, facing south, southwest, or occasionally southeast to soak up the low winter sun. Likewise, cave rooms, such as may be seen at Tyúonyi and Otowi, at Bandelier or Puyé, places Peggy visited from her youth on, were built facing southward. For a time in the mid-1200s, larger masonry pueblos flourished on the Pajarito, constructed mainly in the upper reaches of the piñon zone at a lower altitude from the small, earlier houseblocks.

With the Great Drought (1276-99), the Pajaritans fared better than some Indian groups, as the east slope location was moister than most west slopes. Building their shelters to absorb heat and at lower, less frigid altitudes, they also constructed mesa-top reservoirs and areas used for moisture-retaining mulch on precisely laid-out garden plots. During what some climatologists call the Little Ice Age (1250-1500), the highest mesas were permanently abandoned for reliable streams in lower canyons. During this period, Tyúonyi in Bandelier flourished. By the 1400s and early 1500s, there were fewer villages, but many were immense, with a thousand rooms or more. Though there has been no direct link established between Chacoan Anasazi people and contemporary pueblo people, particularly in the Pajarito area, cyclical droughts, limited resources, and threats from outside assaults or clan warfare precipitated a final move of the Anasazi to the Rio Grande basin where the pueblos remain today.

At their height, the eastern Anasazi achieved a surplus agriculture, the men tending gardens, most often dry-farming corn and squash, and building rooms for storing harvests against times of drought and famine. The clan units became grouped cooperatively in numerous individual settlements. Pueblo skills and artistry included the creation of household utensils and tools, decorative items such as painted pottery, jewelry, and elaborate ceremonial materials for use in fertility and spiritual rituals associated with the kivas. Their ability to adapt to their environment resulted in the major achievement of prehistoric life—the development of agriculture. Their attempt to survive cultural and environmental shifts hinged on their using the plateau, mountains, and valleys as protective barriers as well as trade routes. When the trade ties to the Arizona

Hohokam and the Chihuahuan Casas Grandes peoples were broken, for instance, owing to the cataclysmic changes in those peoples'
environments, the Pajaritans found new trade partners among the
Plains people to the east. Because the Plains people necessarily focused on subsistence, trade was centered on the exchange of goods,
rather than culture. Gradually, such limitations of the plateau took
their toll as the resource base became limited, the surplus depleted,
and—perhaps most notably—the activities that had enriched the
Pajaritans' lives put aside as survival became an all-consuming task.[9]

In addition to its rich human history, the Pajarito Plateau also
offers a dramatic view of the geological past. Located in the heart of
the upper Rio Grande Valley and nestled at the base of the Jemez
Mountains, the plateau gives way to Valle Grande where, more than
two million years ago, two massive eruptions spewed ash from a
volcanic cone. These ash flows cooled leaving the soft tuff rock that
characterizes the plateau. Subsequent erosion carved deep canyons,
leaving the dissected topography of elongated mesas and steep-walled
canyons one sees today.[10] "The place of the bird people" remains a
visual and physical reminder of what Peggy Church internalized as a
girl and returned to in her writing.

No wonder that the full year and two additional summers that
Peggy Church spent with her family on the Pajarito Plateau between
1914 and 1916 became the major formative experience upon which
she would found her life and her creative work. Having moved so
many times during the family's relocation to New Mexico—Watrous,
Roswell, Pajarito Canyon, the Los Alamos Ranch area—and having
attending parochial and private schools in California and Connecticut during this time, she felt more rooted in the plateau area. The
multiple adventures of place—ancient and contemporary Native
American life and cultures, visible historic and geologic wonders—
first attracted her in those formative years before puberty. A preco-
cious but shy girl, she seized the opportunity for free and independent discoveries, riding horseback, hiking, playing with her siblings,
and observing the boys' lives at the Ranch School. These experiences
encouraged her appreciation of solitude and nature, assuaging some
of the separation she apparently felt from her parents during those
long periods she was away, boarded at private schools. When her father bought the house in Santa Fe and moved the family there in
1917, she attended Santa Fe High School, but she would remember

most the transforming education by her governess, during the Pajarito summers. She learned the names of wildflowers and mesas even as she developed a formal knowledge and love of poetry. Her mother also recited verses aloud for the children, particularly passages from *The Child's Garden of Verses* and Rudyard Kipling's *The Ballad of East and West*. Her mother taught her the Greek names and mythology of the night sky above the plateau. Subsequently, her first published poem in *St. Nicholas* magazine when she was only a teenager—"I Shall Take Root Here Like the Pine"—reflected both her early mastery of the forms of English poetry and her direct experience with the Pajarito Plateau. While in high school at Hillside, a private school in Connecticut, she won an *Atlantic Monthly* prize of fifty dollars for another poem inspired by the power of the "place of the bird people."[11]

Peggy enrolled in Smith College in 1922, attended for two years, and then in 1924 married Fermor Church, a young man from Washington, Connecticut, who had come to New Mexico to teach at the Ranch School. As the first faculty wife, the young Mrs. Church was mostly segregated from the activities of the boys, as the superintendent, A. J. Connell, believed that boys needed to separate from the influence of their mothers and other women in order to forge their masculine identities. Ironically, Peggy Church continued to excel and enjoy some of the very activities the boys sought to learn, for example, horsemanship. Finding the isolated mesas anything but dull, she reveled in the "myriad roads to utterness," far from the tyranny of the clock, telephone, or calendar. Though she did miss the companionship of women, she continued to share the natural world with her husband Ferm and with their three sons, Ted, Allen, and Hugh, all born on the Pajarito Plateau. Picnics and hikes became lifelong family habits. The family resided on the plateau in the Ranch School area until 1943, when the school land was commandeered by the federal government for the Manhattan Project.

The Los Alamos Ranch School operated on the premise of rigorous outdoor education, discipline, and fitness coupled with a preparatory school curriculum. A mostly self-sufficient community, the school began at the six-thirty morning bell. Calisthenics, breakfast, and inspection preceded classes. Modeled after the Boy Scouts under Connell's leadership, the school provided each boy a horse, required certain chores around the farm, and included patrols and outings

over the 880 acres owned by the school and the thousands available
through a joint-use agreement with the U.S. Forest Service. Food
and supplies not generated by the farm were accessed through the
narrow gauge railroad at Otowi Switch, twelve miles away. Though
excluded from the boy's activities, Peggy Church nevertheless quipped
in *The House at Otowi Bridge* that she felt rather pleased that she
managed to live her life on the plateau, outwitting her father who
had planned the school for boys, not girls. The school evidentally
prepared its students well. Many graduating alumni went on to distinguish themselves as scientists, artists, and businessmen. Ironically,
Manhattan Project director J. Robert Oppenheimer, though not an
alumnus, had admired the school on a horseback trip in the area. He
came to the mountains of New Mexico first as a boy, for his health,
and had been drawn to return even before the Manhattan Project to
buy a small ranch.

Beginning in the 1930s, Church investigated psychological
study and undertook Jungian analysis, probing her dreams and beginning the formalized habit of introspection. In Church's mind, the
Pajarito's native cultures, both ancient and modern, as well as the
cosmic nature of the plateau's setting itself, were linked to Carl
Jung's psychological theories, particularly to the interpretation of
dreams through archetypal symbolism. She continued this practice,
especially in her journals, for the remainder of her life, seeking to un-
ravel the mysteries of the subconscious, in connection to the mysterious parallels she felt with Anasazi life and to the influences of her
parents and family. Such self-analysis also influenced her development as a poet. Her first two books of poetry, *Foretaste* (1933) and
Familiar Journey (1936), included some poems previously published
in *The Atlantic, Poetry,* and *The Saturday Review of Literature*, and
dealt with themes of nature, childhood, love, marriage, and motherhood. Her third volume, *Ultimatum for Man* (1946), departed from
the earlier themes to examine the consequences of war and destruction. Many of these poems further indicate Church's fascination
with prehistoric and historic Native American life in northern New
Mexico as she observes present communities relating to the complex-
ities of the modern age.

A sensitive and dedicated man, Ferm countered the loss of Los
Alamos Ranch School by moving the family to California where he
could teach in a private school and the youngest son, Hugh, attend

the sixth grade. But the family missed the seasons of New Mexico, and by 1944, they were back in Taos where Ferm started another boys' school, Los Alamos School. By now, the name Los Alamos was so strongly connected with Hiroshima and Nagasaki that some parents expressed fear of sending their sons off to New Mexico, which might prove dangerous. The school closed in 1945. Ferm went to work for the Philmont Scout Ranch, and for the Kit Carson Electric Co-Op in Taos as office manager. He next took a job traveling as a surveyor for an Albuquerque engineering firm in northern New Mexico and Arizona. Like Peggy, he continued to feel the loss of the Pajarito life they had enjoyed. Their family picnics and Southwestern hikes and travels continued to highlight their lives. An environmentalist, Ferm was one of the founders of the New Mexico Citizens for Clean Air and Water. When a 25th anniversary bulletin for his Harvard class was issued, he listed as his occupation ex-schoolmaster. Like their parents, Ted, Allen, and Hugh were well educated and committed outdoor enthusiasts. Each came to work for a government entity connected to the Department of Energy in New Mexico, but the family continued to share a love of the outdoors.

In 1943, Church and her family moved from the Pajarito Plateau to Taos. In 1948, she became a member of the Society of Friends, attended meetings, and published in the Quaker journal, *Inward Light*. Continuing her analysis in Berkeley, California, where Fermor taught briefly in 1956, she saw profound yet natural relationships among the realms of the meditative, spiritual, political, and psychological. During the time that Ferm worked for the Kit Carson Electric Cooperative in Taos and the Philmont Boy Scout Camp, Peggy researched and wrote *The House at Otowi Bridge* (1959), a memoir of Edith Warner begun after Warner's death in 1951 and anticipated in her journal entries previous to Edith's death. *The Ripened Fields, Sonnets on a Marriage* (1957) expressed many of Peggy's readings of her relationship with Ferm in their oppositional but maturing marriage. The poems are a study in how the geologist/scientist and the poet, so different in their orientations, sought unity in a spiritual marriage. The collection demonstrates Church's continual experimentation with and mastery of poetic forms in her desire to voice highly personal yet universal themes.

When the Churches moved to Santa Fe in 1960, they became involved in the life of the city while they continued to enjoy hiking, picnics, and travel in New Mexico and the West. Peggy then began research on another woman writer and early acquaintance, Mary Austin, who had been a famous resident of Santa Fe in the 1930s. At St. John's College, Peggy attended seminars on Pablo Neruda, Walt Whitman, Henry David Thoreau, and William Butler Yeats, as well as lectures by Joseph Campbell, John Holt, and Robert Bly.

In 1975, Ferm died of a brain tumor. His illness precipitated a number of surprising events, including his complete recitation of a poem memorized but never uttered since his own childhood, visions, and vivid dreams. After his death, Church published *New and Selected Poems* (1976), *A Lament at Tsankawi Mesa* (1980), *A Rustle of Angels* (1981), and *Birds of Daybreak* (1985). During this productive period, she also undertook close scrutiny and editing of her journals, some begun as early as 1930, and recorded events of Fermor's final days and death in the "Terminal Journal." She continued her considerable correspondence with Taos friend, Corina Santistevan, and bibliophile and writer Larry Powell, formerly of Santa Fe, as well as with poets May Sarton, Denise Levertov, and editor Roland Dickey. Keeping up with invitations for lectures and readings, musical events, and local seminars, she was often interviewed by radio and magazine writers and honored with awards and autograph parties. After bouts with an inoperable eye condition and acute chemical sensitivity, she died on October 23, 1986, when she took her own life according to the precepts of the Hemlock Society.[12]

The Pajarito Journals are the most comprehensive record Peggy Church kept of her activities and, most of all, her memories and reflections. They date generally from her recovery from a breakdown after her father's death, to her turn to Jungian psychology for guidance, and finally to her reflections as an eighty-year-old. Because the journals function both chronologically and thematically, they provide insight into the origins and shaping of Church's published work, primarily her poetry and *The House at Otowi Bridge*. They also act as a concordance for the key events and influences Church responded to imaginatively. The four sections are arranged in accordance to the author's chronological sequencing, from the original Littlebird and Pajarito journals. They thus express the synesthetic pattern Church recognized in the influences of music or rhythm, geo-logic forms, and cycles of human life. In recording actual events, memory, the text and interpretation of dreams, research and notes for future essays, and metaphoric, poetic writing, the journals offer thematic statements of Church's psychological and spiritual evolu-tion. Church's writing, as was her life, is an adventure of the creative spirit. For this reason, Church refers infrequently to her husband and almost never to her children, which some readers may find sur-prising. Yet in the tradition of American nature writing, the journals are descriptive and philosophical, connecting the outer and inner worlds—a spiritual autobiography.

The first section, spanning the 1930s through the 1950s, cov-ers married life, the influence of Edith Warner, the relationship of Church's direct experience on the plateau to subsequent memories, and the formulation of this philosophy in *The House at Otowi Bridge,* after the Churches' move to Taos in 1943 and Edith's death in 1951. In the second section, the 1960s, the writer examines her own life, inspired by her interpretation of Edith's life. She keeps subjective Pajarito notes, records and interprets dreams, and creates the charac-ter, Quince, through whom the psychology of her girlhood can be worked out, even as she begins an analysis of Mary Austin's child-hood in order to write an adolescent biography.[13] The 1970s section, "The Pattern of Ancient Crossing," is a return to examination of her father and mother's lives, viewed as both psychologically and histori-cally related to New Mexico and the earliest human trails, or patterns of living on the land. Finally, the last section, "The Pajarito Cycles: The Cycles of Selves," reveals Church's very productive and intense final decade of her life—during which she rethought Haniel Long's *Cabeza de Vaca* and wrote her final powerful poems, again against the fabric of the remembered Pajarito.

Part of Church's adventure is the continual effort to articulate her memories. The old, half-remembered, or perhaps even misre-membered selves, adequate to their own proper moments, are inte-grated by the writer into a pattern of the new self. This new self, born of the moment, out of the very exercise of conscious and memory, is ever transforming.

Recall and recapitulation are the twin techniques that effect a transformation of the personality; these are also the essence of great autobiography. T. S. Eliot demonstrates this process in *Four Quartets,* and the poet Stephen Spender speaks of it further in his essay "Confessions and Autobiography":

> The autobiographical is transformed. It is no longer the writer's own experience; it becomes everyone's. He is no longer writing about himself; he is writing about life. He creates it, not as an object which is already familiar and observed, as he is observed by others, but as a new and revealing object, growing out of and beyond observation.[14]

Church's structuring of the journals, the patterns that evolve throughout, reflect this growth and transformation and the universalizing of experience and meaning for the reader.

Moreover, for Church, as a poet, structure is bound up in language—a way to articulate and communicate her felt thought. The seeming fits and starts of her many approaches to telling the story help create a language beyond the merely discursive or rational. T. S. Eliot suggests a realm of semantics for the poet who "is occupied with frontiers of consciousness beyond which words fall, though meanings exist."[15] Suzanne Langer also speaks of "the unexplored possibility of genuine semantics beyond the limits of discursive language."[16] For Church, this area of real meaning, lying beyond the discursive intellect and rational language, can be communicated and explored only through literary devices: through rhythm, image, and metaphor, or through what we may call motif, in drawing the three together. The Pajarito Plateau, for example, is a motif which is designed to re-evoke in the present a memorialized partial self. Church understood she could not hope to capture straight-on, or expect to transmit to another, her sense of self. At most she could discover a similitude, a metaphor, for this feeling of selfhood. A motif is thus adapted to this emotional life, calling forth from the reader a response. By itself it does not represent nor correspond with a statable meaning.

Thus, the reader may want to listen to the work at hand. For the poet, Church, has made rhythmical use of words, images, phrases, sounds, metaphors, symbols, and themes. Her technique is traditional insomuch as it introduces a motif, varying and exploring it in its various contexts so that the essence of the motif is accretional and relational in the whole design of the work. Though journal-keeping would appear on the whole spontaneous and unplanned—perhaps not crafted in the way of a poem—these entries, in Church's hands, are often beautiful evocations in prose. In her natural inclination to metaphor-making and motif creation, Church charges the entire work with these literary elements, even as they stand for her whole self, reborn artistically.

I begin my introductions to the journal sections with poems written during the same period as a way of sensing not simply themes or subjects but more the essence of the search for meanings through language and motif. Likewise, I've included family and historic photographs, most of them snapshots from Church's own albums, which best capture the moment she was experiencing. These photographs are not solely illustrative, but another text Peggy "wrote"—the record of both family events and her own love of image. The images in her photographs, like those in her writing, reveal the way in which recall and recapitulation are at the heart of her storytelling.

On occasion, there are long gaps, up to two years, during which there are no journal entries. Generally, these indicate Church at work on other things, such as her poetry, research, or other nonfiction writing. She was also a consummate letter writer, corresponding for years with May Sarton, Roland Dickey, and Larry Powell. An enthusiastic and dogged record keeper and organizer, Church spent considerable time collecting newspaper articles, letters, photographs, and files on the Pajarito Club, her parents, her Santa Fe years.

Read as a physical, psychological, or spiritual record, as the background for poems and biographies, or as a record of daily influences and imagined results, the journals speak variously and perhaps differently upon each reading and for each reader, even as the writer experienced them as unfinished yet whole within themselves.

Church Chronology

1897	Ashley Pond Jr. graduates from Yale.
1898	Ashley Pond Jr. enlists in Navy, then Army in order to serve in Spanish-American War; enlists in Company C of Rough Riders, but contracts serious fever in Florida, never serves; moves to New Mexico Territory for his health.
1903	Ashley Pond Jr. and Hazel Hadley marry January 21 in New York City, return to New Mexico to begin ranch school for boys. Peggy Pond born December 1, in Watrous, New Mexico.
1904	Watrous Flood, September; Pond family returns to Detroit.
1906	Dorothy ("Dotty") Pond born May 20.
1908	Ashley ("Laddie") Pond III born August 4.
1912	Ashley Pond Jr. takes family back to Roswell, New Mexico. New Mexico becomes a state.
1913	Children begin to attend private and parochial schools in California and in Connecticut.
1914-16	Pond children spend summer of 1914, winter and summer of 1915, and summer of 1916 in Pajarito Canyon cabin with parents; children study with governess when in New Mexico. Ashley Pond Jr. buys Ramon Vigil Grant, along with five Detroit automobile industrialists, for the Pajarito Club, a recreation retreat.
1916	Pajarito Club is disbanded; Ramon Vigil Grant is sold; Ashley Pond Jr. approaches Howard Brook to buy the Los Alamos Ranch on the Pajarito Plateau.

1917   Los Alamos Ranch School established, buys Santa Fe
          house; Peggy Pond attends Santa Fe High School.

1918-22   Peggy Pond attends private schools.

1921   Fermor S. Church, a Harvard graduate in illuminated
          engineering, is hired by A. J. Connell to teach as a
          "master" at Los Alamos Ranch School.

1923-24   Peggy Pond attends Smith College.

1924   Peggy Pond and Fermor Church marry, June.

1925   Ted Church is born.

1926   Peggy and Fermor build new cabin at Los Alamos.

1928   Allen Church is born.

1929   Peggy reads Katherine Mansfield's letters; takes flying
          lessons.

1932   Hugh Church is born.

1933   Ashley Pond Jr. dies. Peggy begins to suffer nervous
          depression, is hospitalized in New Haven, Connecticut,
          November to December.

1934   Peggy reads *The Secret Garden of the Golden Flower* with
          Ferm.

1935   Peggy takes trip to Yellowstone; begins Jungian analysis
          at Berkeley.

1937   Peggy continues analysis in New York.

1939   Peggy continues analysis at Berkeley.

1940   Germany invades France, May.

1942   Peggy reports, "Army men have been swarming all over
          our mesa." Los Alamos Ranch School closes, December.

1943   Peggy moves to Taos, continues dream investigation
          through Jungian analysis.

1944   Peggy continues analysis. Hugh attends sixth grade in
          California where Fermor teaches in a private school.
          Family moves to Taos. Ferm starts new Los Alamos
          Ranch School in Taos.

1945	Allen graduates from Los Alamos School in Taos; Ranch school officially closes.
1946	Peggy works for Citizens of Taos.
1947	Ferm works at Philmont Boy Scout Ranch.
1948	Peggy and Ferm join the Society of Friends, study pacifism. Peggy continues dream logs and analysis. Ferm works for Kit Carson Rural Electric Coop.
1949	Hugh contracts polio.
1950	Ferm's job as office manager of Kit Carson Rural Electric Coop ends; Ferm works as surveyor of power lines in northern New Mexico.
1951	Edith Warner dies, May.
1952	Peggy spends summer in England.
1953	Peggy works in Taos bookshop; attends Hopi Bean Dance.
1954	Hazel Hadley Pond dies, November.
1956	Haniel and Alice Long die. Peggy goes back to Berkeley for analysis.
1958	*The House at Otowi Bridge*, about Edith Warner, is published.
1959	Peggy terminates analysis; sells Berkeley house, moves back to Santa Fe.
1960	Peggy and Ferm move to Victoria Street house in Santa Fe. Peggy and Ferm go to Ghost Ranch for Society of Friends meetings, attend Shalako Indian Dances.
1961	Ferm works in Gallup and Grants, New Mexico. Peggy and Ferm go to London, June. Peggy gets dog, Poli. Peggy begins work on Mary Austin, resumes correspondence with May Sarton.
1962	Peggy goes picnicking above upper Frijoles Canyon; camping with Ferm and Poli, Cochiti Canyon. Peggy goes to Chaco Canyon, July; climbs Picacho where Mary Austin's ashes are scattered, December.

1963   Peggy attends Shakespeare play in San Diego.

1964   Peggy hikes on Goat Mountain; tears knee cartilage snow skiing; goes by train to San Francisco.

1965   Peggy goes to Egypt and Spain, April. "Healing picnic" in Hondo Canyon, December.

1966   Peggy and Ferm hike to Stone Lions, Bandelier. Peggy and Ferm attend yearly Friends meeting in Portland, August. *Woman at Otowi Crossing* by Frank Waters is published.

1967   Mass is celebrated at San Ildefonso to dedicate new church. Peggy takes train to Grand Canyon, August; researches Mary Austin all summer and fall. Ferm goes to Cuba and Gobernador, New Mexico.

1969   Ferm goes to Gobernador, Papecito, Tenneco Wells, Ponderosa, Bisti. Peggy meets John Holt; joins in events at St. John's College, reads at poetry festival, Folk Art Museum, Santa Fe.

1971   Ferm works with Clean Air and Water. Poli turns 10; Peggy acquires the dog Baba, keeps journals on dogs. Peggy meets Mark Van Doren at St. John's College, meets Barbara Morgan at Laura Gilpin opening. Gus Baumann dies.

1972   Peggy finishes early section of Mary Austin biography, types Mary Austin dreams.

1973   Peggy meets with Austin's biographer, Augusta Fink; socializes with Larry and Fay Powell; reads Thomas Merton; begins Neruda seminar, St. John's College; translates Neruda's "Machu Picchu." Ferm becomes ill, November. Peggy reads Plato for St. John's seminar, attends Robert Bly reading, is honored at Los Alamos Historical Society for Los Alamos Ranch School booklet.

1975   Ferm is diagnosed with brain tumor; final picnic at Cañada de los Alamos. Ferm dies February 2. Peggy begins to notice chemical sensitivity that affects eyes;

contemplates moving to retirement village, El Castillo; works on *Selected Poems.*

1976   Peggy begins researching Hadley/Dorsey family history; visits Springer, Watrous, and Valmora, New Mexico. Attends *King Lear* seminar, St. John's College.

1977   Peggy attends *Walden* seminar, St. John's College.

1980   Peggy writes two to four hours a day, working on Pajarito Journals, *Interlinear of Cabeza de Vaca,* Baumann pamphlet; goes to Ghost Ranch for Friends meeting; *Angels* is published.

1982   Peggy works on "Black Mesa" poem; reworks Pajarito notes; gets "hooked" on reading Neruda; copies Quince notes; gives brown bag readings, readings to Jungian group, School of American Research party for Elliot Porter.

1983   Peggy returns to active correspondence with May Sarton.

1984   Peggy receives Governor's Award for Literature, State of New Mexico and Living Treasure Award, Santa Fe.

1985   *Birds at Daybreak* is published.

1986   Peggy dies, October 23, 1986.

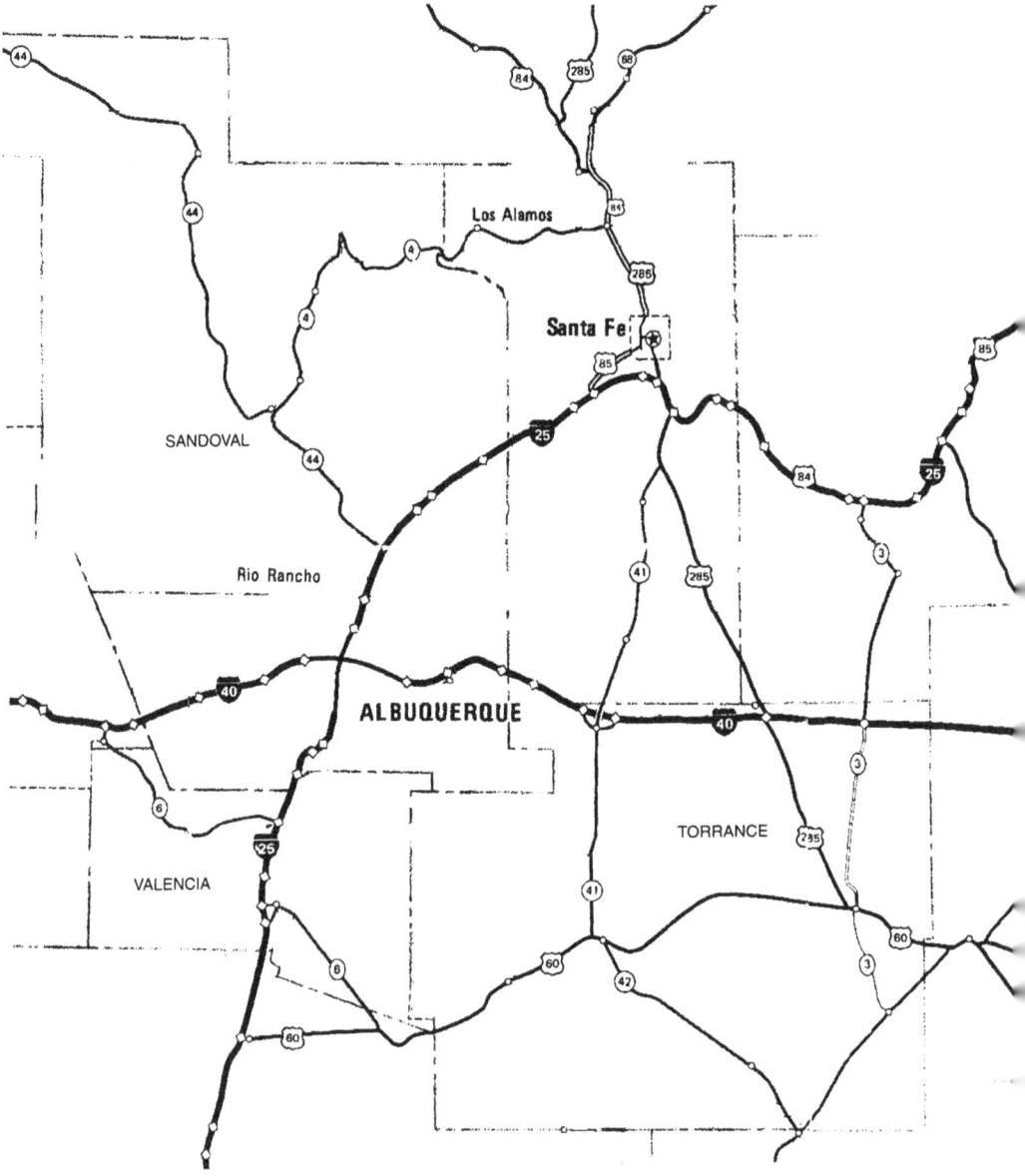

ONE
The Seeds of Wonder

Peggy Pond Church on Benigna, 1935. Courtesy Los Alamos Historical Museum Archives, Peggy Pond Church Collection.

Shattered

A dog barked
and shattered the chrysalis of silence.
I came out of my dream
and found the stars had moved
only a handsbreadth down the indefinite arc
of heaven.
You and I were two people again
contained in two bodies,
and the long wave shattered beneath our hands
and went
on the sands of morning.

(1934)

A lover awakes from her dream to separateness and a wilderness night, where love as a cosmos contains the whole of desert and ancient ocean life. Such clusters of images in this short poem remind us that Peggy Church, between 1914 and 1943, spent almost one-third of her life in the Pajarito Plateau area. The journals from this period, begun as directly experienced yet resonating moments, soon attempt to balance the wonder of the place with the impending destruction of her childhood wonderland, the first home of wife and mother, and the death of her best friend, Edith Warner. As they begin, after the death of her father in 1933, the journals signal Church's turn to the study of Jungian psychology, including dream records and interpretations of their symbols. They proceed to a representation of Edith Warner, who appears as a symbol of wholeness during this shattering period, and to suggestions that inward examination is healing, as demonstrated by Church's membership in the Society of Friends in the 1940s. Few observations speak directly of her marriage or the birth of her three sons during this period. The poet instead writes about her individuality as a process of the creative life, subconscious and conscious, the journals bridging through imagery her actual world and the world of her imagination. In this, one of her most productive periods as a writer, in which she publishes three books of poetry, one children's tale, and *The House at Otowi Bridge,* Church's "seeds of wonder" show the plateau years as ground for the writer's emergence. Though not direct references to the published work, the journals demonstrate the link between the writer's corporal experience, metaphor, and memory.

Also from this period's journals came "Trails Over the Pajarito," a short, unpublished manuscript of the life of a woman in the early twentieth century within the vastness of the Vigil land grant west of the Rio Grande. Thus, Church used the journals to generate short essays about the plateau years, using her own experiences to explore the life of the Los Alamos Ranch School and make observations about Native American lives and ceremonies and the archaeological activities of her acquaintances. In "Trails Over the Pajarito," a playful Peggy recounts the Churches' honeymoon spent in a one-room log cabin at Camp May during which a hailstorm pounded the galvanized tin roof. When the couple attempted to cook, the old cabin range smoked; the creaking canvas cots tended to collapse; pack rats scurried over the roof at night stealing whatever they could and filling the couple's boots with trash the next morning.

In this essay, Church also recalls her first year of marriage in the couple's quarters at the ranch school—a small, slab-sided construction, known as the Pyramid because of the shape of its roof, bordering an Anasazi ruin north of the Los Alamos Ranch School lodge. Here they had a tiny sitting room with an old spool daybed and an upright piano, an Espey that had traveled with Peggy's parents around New Mexico in a wagon or truck. The most noticeable scratches on the instrument were not traveling scars but those of Peggy's fingernails from her childhood piano lessons. A couple of chairs and a fragile Japanese tea-set completed the small room. Water was heated on a two-burner oil stove in the bathroom, shared with another lodger in the Pyramid, who was the school's secretary. Only cold water ran in the rooms, and after the first baby, Ted, was born, heating formula, sterilizing bottles, and bathing the baby all took place in a small enamel tub. The residents' baths could be taken in the guest bathroom upstairs in the big house.

One leisurely afternoon when Peggy managed to enjoy a bath alone, she relaxed in this tub, casually eating an apple. The boys and the staff were out riding horses. Suddenly the door opened, and Mr. Connell, the very proper director of the school, ushered in two lady visitors whom he was touring around the campus. Ever fastidious and resourceful, he managed a quick "Excuse me," and briskly led the ladies back out, as if Peggy in her tub were part of the tour. Such tight quarters and only occasional privacy further encouraged Peggy's outdoor and adventuresome spirit. Despite the faculty wives' being discouraged from such activities, she took long horseback rides alone, napped near canyon precipices, and generally made Valle Grande, Pajarito Mountain, Rincon Bonito, and Garcia Canyon both her home and the site of adventure.

In 1925, the Churches moved from the Pyramid into their first home, designed by Fermor but built with her parents' money. A log building, the most northerly from the school, it offered Peggy a view of her wilderness home, with only a stand of pines between the cabin and Pueblo Canyon. From here, Peggy pursued the great drama of sky and mesa through her kitchen window, as she did her domestic duties. Yet the cabin itself reminded Peggy and Fermor of their fragile existence, particularly during the deep winters. Sometimes the cabin logs shrank, allowing the cold inside. Since the school authorities frowned on burning coal or oil for fear of pollution, the Churches relied on a cantankerous space heater. Like the Majestic cooking range in the kitchen, the heater required regular tending. In "Trails Over the Pajarito," Peggy recalls: "The pine wood sooted up the grates, and I loathed cleaning them, but I loved the feel and the presence of live fire, the sound of the copper kettle simmering gently on sunny afternoons when I was alone, the children asleep. On such mornings, disorder straightened into calm." A living room with a fireplace and facing sofa added to this comfort, "warming the primitive soul in us all." On the back porch, a huge icebox was filled two or three times a week in winter with ice cut from the natural water hole fondly named Ashley Pond, in honor of Peggy's father. With no telephone, the family gathered around a record player/radio for news and entertainment, sharing particularly the Metropolitan Opera and symphonic broadcasts.

This essay, called forth from the period paralleling the elliptical notes in these early Pajarito journals, also connects the world of wife and mother to that of the writer. A major theme woven into the journals brings together the writer's inwardly examined life, her experiences, feelings, and opinions, and her observations about the life of the creative woman. In "Trails Over the Pajarito," Peggy notes: "Besides horseback riding, I must have spent a lot of time sick in bed because that's when I could write a good deal of poetry. It was some-times the only way out for the housewife with even the slightest kind of creative gift, for she can never help being torn between the inward urge that gnaws on her and the demands—the supposed demands—of outer life. I remember how envious I was of my poet friend, Haniel Long, whose wife fed him and kept him and guarded him from all frustrating interruptions. If only the poet in me had such a wife, I used to lament—and still do—though I know that really never solves the problem. The poet in me is an irresponsible creature who would rather go on picnics or walk on mountain trails or read books or lis-ten to music than settle down to work. In spite of all my experiences with real horses, I've had a hard time making Pegasus, my nickname, accept the saddle and bridle."

Surely Peggy's self-description not only reflects the wish to be freed to do her creative work, a privilege she seems uncomfortable ac-cepting, but also indicates another of her characteristics: an inherent shyness that often kept her from claiming the rewards of her talents. Thus, throughout Church's writing, there are not only recurring themes and images, but also a pervasive subtext of the woman's quest. In the first journal, using again the heroic image of horseman-ship as in the playful Pegasus name, she begins with the image of her-self, issuing forth on her mare—an actual experience but also a metaphysical one—the ultimate experience of the moment, "the mare and I, melting, flowing, dissolving in sunlight."

Later, the unleashed writer's voice speaks for the soul-seeking Peggy, ever more intensely as the journals progress, because of the impending loss of the paradise of her youth. Heroic actions must now be seen in terms of her spiritual growth and survival. What was originally directly experienced and enjoyed when she was thirty to forty years old must necessarily become a cherished memory as the Churches move from the Pajarito Plateau to Taos. The plateau expe-riences as subjects of exhilaration thus become manifest in dreams, memories, and in the character of Edith Warner. Peggy's journal entries about Edith show that she had a quiet and nonjudgmental personality, as opposed to Peggy's own sorrow, anger, and bitter-ness over the destructiveness of the Manhattan Project. Church projected in her reflections on Edith her own desire to be more at peace within herself, more demonstratively loving, exhibiting more patience and understanding. Warner shared Church's concerns, but held them differently in her heart. Peggy's reflections on Edith demonstrate how completely Edith came to represent the essence of Peggy's lost plateau.

The progression in subject, theme, genre, and style is considerable when we read the three collections of poems and *The House at Otowi Bridge* in the context of "The Seeds of Wonder," written from 1934 until 1954. Whereas the lyrical *Foretaste* (1933) and *Familiar Journey* (1936) address a woman's attempt to balance relationships, her own creative and independent personality, and her desire to develop spiritual bonds with nature, *Ultimatum for Man* (1946) sharply links the personal and creative quests to the meaning of the atomic age, war, and human responsibility. *The House at Otowi Bridge* is a memoir in which Church intertwines her own journal accounts and reflections with Warner's letters, journals, and friendships. With the loss of Edith, coupled with the loss of her life on the Pajarito Plateau, Peggy seeks in her memory of Edith's humble and settling presence the source for accepting life's disappointments as part of a meaningful whole. She says of Edith in *The House at Otowi Bridge*, "All of her future lay folded still within her, like the Mariposa lilies she came to love—those three-petaled white blossoms with the golden centers whose seed must often wait patiently through years of drought for enough moisture to make them germinate" (12). Peggy comes to see that her own seeds of wonder may sustain her as well.

The journals chart the awakening of the writer to the image as the foundation for ancient metaphors of human thought. From Warner and from her own years companioning the ancient energies of the Anasazi homelands, Church learned that the Pueblo peoples' symbology, based on a petroglyph image such as Awanyu, the Plumed Serpent, signified a larger spiritual reality: "Not the river, but the force embodied in the river; not the cloud but the life-giving energies of the cloud—these are what the image of the Plumed Serpent speaks of to the Pueblo people and to all who know that rain is one of the many forms of deity" (*The House at Otowi Bridge*, 23). In the journals, the poet works in a language that is powered by associations and symbolic meaning. Resonating with the principles of the Imagist movement, some of whose proponents lived and wrote in northern New Mexico, Church's own image-driven work, directed at either the physical world or the visualized interior world, acts to translate felt thought. Thus, ideas, philosophy, and spirituality are conveyed through the suggestiveness of the single word. For instance, in the last part of "The Seeds of Wonder," Church moves from a focus on the meaning of Edith Warner's life and words to reflection about her own life. She does so even as she continues to work out the translation of the simplest domestic acts into the most profound realities using the langugage and metaphor of the Pajarito Plateau. The cycle of stone poems, begun in the 1920s and concluded in the 1980s, illustrates a similar transformation. This poem was written in 1940:

Little Sermon in Stone

The little hill, breast round and hard as stone,
peopled with stones, with dark red stones like blood;
with fist-big stones, and smaller child's hand stones,
seemed at one glance earth's very cinder patch,
infertile, inhospitable to life.
But we stayed there one winter afternoon
hushing our man-proud thought, and stilled our hearts
to the slow beat of time's heart in a stone.

We lay upon the ground and felt the stones,
and saw them with our hands; and with our eyes
tuned to chill light's minute and fragile pulse,
gazed deep into the structure of the stone.
We saw the crystalline flowering of the stone,
the many-faceted complexity,
the light turned back with orchestrated beat
into our listening eyes, the blood-stained reds,
the flush of yellow and the dove-dark greens.

We touched this little fragment of a world
burst from earth's straining heart, this ancient rain
that starred the black night once with splintered fire,
and dared the sky to weep till the sky wept
and rain's fingers quelled the angry light.
This hill became the rounded grave of fire,
ash-cold and ruinous and for an age,
who knows how long, lay obdurate to rain,
all light transfixed and frozen in its heart.

But as we lay
face down, eye close to stone, heart close to stone
we saw the stain of life upon the stones.
The creeping lichens, live and unafraid,
fed upon crystal and transformed the shape
of arrogant rock to supple, pliant dust
and flowered upon that dust. Light became leaf,
and leaf, with who knows what of agony,
contrived its seed to float upon the wind.
The colored lichens take the world apart
in their slow fingers. The bright mold of life
moves like a web upon the unloving rock
and seeks the imprisoned light and sets it free
to live again in seed and stem and flower.

Upon the little hill the frozen grass
stands yellow in the sun. The winter birds
pause and are fed. We too were fed
through mind and heart upon stone's element.

(1940)

Peggy Pond and Fermor Church home in Pajarito Canyon, 1927. Courtesy Los Alamos Historical Museum Archives, Peggy Pond Church Collection.

Los Alamos Ranch School ice house, 1920s; ice was harvested from Ashley Pond. Courtesy Los Alamos Historical Museum Archives, Peggy Pond Church Collection.

Fermor Church with sons Ted (in back), Hugh (left), and Allen (right) circa 1934. Courtesy Los Alamos Historical Museum Archives, Peggy Pond Church Collection.

Peggy Pond Church in the Rio Grande, 1930s. Courtesy Los Alamos Historical Museum Archives, Peggy Pond Church Collection.

Edith Warner at Frijoles, 1923. Courtesy Center for Southwest Research General Library, University of New Mexico.

Atilano Montoya at Tsirege, 1940. Courtesy Center for Southwest Research General Library, University of New Mexico.

Peggy Pond Church at Tsankawi Mesa, 1920s. Courtesy Los Alamos Historical Museum Archives, Peggy Pond Church Collection.

Peggy Pond Church, circa 1935. Courtesy Los Alamos Historical Museum Archives, Peggy Pond Church Collection.

Fermor Church, 1930s. Courtesy Los Alamos Historical Museum Archives, Peggy Pond Church Collection.

Main building, Ramon Vigil, ca. 1914. Courtesy Los Alamos Historical Museum Archives, Peggy Pond Church Collection.

In front of the main building, Ramon Vigil, ca. 1914. Courtesy Los Alamos Historical Museum Archives, Peggy Pond Church Collection.

Ramon Vigil cabin, ca. 1914. Courtesy Los Alamos Historical Museum Archives, Peggy Pond Church Collection.

Edith Warner in the guest house on Rio Grande, 1940s. Courtesy Center for Southwest Research General Library, University of New Mexico.

Edith Warner and Atilano Montoya in the arroyo near her new home, after a heavy rain, 1940s. Courtesy Center for Southwest Research General Library, University of New Mexico.

Edith Warner's second home near Otowi Bridge, 1940s. Courtesy Center for Southwest Research General Library, University of New Mexico.

Santiago (Adam) Roybal, San Ildefonso Pueblo, 1930s. Adam, a friend of Edith Warner, is referred to repeatedly in her work and in *The House at Otowi Bridge*. Courtesy Los Alamos Historical Museum Archives, Peggy Pond Church Collection.

Journals,
1930s–1950s

May 13, 1934

The lively flowing motion of my mare's, Benigna's, slow canter this morning. She lifted herself effortlessly like a wave, and the canyon seemed to be a wide river up which she and I swam—a river of gold. This morning everything green seemed to be turning at the touch of the sun. The oaks on the north side of the canyon were brightest. The leaves of the trees and the pale gold grass and the sandy warm trails and the rocks and the mare and I, melting, flowing, dissolving in sunlight.

July 3, 1934

Today, I thought, watching the thin shower of rain falling at the end of the mesa, oh, why doesn't it fall here? And then rejoiced that some thirsty spot on these mesas was getting it even if not this one. It's all the same earth, I thought. And anywhere that the rain falls is healing for the earth. [This entry and the next were later included in *The House at Otowi Bridge*.]

August 30, 1934

The moon last night made a porpoise or dolphin of the black cloud and haloed it with silver. Today is the most shining green and gold early autumnal day. I walked down the mesa at noon and heard the wind like the swish of a long taffeta skirt in the corn. The tassels of corn, the delicate silk, a deep maroon. I sat at the edge of the growing field of winter rye and saw it moved by the wings of quick little birds and by the wind.

September 9, 1934

On the edge of the hill, the road goes down, overlooking the valley, the mountains, and the heaped-up clouds. It is so silent here at the noon hour, all space and color and billow of wind. Sometimes a bird cries; the cry clashes out into space like the flicker of a small goldfish leaping in a huge, lonely globe of water.

March 22, 1935

I look from my window and see the sunset run up the mountains like a tongue of swift flame, and I have a deep feeling that I must make haste and look deeply on all this, not miss an instant of it, store it up forever in my heart, as one might store up the plenty of his fields against famine.

June 16, 1935

Summer dawn, so different from winter dawn or evening or any other time of day. Incredible that the great globe before us, thickening like a soap bubble and dropping in its own weight, should be the moon. Incredible that the spreading light behind us should be the new day. How pale and dreamlike the rivers shone at that early hour. The surface of the Rio Grande was silvered so that it seemed a new, young, limpid river.

March 23, 1937

On the mesa south of Pajarito today, I walked alone from the others among the trees. I looked down from the edge into Pajarito Canyon and the cottonwood trees, bare and gray, along the river bed. I remembered again how precious the early morning hours of my childhood there had been to me, the long days of aloneness with the wind in the gama grass, the smell of sage and juniper, and that indefinable feeling when one walks alone on an ancient ruin and picks up a pointed stone that a hand, once human, had shaped. It's the continuity of life that's the marvelous thing. By standing where other people once stood, upon the very walls of their home, with the same mountains looking down on us and the same shadows on the mountains, we can have a curious feeling of identity with long-past people. We project ourselves into their past and feel our own immortality.

I rode all day on the mesas between here and the Rio Grande. I rode in a curious timelessness which contained my own childhood and the lives of ancestors of mine I had never known, the ancestors of a race not even my own. Sometimes the boundaries that hem in the human spirit seem to fall. It seems the collective spirit of the world enters into us.

I was all the people who had ever ridden horseback on a lonely journey. I was the sheepherder who walled up a ruined cave and sheltered there by night, following flocks over those bare and ancient stones by day. I was all men who tried to farm in solitary wastes, trying to make a little portion of the earth their own. I felt all their fear of unknown things and all their love of sheltered, inaccessible valleys.

I stood on a high place and looked in a half-circle around the world, north to that wave on wave of towering pink cliffs, east past the barrancas and the strange crumpled hills beyond the river's circle. My eyes were not the first to look on all this and feel wonder and reverence.

January 13, 1938

Toscanini by the Rio Grande. The little house with its clean board floors and the faded Indian rugs, the gentleness of candlelight, the pale moonlight on the cliffs beyond the mesa, that long flat looming horizon, the sound of the river, not quite audible unless we listened closely.

Four people who were silent and listened to the music. Though we said no word, there was an interchange between us; the air seemed to stir with our awareness of each other. We were still, yet we touched one another with the moving current of our lives. Two of us were husband and wife, identified in that relationship, yet separate. One of us was a person wise through contact with earth and hills, who lived much by herself, and was self-contained, who accepted life as it came to her—was like the hill in her quietness. For many years her neighbors had been Indians. She had come to have a kind of Indian reticence herself, a kinship within her with the rhythms of earth and sun and the seasons. The fourth person was an elderly Indian who sat all the time engrossed in his own thoughts and far away from us, inaccessible, and yet not aloof. He smoked a cigarette, not casually or nervously like white men, but graciously, as though it were a ritual, as though he were taking into himself an awareness of each gesture, as though a cigarette were a rare thing, worth the fullest attention in every detail of smoking it.

Music binds people together in a queer way so that they become more collective than individual. We listen to it with our separate selves, and yet we are not able to be entirely separate. Each is merged a little into all the others. Emotion is redoubled. Tonight we suffered and were weighted down, were torn to pieces by Sibelius's 2nd Symphony. We bled and died and rose again. We entered into Valhalla to the sound of the trumpets and the heroic echo of battle. Then the curtain fell and the sound died away, and it was like a great dream ending.

January 23, 1938

It seems I can hardly remember when wars and rumors of wars became a part of the sound of the river. The river in its ceaseless surge and flow seemed always a symbol of human life that channels its way from the far off heights of beginning time to the wide seas of accumulated history.

January 25, 1938

Last night was a strange night in which the supernatural intruded stubbornly on the placidity of daily life. The music we tried to hear was made almost inaudible by a static worse than I have ever heard on the radio. A newscast explained that a tremendous electro-magnetic hurricane had taken place, beginning about one o'clock of the preceding night, and effectively blotting out all short-wave communication for several hours. It was the largest such storm ever to be recorded. A coyote, apparently caught in a trap not far away, wailed and shrieked in spirals of sound that sent shivers up and down our spines and took us back to our primitive history when houses were fragile little islands of safety against which the wilderness beat like a threatening wave. In the middle of the night, I felt my bedrock tremble gently as though registering the beginning of an earthquake. Poor earth, I thought, so harassed tonight by nature and man. Bombarded by electric particles from the sky, torn and bruised by man's devices of warfare, drained of your very blood, fed upon by man. What wonder that you, oh, earth, should dream of shaking loose this plague that has fastened itself upon you and tremble as you dream.

June 30, 1940

We got clear away into a remote and relatively inaccessible canyon, and then, miraculously all the cares and strains of the past weeks began to drift away like the network of ripples on water when the wind ceases. It was as though we realized that we had given up our secure and eternal anchorage to batter back and forth in this current of propaganda, this use other men make of our all too human childishness and craving for security. Here in the canyon where no books of opinion, no newspaper headlines, no blare of radio with its undercurrent of imminent panic. There is only the great sky and the ancient rocks and the stir and surge of wildflowers blooming and the sound of the brook with its uncomplaining obedience to the laws of motion. There are the beaver dams and the mirrorlike water spread out under the tangled thicket, the unhurried wise old fish moving in the water, the early morning dew on the tall weeds and grasses, the birds calling and hurrying, the footprints of bear and mountain cat upon the trail, the sweet masses of wild strawberries under the tall rock shadows. Life and time were woven into this great moment of truth and beauty.

May 21, 1942

This is the first true presence of full spring. It is as though, after pain, the false alarms, the stubbornness, at last spring has become woman, and tender, and we melt like a long-harassed and frustrated lover into her warm, her exquisitely tender embrace. The sky is delicately cloudless, and the wind that has lacerated and tortured us these many weeks is warm and forgiving. The fir trees are full of tiny green new buds at the end of the branches. The miracle of growth trembles before our eyes. Now the oak brush is transformed into a being of delicacy and light; the soft tassel of its bloom is suspended among the sheltering softness of the new leaves. The color is midway between green and gold. The canyon air is festooned with birdcalls.

Why should it seem like a vice to lie under the roof of a tree upon the rim of one's world and simply content oneself with the imminence of summer? Our world goes to ruins, and men destroy their souls to build daily greater engines of destruction. Yet there are these islands of peace and moments of serenity which seem to say that, after all, this is transient. Destruction whirls up out of the sea of all living like the storm which in two hours laid the wealth of our forest low. Yet the great stars acknowledge the ruin by not a flicker, nor the slightest drawing back or shrinking of their motion.

May 22, 1942

Again, reclining between rock and pine tree at the canyon's rim. The wind comes from the southeast today over the shoulder of the mesa, so that I hear it surging like the great waves in the canyon depths and sighing like the ebb of breakers through the evergreens; yet it hardly touches my pine bed. A population of soft, indefinite clouds throngs the sky. There is a haze of subdued light over everything; the outline of the mountains is softened like music, *piano* and *andante*. This is still the hour of birds; the variety of their cries is a turbulence in the gentle air.

The relaxing of the will, the shrinking back into the center, the settling of oneself upon the tide which one had begun to fight furiously, as in nightmares, is a blessed experience. How can one go astray in one's efforts to change the world? Then suddenly we bring our eyes back to the world we have not made and entrust ourselves in willing contentment, suppleness of spirit, to the hand of our Maker.

This is an experience to me as exciting as listening to music: this interweaving of harmony of bird and wind, this sound made by the surges and current of life itself. The invisible medium of air sustains the flight of birds and so enters into our awareness, not through contact with its essence, but through its action, its effect. Eye denies air. Body is subtly adjusted to it so that it senses only air's disturbance; the heart ignores air's presence but becomes frantically aware when the presence is even for brief periods withdrawn. Do we not postulate the presence of the Holy Spirit in the same way? How can we grow more sensitively aware of air, which after all is the medium in which the human organism is rooted far more than it is on earth?

Thunderheads are building up out of the north over Tsacoma [Tschicomo or Chicomo]. They tower and ride like a column of avenging archangels. There is a moistness in the air, a California feel, a seacoast humidity that brings out the fragrances usually unnoticed in dry climates. A tiny spider this moment spins a path from the twig of a barberry bush to my knee and back again. There is nothing to me so beautiful and really thrilling as the light and life in formations of western clouds—watching them build to the maturity of their forms and either vanish in the climax of rain or be swept away in the alterations of day and night.

Here at last she seems to have found her way back to the realm of being she discovered the summer that she was driven from all activities her nature cries for. Why is it so difficult to be contented with the praise of life? Why must she constantly assume disguises that are not her own and rush frantically to and fro in the guise of, at best, a minor prophet; at its worst, a puritanical reformer?

How we human beings have divorced ourselves from earth and air which is our habitat. Houses should be our shelter, to be retired to only when climate and weather are unfriendly. We should resort to them unwillingly, only of necessity, when there is no other recourse. Yet we inhabit our houses as though they were a second skin. We have retreated into them, from the beauty and changeability of the world. Some of us serve our houses as we should our God. We have become cavern dwellers, office dwellers, using the air between us only briefly as passageways from one enclosure to another. And living as we do, certain of our senses close themselves off and wither away, like the eyes of fishes in blind caves.

May 24, 1942

Yesterday we picnicked at Pajarito Falls. There were no falls; nothing but the magic and majesty of the great landscape; the inaudible river curving at its bottom, the history of millenniums pyramiding upward on either side; the remnants of vulcanism strewn upon the strata that monumented the river's history.

The Pajarito Creek has made itself a miniature and hidden in the plain of the level basalt. One rides across the flat mesa, crushing the leaves of the sage and releasing fragrance like an infuriated and living swarm. One marvels at the perfect counterpoint of silver-gray sage and red paintbrush, the two tones so harmonic. Then, suddenly the black slit of canyon appears, and a small paradisal garden is opened beneath one's feet, a climate within another climate, as the moist kernel of a nut is concealed within the dry, crisp shell. Here are cottonwoods and blossoming chokecherry, its fragrant white tassel dangling among the glossy green leaves. Sagebrush, with access to secret subterranean wells of moisture, becomes a tree. There was one old scrub higher up than I, and in it, carefully woven, what I first took to be a cocoon, but on breaking it off, discovered to my dismay to be a nest.

The nest was marvelously fabricated. It swung in the shape of a pouch with the neck narrowed and a small opening on one side of the top. It was braided of the finest filaments of grass and skeleton leaf and plastered with dried leaf, moss, lichen, fern, bits of dried sage from the mother shrub, fluffs of down from the gray and blue of the mother's breast, and here and there a tawny rust from the ruddy-breasted male bluebird. Inside the nest were five nestlings, only a few days old, featherless and naked, all mouth, their only consciousness the need for fuel to fire the enormous energies of growth that filled them. My heart was filled with anguish. Innocently, I had destroyed that architectural wonder, the nest; had brutally terminated the miracle of egg on its way to becoming song. I consoled myself faintly with the thought of the prodigality of nature, the tide of life, of burnished and flooding spring, uninterrupted by the perishing I noted.

Only in my awareness, my own heart suffered, the sensitive heart of humankind that knows its own tenderness and its own despair.

May 26, 1942

On this day most of the oak is at the height of bloom. The fir trees have been for a week or more in new leaf. Indian paintbrush and the common yellow daisylike flower whose name I do not know. But I examined the yucca, both the narrow and the broad leaf, and find them bare or proudly bearing last year's withered stalk, as though not aware it is spring.

March 27, 1944

Early in the dream, I was playing some kind of Run Sheep Run game with some children in the country between Los Alamos and Española. I had to teach them to lose themselves among the rocks and in a cactus forest, which seemed to have sprung up suddenly, to avoid being discovered and caught by the competing group. But it seemed more than a game. In all seriousness, they must get away. They were too young to understand the seriousness of the situation, and I had to let them think it was a game. If they were caught, they would be taken back to Los Alamos by the group that was occupying it, kind of a miscellaneous "they" like the army people who wanted to regiment children and force them into the collective mold, like Hitler, educating them for the state. These children seemed to be going north, toward Taos. If they could safely cross the river, they could be free.

Then it seemed we were on the other side of the river, but the trail was very precipitous and in some places washed away, and we had to climb steeply above the torrent, grasping at the roots. If our feet slipped, we would roll into the torrent below. It seemed a terrific undertaking for young children, but I realized the younger they were, the less fearful they were and that instinct would give them a surefootedness impossible for an older, more intellectual person. I must be careful, I thought, not to let them have the slightest inkling of my own fears. I was especially fearful lest we get into a spot where the way ahead would be blocked, for it would be impossible to turn back.

Then the dream changed. I had been away from the county some time, and I had heard indirectly that Edith Warner had had a baby. I thought it was wonderful that someone who had been so long a spinster and infertile had at last conceived, almost at the end of a woman's childbearing period. But I was distressed she hadn't let me know. I rode past her little house, longing to see her and to discover if it were true. Her house was full of people. She must have many guests for tea. If she'd had a baby, she wouldn't be serving tea, I thought; she wouldn't have time to talk to me. But I wanted to just say hello, so I got off my horse and went in. And lo! Edith was seated beside the table nursing a tiny black-haired baby. I was so excited and de-lighted; it seemed like a miracle. How happy she must be, for I knew she had always wanted a child. I was so moved that I began to cry. Yet why hadn't she told me? She said the baby was nearly a year old (it didn't look like it), and I wondered how she had let a whole year go by without communicating with me?

I have always thought of Edith with great tenderness, as the only woman I know with whom I would exchange lives. She has the kind of life that I would like to have—simple in the extreme. She lives as I would like to live, secure in her own being, deeply related to the feminine forces within the earth. She understands the Indians, and they love her and her friends. She is, in physical being, frail, yet she manages an arduous physical life with such quiet poise. She knows how to say no to the things that do not concern her. She feeds many people, both literally and figuratively—metaphorically—be-cause of her own relatedness. The world of nature is her home, the world that man seems to have forgotten.

April 30, 1944

I dreamed of an Indian who had been married to a white woman, like Mabel Dodge's Tony Lujan. I came with messages and inscribed certain symbols I had seen. He seemed to recognize their meaning. He was one of the Koshare [Tewa *kohsa,* sacred clown of the Pueblo Indians]. He dressed himself in full ceremonial regalia and started back with me.

Then I dreamed I was Edith, walking down a long corridor with a young man who in a rather fastidious way proposed marriage. I—or Edith—at once accepted him. Having been a spinster so long, everyone thought Edith not interested in marriage. The proposal had been half a joke, but she took it seriously. We went down to her house to prepare for the ceremony. Tilano [Atilano Montoya], her Indian companion, was there. I felt his age-old wisdom and equanimity, his oneness with the forces we know not of. The Indian in each of these dreams is a kind of medicine man, with healing and security for me.

I dreamed of being in the Taos Valley, apparently looking for a house. My children and I found that the bridge had been broken and mended with very thin slats. I thought we'd go down later with good lumber and repair it. But two young women who did dry cleaning said they were getting too much business, so many tourists and new residents, they couldn't keep up with it all. I said, half-playfully, that I could stop it all by taking the weak slats out of the bridge so no more traffic could come in.

President Neilson of Smith College was reading to a group of young women about some great test that was going to be given in a few days. We must get ready to take it. When he finished, he looked at me as though selecting me in a special way, as though he already knew I was chosen. He walked rapidly through the assembly and bent and kissed me tenderly on the shoulder as he passed.

June 5, 1944

Then we were in a large hall to look at the paintings. An Indian who had come with us was still boxed up in kind of a crate and very indignant because the authorities had not realized his dignity and position as one of the committee who had arranged for the exhibition. He wanted Mother to sign an affidavit for him, which she did. I wanted to sign it too, but they said my signature would not be necessary. The old Indian was one of the chief men of the pueblo and my friend; but the collective looked down on him, as on an inferior race, treated him as a servant, a peasant, not realizing the ancient, silent, creative wisdom that he represented. It was a kind of association between the introvert and the extrovert that needed establishing, a real reconciliation of opposites, which, as long as they existed separated, had no meaning.

January 23, 1947

I dreamed that I was part of a tourist crowd, and we were walking along a waterfront at the edge of a bay. Some Indians were going on it in a canoe, some kind of very ancient ceremony in which they were costumed mysteriously and bore long feather-tipped wands in their hands, as I vaguely remember seeing in Incan or Mayan illustrations. Then they were on a boat, rather large, like a large motorboat. And when the Indians came on the boat, all the people crowded toward the front and the right so that when the Indians took their place for their ceremony, the boat capsized like an overweighed canoe. I was standing on the extreme rear of the boat, but my weight was not enough to balance it. The people in the front were submerged as under a candlesnuffer, and I found myself standing at the end of the bottom of the boat, and when I realized it had overturned, I let myself jump into the water which was oily and greasy on the surface, like all bodies of water near cities. The people all came scrambling out from under, more angry than hurt, and that is what happens, I thought, to people who follow the crowd.

January 31, 1947

Dream: a pelicanlike bird flew into our big barnlike room and seized a songbird by its beak as a cat might. At first I thought it was no use to try to save the bird, but I opened the jaws of the pelican, and the little brown bird fell fainting on the floor. I picked it up and placed it in a nest on a plate rack that was on the wall. I thought the parent birds might come back to their nest even though their young had been touched by humans.

February 10, 1947

I thought, after my dream of appealing to the authority of the children's grandfather, my father, how, in fantasy, he became a stern but tender "wise old man" of Indian myth. Koshare, with infinitely beautiful gestures of fructification. With what enormous difficulty we disassociate ourselves from the Christian-Hebraic idea of God; how difficult it is to face life on one's own immediate original terms. Because God will not assume the forms we command him to assume, we do not let him come to us in his own form, which for each person must perhaps be different.

March 20, 1948

Then I seemed to be cleaning out old dead branches under a Christmas tree which should have been long ago put away; like an aged Christmas tree, it looked still green, but when touched was dry and brittle and full of dust. How one hangs onto things as though still hoping to have life in them, long preserving that which has given joy after the symbol has become stale. Then hurriedly trying to clean it all up quickly, ashamed of myself for letting it go so long, I grasped an armful of debris from the floor, but one seemed to be a branch from a thorny locust, a wild locust, which also had been saved from an earlier occasion and seemed to have leaves still and white flowers. I assumed they too would crumble, but as I pulled it, a small glass in which the branch had been stuck overturned. I had perhaps tried to root it and given up, thinking the condition wrong, the branch too mature. But it was still alive, supple, pliant. It still had the urge of life in it and needed only to be rooted and tended.

January 6, 1949

In my dream, there was something about pulling apricots off a huge tree which grew just across the fence in a neighboring yard. I felt guilty. Yet perhaps the fruit on the branches that overhung my place was mine, and anyway, I was eating only the rather overripe ones which would soon fall. Then people like Frieda, etc. were with us, also gathering apricots, a kind of Lawrencian enjoyment of the life this was, rich and bountiful. Frieda, we thought, must be extremely old, for D. H. Lawrence had died a long time ago.

Then Ferm and I were going to end our lives. For the time had come and we were not afraid. We sent a kind of map and suggestion of our place to his mother and sister, knowing this would shock them, their attitude was so different from what ours had become; so conventional and full of Christian morality.

June 28, 1949

I dreamed I went to the pueblo to some celebration to which my friend, Wynema, had invited me. On the way to the entrance, through a narrow alley, an Indian woman stopped me. They were turning away all whites, all "strangers." I said I was a friend of Wynema's, and they smilingly let me through.

Upstairs some dog howled or some ceremony of the dead began. They said a baby had been born. Strange, it whistled and sang all the time. "But this must mean it is happy," I said. No, for it was merry in such an abnormal way, excessively so, and soon would use up all its energy, and the reaction would come. The baby when I saw it lay curled like a puppy at the foot of my bed. It seemed sad that it would die soon.

July 10, 1949

J. R., who helps us around the place, looked at me yesterday in the kitchen with the terror of a trapped animal, an animal in pain who may strike out at whomever comes near, friend or foe. The veneer of civilization upon the Indian is so thin that it is frightening, even as it traps them. John suffers for he despises his past because it represents insecurity to him, a way of living which in our competitive realm has failed, and so he rejects it, grasps for some new power. What are spiritual values in such a flux? He is trying to force himself and his people to adapt to a way of life which is itself deteriorating. The whole Anglo-Saxon, highly industrialized, community of man has its own back against the wall, facing its own challenge to adapt or be defeated. "The people," great Asiatics and others, try to regain their lost birthright. Power suppressed seethes and bubbles volcanically among us. The struggle is, perhaps, between the past and present—but the future will select according to its own "instincts."

September 28, 1949

(I have been reading Navajo creation myths.) I dreamed
Wynema had been visiting me, and we went into Miera's cornfield
and began plucking and chewing cornstalks as though they were
sugarcane and were something we remembered since childhood. But
we hear Miera moving about and were afraid he would be angry, for
actually we were trespassing. So we tore ourselves away and hoped we
would find more corn near our place, but it seemed dry and hard,
only there was a sort of tent just outside the gate, and I remembered
we had stored a lot of cornstalks there. They were good, but not so
good as the fresh growing ones.

February 26, 1951

I dreamed I found myself down by the Rio Grande near Edith's
and decided to stop and see how she was. I met one of the women
from Los Alamos, and we went together. I said I knew how weak she
was and how seeing people tired her, but I would just step in the
briefest minute and say hello, tell her I loved her and thought of her.
We went in together. Edith was lying on her bed in a little sort of
perch with windows looking out upon the desert. We sat on the bed
and talked and talked. At the end of two or three hours we realized
how thoughtless we had been to demand so much of her energy, and
we left her to sleep. Then I saw the Indians coming out of the Pueblo
[San Ildefonso] fully costumed for the Buffalo dance, dark-skinned
against the pale desert background, with their green boughs in their
hands. I didn't think it was exactly the season for the Buffalo dance,
but then realized they were doing it for Edith. They were going to
dance all around her house and back and forth in front of it. Their
dancing would impart energy to the earth, would make it holy. I knew
what would heal her would be quiet, sleeping, while the mysterious
healing forces in her body and in the earth wrought wholeness. The
Indians, loving her, were dancing for her, as the Navaho also dance in
their healing ceremonies.

But crowds of people kept coming, all her multitudes of
friends who loved her as we did. I was afraid her strength would give
out; but I saw her lying in the middle of the big bed, apparently

asleep, relaxed. Then crowds of tourists began looking in the windows, and then this made me really angry, and I went out and reprimanded them and told them the woman inside was really ill. It was still a matter of life and death, and they should know enough not to come now. Most of them went, but a couple of pimply-faced young men threw their arms around me, as though to make free with me. At first I was frightened, but then I drew myself together and felt my own dignity, ordered them to leave, as I had the others—and they left.

March 27, 1951

Sarah has just phoned that Edith has gone home to die. And my nostalgia for those wonderful days on the Pajarito Plateau is physically acute. I weep. Symbol of a lost world. With all its tensions, it was beautiful, the plateau. Dear God, how I loved that landscape more than I loved any human, those horseback rides, and the smell of pines, the exploration of caves, the ruins, the hum of grasshoppers in the mountain meadows, the picnics, Tshirege, Tsankawi, and the children growing up there. And everything since as though one had been forever exiled.

May 9, 1951

Suddenly to wake up on a spring morning with the clouds lifted, the chasm, as it were, filled in.

Edith died on Friday, the fourth of May, a day on which I flew about frantically in my little cage, like a wild bird, though I knew nothing of her death until Monday. I do not believe in personal survival, yet somehow we were all travailing with her; we are somehow joined, not pent in our individual bodies as we think we are.

The effort to put into words the meaning of that life. There was a kind of acceptance of life in all that she did. The rest of us railed against it. The world was wrong, people were wrong, this must be done, that must be done. And Edith quietly listened and agreed, or questioned gently and never, never reprimanded. And then she offered for healing the quietness of the land itself, the greatness, the space, the movement and surge and change of the river.

February 9, 1952

When one gets caught in a kind of whirlpool of thinking, all one's energies are devoured.

I only remember a fragment of my dream last night where I came with Ferm to Edith's place by the Rio Grande. There were sandy dunes and drifts we climbed down, and Tilano was living in the little house beside the river. As I walked, or rode, down a kind of isthmus, a ridge of sand, I saw on my left below the ridge grotesque birds, almost like those in Ralph Hodgson's poem, "The Bull," "waiting for the flesh that dies." Yet these seemed to have an ancient patience and wisdom in them. I talked to one of the birds as I walked, but I think it did not answer me, only looked with a wisdom far surpassing that of man who makes an enemy of death. And down to the edge of the river, missing Edith and yet feeling her there and all that she carried in her, and Tilano, the "wise old man" living patiently in the little house, the wise acceptance of them both in life. And Ferm, wiser than I, up there on the bank, talking with him, and somehow a feeling of birds and bird cages. All this a little archetypal, like one of the huts in the forest in fairy tales where the wise man or woman lives. And wanting, somehow, to go to Tilano at once and take his hand.

And so why despair, when the guardians are there always, not talking, but existing. The little house was foursquare. One has the voices within: be humble, be peaceful. Think of the river, the whole life of rivers, the river valley with the ancient levels, the chasms, the rapids, the flat swamps, "the woman who dwells at the place of healing by the river" ["The Woman Who Dwells" in *The House at Otowi Bridge* (121)]. Edith's great concern for man—and her steady stand against being swept from her place by any great collective moment. The humble and the acquiescent. How can one avoid the temptation of anxiety, the feeling that one must do this or that?

Be still and know ["that I am God," Psalms 46:10]. One could talk oneself out against Edith's silences. She was like the rock or the lone tree or the iron stove, perhaps, of fairy tales. She herself made so little comment, nothing more than the murmur of the leaves on the trees. There was a great healing in her silence. Most of us kept trying, like Canute, to bid the waves roll back, but she kept her place, and the waves seemed to divide, as they came to the rock on which she stood, and rolled around, or else rose and fell gently over the surface.

Her relationship with the world was never theoretical—but always human and personal. And to her, truly, all persons were equal—from "Oppie" [Oppenheimer] to the smallest child in the pueblo. She hated and feared the bomb, but she passed no judgment, nor ever closed her heart against the men who made it.

And it is as though the dream stayed with me all day, as though the cleavage between day and night somehow healed, as though where there had been a chasm there was now a thoroughfare, or at least a leafy path, or a fallen tree bridging the abyss. All day Edith's own spirit was with me, so vividly, so tenderly, so completely. And I realized how I carried the house by the river within me. The house with its shade trees—in the dream—like horse chestnuts, two, I thought, in the bare swept dooryard. And Tilano and Ferm, talking man-talk under the trees, and perhaps the "talking bird" there in its cage, not as a prison, but companionably. And perhaps replacing the grotesque birds at the left of the ridge. All day I managed to keep "opinion" from me. Those birds—were they a sinister shadow of myself, a quaking, cawing omen, ominous?

With you, dear Edith, it was a complete selflessness. Your making yourself the channel, that mirror, that kind of bridge, that passage, that nameless connection with eternity. The discipline of your life, its frugality. Not self-imposed, but accepted, beautifully accepting its limitations, working itself out within its limitations.

February 10, 1952

Thinking, as I went to bed, how we are swamped by the tons of "information," the magazines, the radio, the papers, the institutes. Glutted, we are, with newsprint. And, as I cleaned up the debris at the end of the day, I thought, what, after all, is the content? Edith has been so much in my mind. I thought of her life, consisting of contact with the earth and with living people. How firmly she excluded everything not pertinent to such a life. Her communication was with another more eternal world than the world of politics which now swamps us. If one could devote oneself to living as Edith did—to tuning in on that other world.

Edith, you knew who you were, what you wanted, and resolutely put aside every temptation to be or do otherwise. You wished to dwell close to the springs of your own being. Never to take in anything that is not oneself, that is true chastity of spirit. And to all of us who came seeking, you gave quietness, silence—and that other kind of communication we have only when words fail us or when we renounce speaking.

You especially hated women with theories. The anthropologists who visited the pueblo and fitted everything into some preconception.

The white man's wisdom has resulted only in the atomic bomb. But you knew the ancient wisdom that will outlive man and all his bombs, the wisdom of the earth, the mysterious relation we should have, could have, that the Indians have had—with life, with helping the earth to live, with helping the sun. We have made a god of man, and that is not good.

February 17, 1952

I dreamed again of Edith:

1. But first, all about some young girl who was taking steps to adopt a baby. But in the meantime, the baby was stolen and snatched by lawless people of some kind, out of a crowd, and across the boundaries of a stream, into another country, another state.

And then a man came, a kind of outdoorsman, forest or park service, and offered to help. But he said it was doubtful she'd get the other one back. It was best to start looking for another, not keep the heart set on the one that had vanished. . . . And a kind of "health department" sat on a hill above the town, a domed arch of rock, exposing the ancient granite.

2. Then a strange, not quite complete shift, as though we were on a high plateau, in a building like a national park headquarters, a huge castlelike building, and I expected my son, Allen, and went to meet him—or expected someone and it turned out to be Allen. He had only a two- or three-day leave and was driving a Model T pickup. And I was driving a big green Chevy pickup and though doubtful of my ability, seemed to drive it well; lots of power and sturdy work in the low gears to go up the steep hills, and Allen was to follow me back to headquarters, but I got there first. Sitting at a long table, with Ferm at the other end, on the same side as me, and the officials, wives, and

relatives, and at last Allen came, so tall and smiling and happy, and sat at the foot of the table and was given food, even though late, and Ferm, two or three places away from him, began shouting as though he were miles away, trying to impose some plan of his, and Allen smilingly answered, courteously, but holding to his own course.

And we were outside and looked back and saw houses all similar to the left, in a kind of backward L from the main building, and these housed prisoners, but things were being modernized, and the prisoners were to be freed. For it was kind of a medieval setting, a kind of regimentation, a "they" difficult to define, but like the "they" at Los Alamos, that Mr. Connell, the director, stood for, a sort of feudal domination by a "they." And Allen, of course, always the independent individual, driving his little Model T, not powerful and modern, but individual. (Perhaps like the shaggy horse in the fairy tale, which comes to the castle in his simple innocence, where tyranny still rules. This is my son toward whom I feel myself most tender. There is always the Parsifal quality, the good-heartedness of the "younger brother.")

3. And then the dream changes again, and I begin thinking of Edith, and a postcard is brought me from my friend, Ethel Frohman, badly blurred over, that I had been expecting. "This is it," the message said. "Edith died" . . . telling me how they discovered it when they went to give her her bath, and then the scene enacted instead of read. I, seeing Edith on her bare, high bed, emaciated, still, dead . . . and the nurse bringing a tray and realizing when she touched her . . . a heart condition, and then they lift her and put her on a stretcher or litter and carry her past me. But her eyes are open, blue and clear, and I try to say goodbye and that I know how she is facing death. I want her to know I understand. And it seems she was perhaps to have been married. But it is better not, though she and the young woman have been friends, have hardly known each other that long or that well, to have a deathbed marriage. And the three of us talk, Edith now seeming quite vigorous about the treatments and the psychologies in which she had hoped but which had proved disappointing, especially the "we," and I supplied the name of Kunkel . . . All ending in the theme of death, not death; and marriage, not marriage.

The Edith dreams have almost always had reference to her spinsterhood, for she lived and died "Miss" Warner. And yet her influence was great, for she had all the qualities of the (psychological) virgin. She was always "one in herself" . . . And yet—the implication of the dream of the heart. And only after that long look, as she is carried past, does life begin to stir. And Allen, of all my children, is the one who has the heart.

Edith, you knew what you were, what you wanted. You wished to dwell close to the springs of your own being, and many of us have a wish for that, but not many the sturdiness to achieve it. When we held discussion groups at your place, you sat and listened, and never spoke. Did we, I wonder, remind you of vultures, squabbling over the dry carcasses of something long since dead?

Were you brought back to me, in dream, by my sudden revulsion at my own theorizing? Suddenly I see how we have made "man" the individual, the victim, of our theories about "man" in mass.

To whom shall we go? You had the water of life. In your silence were the words of eternal life.

March 17, 1952

This is St. Patrick's Day, "who drove the snakes from Ireland." In the valley between Algondones and Albuquerque, the trees were swelling with leaf; the green was ready to be worn; in the yellow light of the passing dust storm, color was weird and uncustomary—the pale yellow of clouds—the air, all blue, hidden, mountains obliterated, the sky a yellow haze, the trees gray but tipped oh, so invisibly with the green that had not quite been released. "Oh, Lazarus, come forth!" And the resurrection myths of so many people surging in the background of awareness. This death and resurrection of life that is so tremendous a unifying factor of all myth. Persephone's return from Hades; Jesus risen from the grave; Changing Woman of the Navaho; the rebirth symbols of the mysteries, the pulse of life, springtime—and it is curious that the celebration of this phase has belonged always to the woman's mysteries. Even in Albuquerque, in the shops, the spring fashions on the complacent dummies: it is the woman who is reborn in springtime.

And I think it is important to realize, to be aware of, to take our part in the cycles of the year. To have lived on the earth is to have experienced its spring and winters, its rains and snows and droughts, the return of the birds, the sap stirring in the trees, the blood too moving differently in the heart.

April 14, 1952

Blake believed that Jesus taught above all else the forgiveness of sin.

It flashed upon me as I thought how we all in a sense become tainted with "original sin." The nations into which we are born—not one but which is, in its way, a piracy. Yet we—none of us—can make atonement, except by beginning here, now, with our own lives. I think somehow we have to overcome this tremendous sense of sin that our Christian culture has hammered into us. Cultivate the faculty of awareness—of wonder —instead of criticism. The heart leaps on mornings like this to hear the meadowlarks singing. I pause at night to wonder, beholding the marvelous order of the stars—and when a man overcomes his own grasping self, when an act of love is done.

April 16, 1952

Outside a brisk wind whipped daffodils into bloom. Birds sang, a chorus, almost of meadowlarks. She noticed the pale, blue small flower on the creeping phlox, pale lavender with an outline of purple. Great, gray-bodied bees come to it, piercing it with a kind of elephantine, woolly proboscis. Not only the sea around us but the earth around us. The holy mountains of the horizon—deities? Or the residence of deities?

And now the ferocity of the rivers of America. The unleashed power of water, the tremendous potential. The images of Yellowstone awakening from winter. She has stood at the head of the Missouri. Three Forks, where the headwaters come together, itself another tributary, foams and rushes through the golden canyon, the jade-colored water, the ospreys soaring. This is the heart of America, this high silence, with its dreaming lakes, its subterranean fires . . . (The secret passion I have always had for the headwaters of rivers.)

One thinks of the deities of America waiting to be discovered. Before man came, did the finger of God move? A wonder to think of the silent land, of the storms moving over the silent land, of the splendor of sunrise and sunset and no human eye to see; the lichens creeping upon the raw rocks; the tidal creatures, depositing their shells in the basins of the long dead seas. The animals emerge from the waving forests and fight and devour one another. Man comes, the greatest carnivore of all, the greatest mammal, the most helpless infancy, most invincible in his maturity.

Wednesday, after Easter [1952]

The snow-covered mountains seem to lean against the rounded blue of the distant sky. The plaza of Santo Domingo Pueblo is at the center of the world. East and west, north and south, the mountains bound the world. Above, the sky arches over, and the white clouds are curved and curled and interlaced like ripples upon water. Under the horizontal surface of the earth is mystery, darkness from which all growing things have emerged and from which man himself now emerges to take part in the ritual of growth. The two great kivas stand, one at the end of each of the two plazas, round as ancient watch towers, earth-colored, symmetrical, the ladders leaning upward in a strong diagonal, poised against the sky, uniting the dark world with the bright.

The dancers in the plaza all hold branches of evergreen. At first one is aware simply of that great mass of moving green, dark against the bare yellowish earth, cool under the blazing sky. The plaza is a long rectangle, and the rectangles of the houses as though they have been drawn by a child's hand, the broken perspective of the roofs, and beyond the roofs, the faint aureole of trees in their new green and one great delicate mass of peach blossom against a dusty, spotted hill. A windmill turning, also is symbolic, the disk of the great fan, the pyramidal undercarriage, the horizontal motion of the wind transformed into the vertical motion of the piercing rod, sucking water up out of the silent ground.

The women who are not dancing lean against the house walls, or sit under the portals with babes in their arms, or cluster upon the rooftops, bright in their Easter clothes, shawls of all colors and every variety of printed and commercially dyed cotton cloth. Some of the dancers, those of the other kiva group, for whom this is an intermission, wait in the doorways, their black-embroidered mantels fastened over one shoulder, bare feet, loose hair, the blue-terraced *tablitas* upon their heads, heavy necklaces of blue turquoise and silver about their necks. This is midafternoon, and each group must have gone through the pattern of the dance several times already. The girls' faces are dusty, but they stand poised, not as though particularly fatigued.

A medley of bells and shells; men's voices chanting. Then suddenly one is aware more than anything of the drum, the pivot of sound upon which the whole pattern of sound and movement turns.

There is nothing, no nothing in all our civilized experience to equal the spell, the ancient irresistible magic, of the beaten drum. The whole of man's strength goes into it. One hand holds the great weight, balanced, a little against one knee, against the leg below the knee. The right arm brings the wrapped stick down against the taut surface of the drum, not lightly, but with continuous full power. The man's whole body and breath and being goes into it, without reservation, without ceasing, without interruption, without rest, except for a brief interval of no more than a moment or two between the differing figures of the dance. At least once during each complete performance, the drum is reversed. Steadily, without losing a beat, the drummer lays it on the ground, catches the looped handle at the other end, flicks it into position, and all one knows is that the pitch suddenly changes, while the rhythm continues and the strength of the percussion never alters.

The rhythm is not the monotonous one-two-three-four that it seems at first to be. There are repeated intricate caesuras that break up the measures which the feet and movement of the dancers must follow. And always among the long opposing lines of men, of women, of tiny, solemn, and sometimes giggling children, the Koshare weave with their supple and eloquent gestures, their painted clown faces, part ridicule, part endless mystery, a blend of mockery, of solemnity that is as remarkable as the tears of the men who sometimes weep for joy—an assurance, a poise in their hands, as though they were the eternal hands which summon life out of the brimming sky, which draw life up again out of the brooding earth.

But perhaps it is the chorus of singing men that one can never tire of watching. Their rather full-flared trousers are gay cotton, like the women's shawls, and most of the shirts, belted and hanging

outside the trousers, are brightly colored. Some of the faces are
young, but the ones we notice are the old men, who all afternoon
long sing and gesture, some with rapture in their faces, the joy of an-
ticipation, participation. . . . I am so grateful that the pueblo and the
dancers are part of our environment, part of our lives. We can't help
but have a different relation to them than the ordinary tourist. They
speak to us constantly in a language without words; they remind us
of the cosmic setting of our lives. They are a treasure, [by] which we
are reminded seasonally, [that] the life of reason, of intellect, of fact,
is not all, not the whole of life.

April 20, 1952

This morning the sky is all soft, sorrowful gray; the tops of the
mountains misted. We are hidden from the sun. The phoebes crying
endlessly their mournful note—like a warning? like desperation?—
and yet they go about their daily lives calmly.

Yesterday, on the shoulder of the mountain, high above the
plain and solitary, the grains of shining sand in the flowing water, the
pool backed up by tree roots and the burden of dead oak leaves. At
the base of the huge scarred pine tree, the root, gnawed tender, and
across the scar, the reflected sunlight flickered, mirrored from the
bright surface of water, a pattern of shifting light and shadow as in-
substantial as smoke, yet lovely and touching in its motion. That into
this dark cavern of the wounded tree, sunlight should yet come, as
though for an hour or two a ray of light should enter a prisoner's cell.

When we were young, we were taught to think of "eternal
hills," and yet to look upon the mountains and the plains is to be
aware more than anything of constant change, of ebb and flow, of
form and elevation.

It is not only with my eyes I am becoming conscious of the
earth, but through my eyes the earth itself becomes conscious. To
learn of the past of man's life in other lands is not so much to accu-
mulate fact, but somehow to awaken memory—as though all this
were stored in the cosmic mind, a mind that sometimes slumbers
deeply, sometimes dreams, sometimes wakes to bright awareness,
and then sinks to sleep again.

There is a world, a universe, that is formed in each one of us, where all the fragments of our partial experience are somehow stored to make a whole—a unity.

April 28, 1952

It was the day a painter [Gustave Baumann] died. The world, that is the world around us, was beautiful. The sage was that deep new blue-green which he had translated to canvas. Clouds rolled and sprang upwards around the horizon, always bolting upwards, as the warm air of the earth formed against the cold air of heaven and at the area of contact, became visible, though so still, surging, moving.

We had driven far and picnicked in a cluttered tumble of igneous rock, granite, and crystalline early crust of earth, here a vein of quartz, or pegmatite, and pure shining mica layered below it. Oh, monument of ancient furnaces, of heat, of cooling. These rocks, as our human eyes and hands passed over them, suddenly becoming, as it were, conscious, receiving memory through us.

On a sharp cliff of granite grew piñon trees and thrived. Trees everywhere reached, reached toward the sky and light. Everything was energy and the discipline of structure. Why have we made an enemy of death, we men, when death ends nothing, but only brings change? And what fierce, huge energies are locked within the atoms of our dust?

The energy within the crystals of granite which the growing tree unlocks and the birds and squirrels feast upon, the energy within the clustered seed, and we men, burning the slaughtered wood, are warmed by the pent energies within the logs.

"All flesh is grass"—and what is grass but earth and sun?

"Energy," says Blake, "is eternal delight."

May 8, 1952

Strange and beautiful the day with Ferm and Allen beyond the Pueblo [San Ildefonso] near Lucero Canyon. The tangle of wild plum along the road, the scent of it, Indians plowing their fields, each his own field, each set off from each other by the plum thickets, the loneliness—perhaps I should say the solitude of each man as he plowed or irrigated, the relation, I thought, between man and earth, something so ancient, so touching, this border of fertile land at the base of the mountain, the apronlike outwash, tapering off into the flat and arid valley, the mountain itself, rocky, and the rock itself split into veins, and cracks along the sides, each vein a sort of vent from which issues the delicate feminine green of spring growth.

The relationship between man and earth here a holy and reverent thing, the horses with their jingle of harnesses, the knifelike thrust of the plow; in some fields, mounds of stones half the height of a man that had been taken from the ground before it could be cultivated. The beauty of the earth, the fertility, the wonder, not only that all flesh is grass, but that all grass, and so all flesh, is rock, and rock is sun stuff, torn violently from the globe of fire that is our sun.

And so in some mysterious way, inherent in the dust from which our flesh is made, is all our consciousness, our intellect, our emotion, our will. And so, through the convoluted brain of man, the earth becomes slowly conscious of herself. The sun beholds and measures and rejoices at the phenomenon of light distributed in rainbows.

May 20, 1952

I dreamed I was in a canyon with Ferm; upon the shoulder of it, a large, detached rock (lava) and on the side of the rock, a large pictograph of the Plumed Serpent, like the one at Tshirege, only larger. I climbed up an old trail, hand and footholds, and came to a sort of cave, and on a slab of rock, two more symbols, a serpent (I think) and a very small, delicate sheaf of corn (like the one on Inscription Rock [El Morro National Monument, Cibola County, New Mexico])—the floor inside very clean, a basket in the floor. This is where the old men of the tribe had come, I thought, when driven out of the valley or main canyon below, and how long had they lived here thus secretly, a kind of "underground" life. And I called to Ferm who came around another way and couldn't get to the cave and had to go back and around. And we saw some children playing in the canyon, watching us as "natives" watch tourists. And I suddenly had a feeling of suspicion. We pulled up the basket from the floor, and underneath, or attached to it, a paper or a picture of people in Victorian clothes standing under gaslights. So if the basket belonged to such a late era, it must have been "planted" here, and the whole thing was a hoax. I should have suspected, as indeed I knew I had, because the floor of the cave was so clean, swept and not deep with debris and the musty, dusty smell of the cliff dwellings, the cave remembered so well from my childhood, the smell of old twigs and dried animal dung. How disappointing it was and yet having a meaning of its own—the Indians "exploiting" the tourists, their secret revenge to make fools of us, and we do not take graciously to being made fools of. I should not have been taken in so easily. I should have "known better"—the ancient treasure never to be found in so conspicuous a setting, so plainly labeled with obvious symbols. Always it is, I think, obscure, and to be come upon alone, and not somehow with searching—the small animals have guarded it and know the way to it but do not lead you, and then one digs beneath the dry, powdered dust of time.

June 1, 1952

"There is a new fetish, the standard of living. . . . Surely it is time to recognize not a standard of living but a standard of values in which beauty, comeliness, and the possibility of solitude have a high place among human needs.
. . . In America vast stretches of countryside have the lack of form and sanctity which show it only to have been tilled since the age of exploitation; the American people, the most successful materialists in the history of the world, are now often to be found speaking with loathing in their own life, and with nostalgic envy of the happiness of primitive people."—Jacquetta Hawkes[1]

February 10, 1954

Took my quick walk as a form of worship and thought of the delusion of comfort. Perhaps it is the need for comfort which more than anything has betrayed us.
And thought how the spirit is distilled from everything we eat, and how the plants distill it from the rock; and has the rock not distilled it from the sun, the source of life?

Oh, Edith and Tilano, teach me how to find the god within the stone.

Thinking, the antidote to materialism may be to regain the worship of life.

February 11, 1954

More and more to find a side of life mirrored in you, Edith, that calls to be reunited to the life of western man. We can't, most of us, go back to the simplicities and rigors of natural living, but we must regain the relationship to the earth that we have lost.

February 13, 1954

Edith had a firm self-will, a real stubbornness of being, as well as obedience. But there was never a hint that she thought the Powers would do her will.

For it became a study in the use of power. "The force that through the green fuse drives the flower" [Dylan Thomas]. The wordless power that surrounds one in rock and stream and sky. There is nowhere energy made more wordlessly visible. The energy of heat, of light, of motion, and finally of life itself. Tilano taught Peter [Edith's goddaughter, whose nickname was Peter] to find the God in the stone. John Boyd taught Edith to see the significance in a stone. . . [recorded in *The House at Otowi Bridge*]. What of the scientists tearing apart the atom?

Strange that too should take place upon these mesas where in the kivas the "force that through the green fuse drives the flower" was so long worshipped.

The belief that dancing men could transmit power to the earth. My dream that the Indians did their Buffalo Dance all around Edith's house as she lay dying, to fill the earth with power for her. At the end of her life the power of atomic energy itself was enlisted in her service. Atomic energy, knowledge without love. The symbolic relationship to life, the ecological. That is what the Indian has that the white man lacks—altogether lacks.

February 21, 1954

About Edith: This intuitive feeling of oneself into another's being. The "secret" was she made a god of something other than "security." She trusted in her inner voice. She had that combination of
trust and determination. Yes, one felt that Awanyu, the Plumed Serpent, was the god—the divinity that enthralled her. Her being
driven into this utterly strange land a little like Myra Behn's going to
Gandhi. The sudden recognition, in a woman, of her fate. She rejected the mold of her external life, the collective pattern, the tradition, and strikes out, choosing her own way with complete devotion.

Niels Bohr called it her "bravity"—There is that moment as she
sits on the steps, the first night in her new house, facing the unknown, and accepting it. Where did she begin to learn the secret of
"keeping herself clear"? "If our hearts are right, then he must come,"
she said.

This is the religious motive. She had no "mission" but that of
learning to keep her heart right, "clear, not clogged by ideas of what
we think ought to happen," she writes.

The "power" she invoked—the power she was aware of—the
physicists seeking for it with their minds, the energy at the heart of
the matter.

The first physicists were themselves poets, sensitive men, as
dedicated in their way as the men are in their kiva. But the trouble
was, they were not free men; they were controlled by the statesmen,
the military. And the statesmen were seeking mastery, knowledge
without love.

The tragedy that all their knowledge could not save this one
person dying. But hers was the victory, the victory of the spirit that,
having been obedient to life, faced death without fear. She was like
the "blade of grass," as conceived by Blake; she was the link between
the ancient instinctive knowledge and the new. The "power" is there,
but whether it benefits or destroys us depends on whether our hearts
are "right." Does this mean the utter casting out of self from the
heart?

The mysterious effect on mankind of those few isolated persons
who have abandoned personal security, the guidance of the striving
will.

In rejecting that which says, "All these things will I give thee"—they threw off the servitude, the bondage. Daily bread, that was all she asked for. No, peace and beauty were all she prayed for.

It was her "poverty" that endeared her to the Indians, and that they were able to help her; her humility, her unassumingness. I remember her willingness to accept without being either superior or inferior.

The mountains and the mesas befriended her, as they never would me, because she came among them naked, empty-handed, and asked nothing.

February 26, 1954

"If when we dance and our hearts are right, he must come."

You [Edith] never talked to me about any of these things, and that has always been a kind of hurt inside, as though I had been rejected. But when I look back, I see how proud, how full of my own self I always was, how defensive and rebellious and incapable of giving my own self up. I haven't learned yet, Edith, I haven't learned yet—but I grow more conscious and attentive to the struggle each day.

Always wanting everything my own way. Filled with fine intuitions of the god in the stone, worshipping "nature" in an intellectual way, but using everything I knew in my own struggle for power over myself and everything else. Through Quakerism I have come close at times to the Force that flowed into you—but I practice it too rarely. I haven't learned to keep that circle of silence with me at all times.

One needs ritual to focus one's attention. How different your humble, silent seeking, and the noisy, ostentatious evangelism of us all. The mysterious religion simply is not evangelical. It is taught only in secret by one to another.

March 6, 1954

The moment today when I realized that to live here we must not only think the mountain is holy, but know it—think of its holiness each time we look at it—focus upon it the spirit of all holiness which we feel in us. A mountain is made holy by men who endow it with holiness. And so I thought this, and looked; suddenly rays of light came through the western cloud, and the sharp-rocked fins of the mountain glowed with a kind of joy. It was holy, and something joyful passed between us in that moment of recognition. It has been stamped with holiness by all those who have seen it so.

We know it is the relationship between earth and sky that creates our summer rains—in truth the heat of the sun and the cooling of the mountains. There must be evaporation—condensation—precipitation. Rain in the summertime is never gentle—it begins with the blackening of bright clouds and the streaks of lightning, the roar of thunder; all demonstrations of hostility, of violence. And the fallen rain rushes in a torrent through the dry riverbeds and pours with fierce energy off the lips of the mesas. Demonstrations of energy, of power, of force.

Force which the Indian does not, in arrogance, seek to master, but to adjust himself to in harmony.

How strange that the development of the atomic energy at Los Alamos demanded the most unstinting cooperation from all nations. As the Indian men gather in their secret kivas, the wise men of our time gathered behind the barbed wire on the mesas and probed into the mystery. Was this knowledge without love?

March 18, 1954

Yesterday morning they said, "Wind and blowing dust by afternoon," so I went outside about eight thirty and started tidying up the inner garden. It was warm and bright and calm until nearly eleven. I planted the sweet peas at the upper end, where the clematis used to be, and gave mulch and water to the rhubarbs unfolding bold and vital out of the dry earth.

In the afternoon the wind and dust became terrific. The sky was so yellow one could hardly see to Llano, and all the mountains were obliterated. The wind quieted around six. The dust cloud passed and leaned, black and heavy, against the flanks of the mountain. Then a little snow fell, just lightly and mercifully feathering the ground. In the night, the wind came up again, fierce and angry and cold. The sky is a billow of gray cloud—but no dust.

I had been meditating about Edith—and in the dream I saw her. She was seated at a table, a shadowy figure, yet I knew it was she and [I] was speaking to her sister of her—knowing how far I was from the attainment of tranquility which had become hers.

She represented a spiritual height, or state, to which I aspired with all my heart, and yet still partly unconscious, because she was in shadow, and because I could not communicate with her directly but only with her sister. The table was an oblong one. She sat on a bench near the end of it. It had something to do with her great capacity for nourishing others.

Remember [as Edith had said] "I was but a channel"—remember that utter self-effacement—not obliteration—but the self giving it-self away to form a channel for a greater thing than self. I think I must try to write the book by creative imagination entirely—in the form of meditation or contemplation—of communicating love.

Two
Time Buried in Oneself

Hazel Pond, Ashley III, Peggy, and Dotty, ca. 1912. Courtesy Los Alamos Historical Museum Archives, Peggy Pond Church Collection.

Alas

Alas, my love I grow older.
The nights seem colder.
Morning no longer
sings me awake as it used to
with birds
or the sounds of fish leaping.
The nets that I cast for my dreams
are torn and too heavy
to lift out of the draining water.

Day breaks
and I lie in my bed
like a chick
feeling my warmth curved
close as a shell around me.
There is frost on the window.
Ice crystals live and
growing into forests.
The sun will rise soon and melt them.
The slow fires that burn in my blood
even while I sleep, and keep it moving
do not warm me as well as they used to.
The stars seem colder.

I do not dream of love anymore,
only sometimes of death in deep waters.
What will it seem like, I wonder, not to waken?
The world will go on, I know—
summer and winter,
morning and evening,
birds coming back in spring,
and rivers carving valleys
and filling them up again,
seas rising and falling.
But what when the eye does not wake
to see or the heart to sing it?

How I begrudge the body's slow death;
would rather be seized and eaten
by an eagle or a sharp fish
than by this inward worming.
Must we live at the last in a house with dirty windows
and doors that will not open,
and chimneys clogged and the hearthfire grown too
    sluggish
to make real flames anymore?
To desire nothing anymore
except sleep?
If one could only
spin some kind of cocoon
and then wait mindless
as a caterpillar that winters on a bare branch.

                                        (1963)

Whatever it was in Edith Warner's life and in her writing of
Edith's life that prompted Peggy Church to rethink and revalue her
journals in the 1960s also influenced her use of the journals in new
ways. Turning sixty years old during this decade, she "returned to
landscape," using memories of her parents and analysis of the Pajarito
experience as antidotes for aging. For if loss of her friend Edith
Warner and of her daily life on the plateau marked the earlier
Pajarito journals, the physical realization of the loss of her own youth
prompted the recollections of the 1960s. What confluences of genet-
ics and social shaping had generated such different responses to the
New Mexico wilderness in her father and mother? Indeed, what were
the elements of the deeper psychological makeup of each and how
may they have influenced her own personality?

To answer these questions, Church originally entitled the 1960s
Pajarito journals "Littlebird," playing not only on the Anasazi "place
of the bird people," but also on the multiple ways in which the bird
metaphor represented ancient influences, the classical mythology
of her education, and her father's playful "a little bird told me so"
responses to her questions as a child. Indeed, Church was deeply interested in the relationship between the magical (and to adults,

seemingly mystical) world of children and the more traditional, arduous, and rigid adult world.

Church turned again for understanding and possibilities of interpretation to the principles of Carl Jung, whose psychological theories suggested personality might be understood through identifying recurrent symbols or archetypes, which became metaphors for understanding so-called male and female attributes and actions. These archetypes included what we might call character types, such as the Terrible Mother, as well as archetypal experiences, for instance, any cultural rite of passage from childhood to adulthood. Further, the active creation of one's identity, in Church's interpretation of Jung, involved the balance within the self of the animus and anima, attributes of the male and female within one person. Thus, in Church's attempt to reconcile the idealistic dreamer, her father, with the sometimes buffoonlike and physically overwrought actions of the same man, she admitted to a "shadow" side of his personality, the dark side, the Terrible Mother, who could be controlling and even mean-spirited. Because Church, as a child, reveled in the free-spirited life of seemingly endless adventures, less restricted in the outdoors than had she been in an urban society, she wondered as well about the origins of her own dark side, when as an adult she lost her temper or felt hostile or rebellious.

These journals therefore contain Church's own attempts at interpreting behaviors and events on the basis of her reading of mythology, folklore, and Jungian psychology. Such analysis employed dream recording and "interpolations," as she sometimes called them. And within this cross-cultural, yet Western psychological reading, is her creation of the child character, Quince, who as alter ego allows Church to write of her youthful, freewheeling nature in opposition to her family and society's expectations of girls and women.

No doubt the journals' reexamination of childhood and family and the creation of Quince parallel her new research project: a youth or adolescent biography of the writer, Mary Austin. During the 1960s, Church took on another woman's life, one very different in personality and public accomplishments from Edith Warner's. Peggy's goal in the Austin biography was to discover through re-reading the childhood of Austin how such a talented and gifted writer also possessed what for Church was an ego-driven, reputation-seeking, and dominating personality. The influences that Church sought to discover and evaluate in her own life were also those she treated as a biographer of Austin. She kept separate Austin journals, including a dream log, but though she rarely directly refers to the Austin research she is doing or the materials she is reading on Austin during her 1960s journal period, the work is necessarily an analog to the Pajarito Journals.

Ultimately, the creation of a point of view through Quince (that is, third person limited, yet obviously fueled by an autobiographical intent that suggests first person) allows Church to objectify herself. And this point of view is directly related to the Pajarito as place. Eudora Welty has explained this phenomenon well in her own attempt to assess how sense of place and point of view are linked. She writes:

> It may be that place can focus the gigantic voracious eye of genius and bring its gaze to point. Focus, then means awareness, discernment, order, clarity, insight—they are the attributes of love. The art of focusing itself has beauty and meaning; it is the art that continued in, turns art into meditation, into poetry. The question of place resolves itself into point of view.

Peggy Church accomplished this focus, not only in the implications of Quince and her obvious rebellious or dark side, but in Quince's metamorphosis as symbolized in the shift in imagery from a westernized, social view to that native to the place she lived, the American Southwest. For example, the Native American and Spanish words, myths, and legends that Quince learns experientially replace the conventional European ones. Possibly Church's recollection of her need for more demonstratively expressed love from her mother caused her to understand some of Mary Austin's aggressive behavior as compensation for feeling unloved or accepted. Therefore, Church objectifies some of the traditionally accepted thoughts, feelings, and behavior in writing about Quince as "she," allowing for distance to analyze her own rebellious behavior and the freedom to create a unique, not conventional self. That the Quince character is an exercise in self-acceptance is very telling and interesting as we think about the writer's need to revisit the sanctity of childhood landscape and its modeling effects on the formulation of her personality and values. Implicit in this section of the journals is the mission of the awakening eye to review one's psychological growth, perhaps most especially in one's waning years. All the more reason to realize one's own transformation through the "time buried in one-self," directly lived, remembered, or imaginatively reconstructed, as Church alerts us in this poem of the same period:

Among the Holy Stones

The world I moved through
all day
seemed as much inside me
as it did all around.

Shakespeare's "delighted spirit"
got mixed with Blake's bird,
that "vast universe of delight" our senses
most often keep closed out.

These were
once fiery New Mexico mountains we walked on.
Inside, a mountain of transfiguration
became their reflection.

"In your own Bosom you bear your heaven
and Earth and all you behold."

We drank our thermos of coffee on a hillside
among the holy stones.

(1965)

Ashley Pond, when he first came to New Mexico. Courtesy Los Alamos Historical Museum Archives, Peggy Pond Church Collection.

Peggy Pond, center, with siblings Ashley and Dorothy, ca. 1914. Courtesy Hugh Church Family.

Riding party at Guaje Mountain Lookout; Hazel and Ashley Pond are at left on the back row, 1910s. Courtesy Los Alamos Historical Museum Archives, Peggy Pond Church Collection.

Mary Austin directing the play *Fire,* in Carmel, California, July 26, 1913. Author's collection.

Peggy Pond, 1923.
Courtesy Los Alamos
Historical Museum Archives,
Peggy Pond Church Collection.

Peggy Pond and Fermor Church in
1923, the year before they married.
Courtesy Los Alamos Historical Museum Archives, Peggy Pond Church
Collection.

Hazel and Peggy Pond, with Boris, Pajarito Canyon, ca. 1915. Courtesy Los Alamos Historical Museum Archives, Peggy Pond Church Collection.

Peggy with two unidentified friends. Courtesy Los Alamos Historical Museum Archives, Peggy Pond Church Collection.

Three students at the Los Alamos Ranch School for Boys learn the art of becoming robust young men, ca. 1920s. Courtesy Los Alamos Historical Museum Archives, Peggy Pond Church Collection.

Left to right: Hugh, Allen, Ted, Peggy and Fermor Church, 1930s. Courtesy Los Alamos Historical Museum Archives, Peggy Pond Church Collection.

Peggy Pond Church at play with Hugh, Allen, and Ted, circa 1936. Courtesy Los Alamos Historical Museum Archives, Peggy Pond Church Collection.

The Church family, Thanksgiving 1960, in the backyard of Hugh and Kathleen's first home in Albuquerque. Back row: Elizabeth, Ted, and Malcolm Church; Kathleen Church; Margie Wakefield (Carolyn's mother); Carolyn and Allen Church. Front row: Hugh Church; Allen's daughter Nancy; Ted's daughter Robyn; Peggy Pond Church with Janet. From the Kathleen Church Collection.

Journals, 1960s

At an altitude of 7000 feet the sun is indeed lord. The sun fills the deep Rio Grande valley with heat; the waves of heat rise upward. Heat waves shimmer. Clouds begin to form over the mountains, very white at first, then becoming shadowed from their bases upward, rounded as thick leaved, closely curled cabbage roses, full of movement, towering upwards, seething into the immaculate blue sky. Around midday or earlier, rumbles of thunder deep as the voice of a nursery ogre, the blaze of lightning.

June clouds are mostly sterile, lazy, so-called "cumulus of fair weather." They hover lightly over the horizon, decorative, innocent, and sexless as children, scarcely creating any shadow. The sun pours down its arrogant and merciless light. Grass becomes brittle; the lupines stop growing; the earth underfoot grows hard and crusty as the scab on a half-healed wound. The soil bakes and splits irregularly around the margin of shrinking waterholes. The stream which has been flowing brisk and clear since spring, subsides and vanishes under its sandy bed. Pine needles grow slack and darken.

For those two years I began to experience the earth and the rhythms of the earth as an Indian would. There were the two years just before puberty when I was, perhaps, as much a boy as girl. The incipient breasts had not yet begun to form, nor body hair to emerge. I was conscious of the desire to be male rather than female, to be hunter-on-the-trail, to be tried as warrior.

I already knew about horses and the bodily agility that comes of adapting oneself to the motion and care of an animal. I saw young horses being broken and was given a colt myself to raise. I watched my father training his puppies, saw them cower and whimper when he shamed them for making their puddles. I used to beat my own pony furiously with the end of my bridle when she would not mind me.

The pine tree which I could see from my window at night, which became the landmark, fixed and steady, against which the stars moved in procession, streaming up from the sky from the east, as through a great canyon. My mother taught me the names of the stars and of the constellations, Greek names, so that the Greek myths were always present in my mind. Cassiopeia's Chair, the square of Pegasus, the sky so overwhelmingly pagan.

Our Christian mythology began with a star—but gave no Christian heroes to the heavens.

At the same time that I was learning the stars by their Greek and Arabian names, I learned that the Plumed Serpent was a god of the Indians who in some way offended him, so he left them, throwing himself into the heavens, becoming what we now call the Milky Way.

I, like the ancient people of the plateau, had my mind formed in response to its geographical features. That first year, living in a canyon whose axis was East and West, so that the sun and the stars came streaming up it. The perpendicular and the horizontal were accentuated, gravity and grace. It was a world of intense geometry, angles and plane surfaces, and over all the marked circumference of the sky.

If I had not already been given a mythology, I would have had to invent my own! The earth itself was a deity, an enchanted being. "Oh you who say I am pagan/come for a while with me/I will show you the beauty of dawning/and the wind on the sea."

September 27, 1960

South of the Valle de las Conchas, in a forest of aspen and pine, the wind far off like the rush of strings in an orchestra—sharp, delicate rattle of drying aspen leaves.

Radiance of slender aspen trunks wearing their golden crowns like the metallic headdresses of the queens of Ur.

Marvelous mountain solitude, rare, and one had thought, almost lost. The crisp autumn air, constantly moving and changing in pressure. As the sky clots with thin clouds comes a thin whisper of frost, and a dimming of the blue end of golden light.

One is carried back and back into time: time that lies buried in oneself.

P.M.

One thinks of the child into whom the life of the mesas and mountains entered. There is a story here crying to be told.

The transference of Nature. I can't find a form for it.

The secret life of nature that goes on of itself without us. The teeming life, the existence of the creatures in the holes in the rocks, the tunnels in the banks of the arroyos, the submerged water in the dry stream beds, the gunmetal grey and smooth surfaced water in the flat meander of the great Valle.

"Great wide beautiful, wonderful world," the child used to sing to herself as she wandered intoxicated with the scents of this world, the dry-sharp scent of the piñon twigs and needles mixed with dung in the blackened crevices where the squirrels or bats had stored their littered treasures.

The seeds of time: hearing the adults talk vaguely about Mexico, Pancho Villa, Caranza, the bandits of those days.

She becomes aware then of the gulf of insecurity, the fear of revolution in her father's mind. She blindly is aware of great opposites in his nature. His overwhelming power over animals, sheer muscular force, and at the same time his real fear of life. She herself is "beaten," spanked, often, and terrified of the suddenly bloated face, the maddened eyes that bent above her, the tongue protruding a little, a human being beside himself with rage (and perhaps she thinks now, it was an epileptic seizure, unrecognized, that so often disfigured him).

She looks askance at the life of the adults, their fear and resistance to ever being alone. Always there are gatherings, picnics, the smell of roasting corn, her compulsively gregarious father, her mother, who, she suddenly realizes now, was really the introvert of the family, bound by that mask of duty.

The father's real insensitivity to feminine values. The mother struggling to grow her careful gardens. Who said, later, "I never did anything for love, only because I felt it was my duty."

The two ways of looking at the land: the woman hating it because, I suppose, in a way it is her rival. When women are so identified with the earth how is it that it seems so hostile to them?

The child always envying men their strength, their freedom; only because of their weapons can they go freely into the wilderness. And because they are men, for them there is no dread of rape.

A female animal is toothed and clawed, but a female human is vulnerable and usually weaponless. This is when we most feel the need of man at our side; the great darkness at our backs—the quiver of fire as he bends to replenish it. The flare of light that has an effect of intensifying the darkness. The rainy continent infested with enormous beasts.

"Do not play alone in the park."

"Never, never accept a ride with a strange man."

All these warnings and terrors are part of her experience with the wilderness.

And her resentment that the sexual act results in bondage for the woman, the child implanted in her becomes her anchor.

She is actually never quite at home in the forest unless her dog or her horse is with her. Behind all her experience has always been the presence of a man, a father, husband, sons, the doctor, the analyst.

Beauty and the tenderness of flowers, staunchness of trees, but always the mixture and echo of danger, of threat. Fire! and the helplessness of nature. The naked stump and stubs, the fallen branches among the live green trees. Drought—the withheld rain and the withering of grass. The predatory creatures. And no way out of it, apparently, but by a vast fecundity.

In the autumn the increased awareness of death, the withdrawal of summer's wrath. The ebbing of life from grass and trees, withdrawal into the root, falling of leaves, silence of birds. The catastrophes:

She remembers the windstorm that blew the mattresses into the lake.

The forest fire leaping out of control from the matches in her hand.

The Canadian children who came to school with scalps lacerated by the claws of a puma. Vulnerability of flesh. Bee stings, leeches.

The colt, shoulder torn and bleeding from lashing against a barbed wire fence.

The indignities of flesh. Prying fingers in the secret places.

The humiliation of childbirth; the propped positions, the opened knees, the doctor standing opposite, the obstetrician.

The bloody rags and napkins.

Alien tongue prodding with the mouth, wet lips, the belly wet.

The animality of the body could be tolerated, but all her training has been against it. One's body is one's own.

The bees and flowers much more delicate.

And all the poetry she reads mystifying her by the constant reference to the other, the "thou," the "you."

One finds, returning in later years to childhood or youthful scenes that there is a resonance within oneself—a long-forgotten emotion rises to meet the scene, as it did when today I passed the stump of an old tree covered with an avalanche of scarlet vine, and remembered how those combinations used to move my heart. It is not so much the thought as the physical sensation that arises. It is as though the bodily senses respond to a certain imprint which long ago formed those sensations and which still lies latent. The recurrence, or recollection of physical fatigue at a certain point on a horseback journey—is brought back by the constance of the road's curve.

"That is why only involuntary memory can adequately restore the past."

Germaine Bree

January 18, 1961

I was thinking of the little girl in Pajarito Canyon, trying to read the symbols of her inner world in the rocks of Pajarito Canyon. She who already had encountered Norse and Greek gods in readers and picture books, who had been indoctrinated in the ritual of the

Catholic Church, haunted by the lives of the Christian martyrs that were read to the little convent girls, resting under the shade of the passive vines along the hot tar oozing road of southern California: memories of the Host carried in procession and exposed in the ornately rayed Pyx; meditations on the Sacred Heart, red and oozing blood.

Now encountering everywhere a living paganism, evidence of a people to whom the rising sun was sacred. Why should it not be, she thought, watching the magnificent spectacle of dawn breaking over the blue and thrust-up mountains, the wonder of the hours when dark gradually gave place to daylight, the movement of color, like music, and then suddenly the brilliant charge of light, the smell of the morning air, summer air, cool but not too cold, vivifying as the taste of fresh water; the sudden awakening of birds, one by one, then a full chorus! Remembering now the pulse of that turning moment, like a wave rolling up out of a smooth sea, curving and then breaking in a deluge of light. One has forgotten how much more deeply engraved the experience of dawn and evening than the seasonal changes. And how we project the rhythm of our own being into them.

Mother: There are surprising memories of her that haunt me— the mechanical drawing she took (I think by correspondence); the box of measuring implements she used, austere triangles, arcs, straight rules; the big sheets of blueprint paper. Order was her middle name. How clever she was at sewing. I remember the mechanical mysteries of the machine, the treadle communicating its motion to the wheel, the revolving wheel to the needle which went up and down while the bobbin locked the thread beneath the cloth. As the bobbin was wound, the spool leaped up and down on its spindle as though it were a dancing elf. My mother's feet pressed the treadle with a swift, rhythmic motion, like a quick march step. Her fingers fed the cloth under pressure foot without once swerving. She was altogether mistress of the machine understanding all its adjustments and what to do to keep it in running order. I believe her great gift was the essential common sense of woman, a common sense which I, alas, scorned, preferring my own flight of fancy, and so came to hate my resemblance to my mother and to fight against it.

January 1962

Talking with the Indian girls Saturday evening: I realized how the Pajarito years were important because the land itself indoctrinated me with what the Indians both had learned from it and taught it. It was like fertilization. How different their father image was from mine. The father who told them stories and played with them and carved toys for them.

In the deep recesses of the mind, behind the heavy oak door, sits the image of Stone Ashley, my father's father, like the skeleton in the family closet. A little bird told me—implying all the symbolism of the bird, the pajarito. What we learn from animal contacts. In contrast to the law of Stone Ashley, which is rational.

The conscious experience begins in the grandfather's house in Detroit. There was, one might call it, the den of Stone Ashley, where she climbed once upon the knee of one whose word and whose mood was law, and where this great being once let her play with his great gold watch and his magic paper clip with its intricate twists and turns. This was where she first learned that everything spontaneously gay and feminine must subdue itself in the presence of the great ruler of household. The darkly bearded, usually grim-faced old man (but I did not know then that he suffered continual pain from a broken hip that had not healed correctly), smelling of stale tobacco, whom everyone coddled and obeyed, for his word was law, and his need for comfort was supreme. She wonders if her father ever overcame Stone Ashley, or if he continually had to keep on running away.

The father, brought up by a doting father and all the protocol of a recently upper class family. Protective women on the one hand, even more protective because of the loss of the first born in childhood, and the father whose emotional life was centered on the surviving son. The dour old man, who, like Yahweh, hoped to make his son in his own image. His wife, the mother, whose life consisted in traveling with her husband in his private railway car from one fashionable spa to another and who must finally have died of ennui, having no nourishment at all for the heart.

Pictures of my father as a young man. Tall, blond, a cleft chin, a look almost of feminine beauty, enough to have set Shakespeare brooding on his master—mistress. The picture of a hero, of a young god in his military cape and cap. But he is also, unconsciously, governed by the power of the irrational woman in himself. He might have been, if he had had another kind of training, a Walt Whitman, quick with an almost feminine sympathy. One of the earliest clippings in the family scrap book tells how as a young man he had beaten up a carter who was whipping a horse up a stony cobbled hill.

Our childhood existence was no paradise, no bed of roses, but we nevertheless harbored a dream of paradise, unconscious, an archetype built into our dreams, and with this we contrasted the actual situation.

Coercion by parental authority we loathed, all of us: the paternal representatives, but perhaps most of all the mother's animus—the masculine elements by which she enforced her will, her rule, her masculine authority by which she continually castrated the father psychologically.

April 3, 1963

To think of the child by the lake in Michigan, learning the sound of water, the fish leaping, the kingfisher. She did not know it then but she lived in a world filled with mythology.

Fear of the dark; fear of deep waters.

The child and the dove with the wounded wing.

She finds it on the stony hillside, fluttering, with one wing dragging. She is a usually fierce child with a dark bang slantwise over her left eye, angry, sullen half the time, full of bravado. This is the first time she has ever had a bird in her hands. The lid drooping over the circular eye with its iris ring-formed. She feels the heart beating thunderously in the palm of her hand—*agitato furioso*, the bird captive between her palms, too exhausted and terrified to struggle.

Games: Heaven and Hell. This was the game we used to play, a little afraid of ourselves, climbing down into the sharp-angled ravine by the sea, the smell of geraniums and nasturtiums, the slipping shale, a step up, two steps back. If we went down too far, the bottomless fires would get us.

And always in the background, the fascination of the threat of danger or of the uncanny, as though one tiptoed always on the edge of it, always trying to do just as much as one dared and daring each time a little more.

The old man fascinated with circuses who tells her about the acrobats. The circus her first experience of controlled danger.

Everything, in those beginnings, that sets the theme for development in later life, as in music.

My feeling that children do not live so much in the adult world as in a world of the archetype. The games they play—or used to play—with such passion. Are the games taught to them by adults, or by other children? How is the peculiar wisdom of the child handed on?

The passion for secrets. These are the little mysteries. If one does not have a best friend, then one cannot have secrets; such sorrow. Then come the codes and the writings with lemon juice.

Why don't grown-ups understand us? Why do they live in a world of such rigid rules? Rigidity! The children are torn between such opposites, the formal rule of the mother, the chaotic tenderness of the father. Father was fun, but could not be trusted.

Is there anything that binds a life together, that makes it a unity? Jeanette says the old women in the geriatrics ward endlessly reminisce. They go far back in exploration of their childhood, and sometimes they seem to resolve certain things about themselves that give meaning to their present stage of life.

The child she still is embracing the wise old woman.

How the child creates her own mythology in relation to the physical world. So the child Quince in the year in Pajarito Canyon learns the rhythms of the seasons. Sunrise behind the mountain in the east—its disappearance behind the mountains in the west. The cool strange mornings, filled with shadow, the dew on the grass blades, the prevalence of birds, horses feeding, the milk of the cows.

The heat of a June day at the time of the summer solstice; the coolness of the milk room built half underground.

January 21, 1964

Thinking again of Changing Bear Maiden—the enchantingly beautiful girl who kept house for her brothers until enticed by Coyote—and becomes a monster with all the attributes of the Terrible Mother, tusks, claws, rending snout.

In a way she does, perhaps, like Psyche, marry a monster, becoming one herself.

Newmann: The overwhelming might of the unconscious is seen figuratively as the evil mother, whether as a blood-strained goddess of death, plague, famine, flood, force of instinct, or the sweetness that lures to destruction. The cult of the sow as a mother-goddess has left numerous traces.

The domestic and the nomadic: The matriarchal group, strong local ties, greater inertia, bound to nature and the instincts, women's vegetative nature, the powerful earth tie which arises with the development of gardening and agriculture by women, and dependence of these arts on natural rhythm. The male group given to hunting, and moving, and making war.

January 22, 1964

Quince is not Changing Woman but she has to be initiated by or through Changing Woman. This may mean experiencing or recapitulating Changing Woman's biography in herself. Changing Woman was always good, but her sister, Bear Maiden, was more of a monster. There were always at least two figures. You had to learn and understand Bear Maiden too and her part in you. You had to learn that opposite things always went together, that you couldn't have one without the other.

> As if a man fled from a lion
> And a bear met him;
> Or went into a house and leaned with his back against
>   the wall
> And a serpent bit him

Bear and big snake . . . were the guardians of Changing Woman's first sordid home on earth.

The Terrible Mother is the irrational, the uncontrollable, the destructiveness that goes side by side with life. The unconscious that keeps frustrating our conscious purposes.

Evil is, to the animal, hunger, the hunger that devours them from within, wasting their flesh and tissues; animal hunger, the hunger of other animals that devours them from without. The universal quality of all living things. Life feeds itself by devouring life. There is no escape from it.

Quince will try to find out whether there is anything that lives without feeding upon another. Not in the animal world. She will see the little chickens pounced on by the cat, by the hawk. She will watch the swarming minnows and the kingfisher. She will watch her father put the minnow on the hook and with it catch the bass which that evening, baked, appears on the supper table. In the same summer, she nurses the wounded dove to recovery whose wing was broken when the dog caught it and pets the lamb on which they later dine. She stands by when her mother's brother's son, her cousin, shoots the duck out of the line of flyers so skillfully it falls at her feet. She sees the great teeth of the horses crunching at the carrot in her hand, then strongly crushing it. The fox in the hen yard; the dog with the dead chicken by the neck.

She will experience the ravenous lips of her child, furiously fastening to her blue-veined breast; the child that grew within like a little parasite, like a clump of mistletoe, taking its sustenance from its host, the tree. A flashback, then, to the Host exposed on the altar in the convent on high feast days. This is my body, this white wheaten wafer, pattern of which at communion was tasted on the tongue, the body of one's god, or so the prayer book said.

This child still so much in the clutches of the Terrible Mother, wanting its own way, its hand against every man. But perhaps one reason is that when she truly needed mothering she didn't get it. Rejected, she turned to nature, the archetypal mother, and I suppose you don't experience your mother in a human way if the infant is rejected by its human world, thrown out into the cold; then the archetype, the Bear Mother, brings it up and it grows up a kind of animal instead of a human. Remember Changing Bear Maiden in the Navaho mythology!

January 26, 1964

More and more the book should show Quince's development into consciousness away from the grip of the devouring mother.

Rather, what one does is to develop the feminine through its stages. How to be a woman. How just to be yourself.

Think of the daughter of that house, imprisoned in the laws of the household, in rules of etiquette, social protocol; her fascination with very important people. Her father a man of brilliant rational intellect and completely undeveloped feeling. If the mother's sister is archetypal symbol of matriarchal authority, what place in the hierarchy does father's sister hold? She is completely a prisoner of the collective; her power, her prestige, was in her wealth. She served the patriarchal law; her will to have her will obeyed was adamant. Though she was no mother, she ruled as a matriarch; she seemed a kind of iron maiden, this spinster aunt of theirs. She came to play, in Quince's dreams, the role of collective tradition, inherited standards and concepts, which ruled her from within.

There had, somehow, somewhere, been a poisoning of this woman's feminine life. She seemed an embodiment of Cinderella's sisters who tried to shape their feet to the glass slipper. She seemed a kind of ogress to the children, partly because the father's unconscious attitude toward them was sensed. She represented to him the bondage of patriarchal tradition against which he had rebelled by going west, by obstinately and conspicuously flouting social laws whenever he could. Yet like a tyrant demanding conformity of his children. In both of them the energy of Eros was strong—but in both of them Eros was chained like Prometheus to a rock high above the snowline. There was a terrible split in them both between reason and emotion.

February 23, 1964

Again I think of the problem of my mother's animus. Does a girl inherit her mother's animus? The first stark naked sketch of him in my own life was the dream of the Puritan, Mr. Litchfield. He was so many times the school dictator. The side which has no use for feeling. Or for individual relationship. Pharisees from the Bible. Shylock, too, who demands his pound of flesh as a kind of vengeance for his own misery. The generals and colonels of the American army in the first days of the military occupation of New Mexico. General Carleton with his bitter and disappointed face. Cruelty. The lines in his face might have been drawn by knives. Power. The will.

She, my mother, preferred to live by a man's code. Her heroes, strange to say, were out of the Zane Grey and Edgar Rice Burroughs mythology. She would like to have been a man and live wild and free. She hated housework and passed her hatred to her children by demanding they do it. There was some kind of tyrant that lived in her. Perhaps she was after all a man-hating matriarch—at the bidding of her negative side, she slew Eros in herself. In her unconscious, something wild existed—wild as Tarzan and Jane, wild as the horse-thieves she loved to claim among her ancestors.

I suppose all the women of her family hated the tyranny of existing as housekeepers and breeders for the men they were chained to. Of being chained to the household when the men were out and riding, taming and breaking and branding horses, making big deals. Perhaps it was the jealous male in herself that made her complain about her husband's fishing and hunting expeditions, made her chain him to her. If she could not be free, neither could he. It was the strong irate animus of a woman forbidden in its own existence. Her rebelling reminds me somewhat of Mary Austin. I remember that she wanted to be an architect, that she took, at one time, a home course in architectural drawing. And how during World War I, she was one of the first in her community to take a class in automobile mechanics. She never really found an outlet for the masculine side of her creative energy.

She, my mother, had no real instinct for maternity. It was father who mothered the puppies and kittens and newborn colts and babies. My mother who drowned or gassed small puppies. She loved flowers, though, and her garden was a masterpiece of order and composition. This must have been where her feminine nature all came out. She claimed that she hated to cook, and yet she was a good cook. She was proud of her white cakes and icing and of setting vegetables on the table which she raised herself.

This is taking me away from the problem of Mr. Litchfield, a part of the American psyche, perhaps. An inheritance from our Puritan ancestors, Stone Ashley, my grandfather's rules of order of his household. What a demanding man he must have been.

On what pattern is a young girl's animus formed? What Quince was constantly dreaming of, of course, was someone she could talk to, someone who would understand her introverted feeling side— and yet she herself made no effort to understand the Logos side of life. Perhaps her hatred for all that side stemmed from her mother's rejection of her female children in favor of the boy. Service to a man she could not understand. There was always a spirit of strife in her, a feeling of competition that made her try to prove she could do anything better than a boy.

Perhaps what one hates most about woman's work is that it takes one away from playing—from the carefree following of nature's trails, from the freedom which boys seem to have. How little one is aware—how little she, Quince, was aware, of the effort someone else had put into producing her daily bread. She wanted to be the colt following at its mother's heels. She resisted the yoke, the saddle, the bridle, the burden of existence.

Well, of course, the men too had run away west to escape from the daily drudgery, seeking danger and excitement rather than safety and success. Kit Carson, apprenticed for so brief a time to a saddle maker. The fur trappers who were almost another kind of wild animal. Is it women who are always trying to tame a man's wild nature?

The earth beareth fruit of herself—but really, it is not so easy as all that, is it? The earth bears fruit with much effort and uncertainty.

Quince, 1964

Father and Stone Ashley: thoughts. From *An Appreciation of Ashley Pond,* by Francis C. Wilson, "Ashley Pond's devotion to his fellow-citizens." The dramatic instinct, highly developed. The alarm of whistles, of clanging bells, of frightening sirens, of excited clamor was music to his ears (his founding of Santa Fe's volunteer firemen). The challenge of danger and of opportunity for heroism thrilled his soul. His self-abnegation knew no limits.

His zest for living was unlimited but this material world held many enigmas. The riddle of human conduct he could not read. . . . To his way of thinking, everything should be reduced to obvious standards of right and wrong conduct. The in-between gradations between which men and women hide to cover their wrongs, to disguise motives, and to injure each other, confused and mystified him.

No one ever called upon him for aid who did not receive all that Ashley Pond could give of himself or of the means within his reach. The worthiness of the request was his last, not his first subject of inquiry. He had a passion for service which was unquenchable and embraced his community and all within it. It was that quality which will remain in our thoughts of him long after his failures and his faults have been forgotten and forgiven. He was impatient of those who could not see eye to eye with him in his visions for the reformation of the world, for the punishment of the evilly disposed and the wrongdoers. The difficulties in the path of attainment were unworthy of thought. He disliked details as whole-heartedly as Nature is said to abhor a vacuum. The wisdom which is involved in careful preparation for all ventures was not his.

The great extroverted passionate intuitive! So his daughter marries the exact opposite—an introverted sensation type. His undiscriminating compassion.

Shall Quince write a chapter called "Portrait of My Father"?

Jung: "When the image of the father is too patriarchal, it is apt to become psychotic."

How was it that he was over and over again imposed on? He really had no discrimination. He was not really related to the inner Logos. He was always tied to Stone Ashley by money problems. His sister continually helped pull his chestnuts out of the fire. The money he gave away and used for promotion, of course, was never his own—never earned by the sweat of his own brow.

His introverted, unconscious sensation became the renegade. His unconscious ruled the roost at home, his physical appetite, his snorting passion. Blinders of conscious virtue so the ego cannot see what the shadow is doing. The dragon—he did not kill it but fed it.

But in contrast to the devastating psychotic image of the patriarchal father, Quince has the "wise old man," and always has.

He who taught her and guided her in the world of nature. She perceives him now as Pan—as in Psyche's quest according to Newmann, the old God of nature who holds Echo in his arms—a bit like Merlin and Niniane [possibly, Nimue].

From her father, or from her mother, or from the Self, there has always been someone, the wise helper, who has shown her what the footprints mean on the trail; the arrowhead, when she utterly was lost. Where the actual father was rudderless and failed her, both in showing the meaning of Logos and Eros, this inner guide was always somehow with her or within her.

Father: Her real terror of her father was her terror of the masculine and her resistance against being feminine. For if you are feminine, you are vulnerable. You couldn't help but feel it all around you, the way the female creatures were victimized by the male creatures. There is something extremely awkward and ungainly about copulation in nature: the awkward assault of the four-legged creature upon the female form; the hooves of the stallion leaping and pawing; the bull ascending the cow; the conjunction taking place right there in that messy place beneath the tail, the place of dirt, of urine, and excrement. The way the dogs pursue and leap upon the bitch, one after another; the silly casual look with which she stands there; the way the hen ruffles her feathers and puts herself to the rights when the cock lets her go from under him; the prolonged clasp of the male grasshopper upon the female; the horrible howling of cats in heat and at their lovemaking.

It was a mystery to her, too, how in the movies, the silent films, encounter between the sexes seemed to consist of so much wrestling. Everywhere in nature the male pursuing the female, the struggle, the few seconds of copulation. No wonder, thought Quince, that when parents tried to explain about sex to their nubile children, they went off into stammering sentimental descriptions about the bees and the flowers!

She was terribly innocent at her marriage. She really had no idea how the sexual act between a man and a woman was performed. She knew nothing at all about the tensions of the kiss, having known only childishly chaste parental kisses on brow or cheeks: "never, never kiss anyone on the lips," she had been taught since the age of five. In the mouth is where germs are and the slime of saliva—old men expectorating on a sidewalk, or the phlegm coughed up in catarrhal nights.

So when her husband's tongue first penetrated her lips she was filled with horror and a kind of secret nausea. The violation of her mouth was a shock for which she had been in no way prepared. It aroused nothing in her but revulsion, for in her mouth was the source of her purity. Had she not even been warned against lies which could dirty the mouth so it has to be washed out with soap? She was indeed a violated victim. It was years before her sensory perception woke and she learned to relish the kisses of the mouth to give them as well as to receive, and to enjoy the caresses of the lover's body.

Ah, never to have been brought up like any puppy on caresses, to have been taught so early that bodily contact was evil—to have feared even to hold her children lest holding and maternal tenderness "spoil" them.

Can you ever go back and change those things, Quince wondered? Is it possible to go back and redeem the past simply by being changed oneself in the moment now? To be cleansed of all one's ghosts? To become whole?

Her real father, husband of her mother, demanded that his daughters be treated, like boys, in the Spartan manner; they were never allowed to luxuriate in a half-dream between waking and rising but had to appear promptly for their breakfasts by seven. Later, in the convents and in the secular boarding schools to which she was so early committed, there was always the inexorable strident bell which they had to obey as though it were the voice of doom.

Disappointed too, Quince realized. The disappointment of the dreamer who can never forgive reality's failure to conform with his own dreams. Disappointment when her mother, who could not encourage his fantasies, always turned out in the end to have been right about everything, to have known that the trusted ex-jailbird would betray the trust, that the stock in the silver mine would prove worthless, that the traded horse would have a blind eye, that the paradise retreat would dissolve in bankruptcy.

The man in her mother was annoyingly always right, yet was it not this same masculine quality that enabled her to maintain order in what might otherwise have been a chaotic household?

In order is security, Quince very early learned; the calming tempests lay in her mother's skillful hands. She, too, provided the cooling shelter from the blazing fire of the father's emotions, like the eruption of volcanoes, or like those cyclones that erupt from the face of the sun. No way to combat them, only a way to hide, as Psyche was instructed to do by the supple reed in the old story; the mother would set her child another task, or send her out of sight until the wrath had cooled. The mother was always just, sometimes too just, like old Shylock, insisting on the letter of her law.

Quince was never, in reality, her mother's darling, but in secret, perhaps she always longed to be one. She adopted trees as mothers and flowery meadow. Rainfall and snow gave her a feeling of womb-safe closeness. Going to bed in the over-spreading darkness, along with the fantasies where the demand for "reality" did not enter. Was this the meaning of her long bedtime fantasy of entering a mountain fastness to rescue a girl who had been imprisoned in a tower by a tyrant father?

Remember, I tell Quince, that when you were born your mother was only eighteen. Snatched roughly as Persephone from the circle of her maiden companions, the "spoon aunts" (named for the dozen silver spoons with each name engraved in the bowl that were given her by her close school companions at her wedding); confronted all at once with the completely patriarchal world of Stone Ashley and the vigorous lust of the half untamed creature she had married, the "bull in the China shop" who carelessly floundered among her delicate tea things, who incessantly got her with children which her unwilling womb tried over and over again to reject. She perhaps rejected the woman's role that had been thrust upon her, for which, at her fashionable "finishing school," she had been only superficially prepared.

On the other hand, Quince, remember your mother's affiliation with these "maidens"; on the other, her adoration of men— father, brother, the two little brothers that died. She was in some ways a young and willful Venus who was never so happy as when entranced men were lying like tokens at her feet. Yet always within her, in the earliest days, one discerned the young hero, as though the woman's part were really being played, as in the days of Shakespeare, by an agile boy. In her school days the young girl, Hazel, had allied herself with boys, had escaped as often as she could from the traditional feminine role, had cut short her auburn hair, had ridden bicycles, worn divided skirts, rode astride on horseback, swum in daring, close-fitted and subtly revealing costume, daring for her period, that is. She had a masculine cleverness about her without, however, losing her look of feminine daintiness and charm.

Even at sixteen, Quince thinks, turning the faded picture around and around, the face of an incorrigible four-year-old, an arrogant assurance of power that little girls sometimes show who have been their father's darlings, who have early learned how to use their feminine wiles to get their own way and dominate the male. As she stares at the photograph, she finds it suddenly changing. From the look of the fascinating young witch, it becomes all at once the face of the wicked stepmother of all the fairy tales, she who replaces the father' s dead wife, who persecutes the father's own children, who persuades the father to expose them in a wilderness or to have them killed. Her own daughters must become queens and marry the king's son; the true princess must be sent on an impossible journey, or married to a beast, or entranced into a deep sleep from which, the stepmother hopes, there shall be no waking.

So it is, Quince, the Terrible Mother appears to us from the beginning, continually driving us out of paradise, and continually we keep trying to creep back again under the hem of the garment, beneath the comforting feather-soft wings, into the cozy bed that received us as a nursling.

March 24, 1964

Quince remembers, on the one hand, tensions that existed, though unspoken in the children's presence, between father and mother, the human family. On the other hand, the world of animals. Even there was obvious conflict. My father surrounded himself with dogs, with horses, with herds of cattle, with trophies of deer and mountain lions, with a fisherman's lures and hooks and rods.

My mother was mistress of the chickens, the setting hens with their ruffles of red feathers and beady, apprehensive eyes, their warning clucks if a child came too near. There was a formal chicken house, but it had, for some reasons, fallen into disuse. The hens were temperamental and liked to choose their nests in different parts of the barn, sometimes they absentmindedly, or with special malice, laid their eggs in the boxed-in end of the mangers where horses mumbled before their oats before munching the tougher hay. If an egg were left ungathered in the oats box, a horse might eat it as a special delicacy. It was the children's job to make sure this did not happen.

A setting hen was a special mystery. (I have just made an odd discovery that the word clutch is no relation to the one that means "to grasp" but is from the same root as "galaxy," the formal name for milk!) I forget how many eggs it took to make a clutch. By the time I took to keeping my own flock of chickens, it was rare to hatch eggs beneath a hen. My mother sometimes used an incubator—I think not at Pajarito, but in Santa Fe. More often she, and most certainly I, bought baby chicks which came in squealing boxfuls via the post office. Peep! Peep! A sure sign spring was here. These we kept at first in a brooder, huddled together in a fluffy mass under some source of heat, until, I think, their fluff vanished, and they were able to run about, awkward and gangling, in their juvenile feathers.

Hens did a better, though nervous, job of mothering. When the eggs hatched, they followed the hen around the barnyard, or maybe a fenced enclosure of some kind, in the hopes of keeping out from under the feet of nonchalant horses. How adept and fearless they seemed as they ran after her, pecking at bugs and grass seeds, even at non-bugs and buttons, until a shadow crossed them. Then they fled scuttling under the hen who fluffed her feathers to indignant size. The hen always seemed an example of mindless, automatic motherhood. Without a glint of affection in her eye, she was none the less possessive and commanding. No adventuresome chick could stray far from her attention. Or was its attachment more to the close congregation of fluffy siblings? A hen thought its main duties were to care for the chicks. Really, it existed, we thought, to produce the daily egg for the family table. How we loved to gather them, warm from under her, filling the basket we were entrusted with the dozen or so expected each morning.

The roosters, the young cocks, were another thing altogether. How macho they tried to be with their bright combs and their strident tail feathers—little dreaming that it is a cock's fate to be guillotined and plucked and eaten. Our barn man wrung the necks of the cocks rather than decapitating them. With what repelled awe, we observed the truth of what we were told, that the headless body of a cock would flop about for sometime after its lordly head had been severed, a gruesome fact of life like the squirming and writhing of a decapitated rattlesnake. Did they really writhe until sundown, or was that one of the folk stories, the fictions we absorbed along with the everyday reality without exactly discriminating as to which was what?

The episode when Quince and Sophy, her sister, were both spending a Christmas holiday with Aunt Frances in her elegant 72nd Street apartment. Aunt Frances so completely enslaved and imprisoned by the cultural canon, by the ghostly presence of Stone Ashley— dead for over twenty years, who would not let his daughter go. The aunt was chaste and elegant and dominated by an aching compulsion to do everything correctly. Everything to do with sex was unclean to her. Later, she reprimanded Quince soundly from her enthusiasm for Thomas Mann's story of Joseph and his brother. But in the hours of darkness queer things got loose and prowled the apartment.

Quince and Sophy, the two nubile children, began secretly collaborating with each other in writing a "novel." It was a continued story, penciled in a lined composition book. They hid behind the Louis Quatorze sofa to write it, and every few days in panic destroyed what they had written.

The story had to do with western "bad men," horse thieves, gross and low-browed, who took captive and abused the young girls, owners of stolen and fabulous horses; half buried them in manure and mud in a watering trough; filled their mouths and ears with mud and filth. Of course, the girls, as in the serial movies of their day, managed to escape in the end and rescue their fleet-footed silver-maned steeds as well. But what stays in Quince's mind is the downright masochism of the details, the children's endless fertility in imaging degradation. And the fact that there never seemed to be a hero to rescue them; they rescued themselves and outwitted the tormentors by nick-of-time ingenuity, escaping, though never destroying the villains, those Calibans, whom they themselves created. Whether from the depths of their own undeveloped psyches, or from the dungeons of respectable Aunt Frances, Quince can never quite be certain.

Quince and the Seasons: Interpolations . . .

Summer and winter: which does she know first? Lilacs are blooming, heavy, sweet, the little four-starred flowers with the long tube; bite off the tip and suck the honey out; pull the flowers out of the cluster and make chains. Looking back, she remembers how the bushes towered over her like trees, the presence of twin goddesses, the lilac and the white. Which would you rather have? Which would you choose? Gold or silver? Oranges or lemons? London Bridge is falling down. She is caught in the circling arms. Which will you have, demand the voices? Will you choose gold or silver, day or night, your father or your mother?

The lilac grove is full of bees. They hover everywhere among the blossoms, then hump themselves into frenzy to suck the nectar. One afternoon when she had run away from her nap, barefooted, to lose herself in the lilac forest, a bee stung her on the ankle. The sharp jab, the sudden burning, the wounded foot swelling in its own anger. If she runs home to Mother, she will be punished, ostracized, and put to bed without her supper. But mother she needs now, and so she runs to the sleepy house where mother has only just awakened from her own heat-shunning nap. To Quince's surprise, her mother does not scold, not take her in her arms either. She does the practical thing, brings a basin with hot water and soaks the foot. How strange it seems that this is the first time Quince can remember discovering that a mother can be kind as well as judging—though I suspect that, foot bandaged, face washed, the child was put to bed and the door closed upon her.

There was an oil painting of a fish, curved in the arc of its leap out of the water, brownish-black, pale flesh-colored undersides; as long ago as I could remember, this painting hung in the dining room of whatever house we lived in. The gray-green of the water matching the brownish-green and the pinkish spotted underbelly.

In the lake near which she lived at the dawning of her consciousness, she used to watch the fish jumping out of the placid water, then vanishing leaving only the concentric rings that spread and widened.

My father was, as long as I ever knew him, a fisherman. He was proud of me when at six or seven I caught, all by myself, from the dock of the resort where we were staying, a bass that weighed nearly five pounds. I remember still the thrill of the quick nibble, then the arched rod as the hooked fish struggled to swim free. I could never have lifted it from the water if a man standing nearby had not helped me a little—and then when he ended up buying the fish (from whom? from my father?), he took it away for himself. I was somehow persuaded to feel honored rather than disappointed that he wanted it.

The watery medium that was always a puzzle and enchantment. Quince, of course, could not remember she had been a fishlike creature in the uterine waters or later a curled salamander shaped, tailed, with nubbly flippers that were budding arms. Almost as little could she remember the three times her own body had ballooned with a little spherical sea in which sloshed successfully the embryonic forms that were to become her three sons, eventually gliding slippery as fishes, between her thighs into airy life.

Lake fish and river fish. Along the shore of the lake, shoals of minnows drifted and darted. Her father used to catch and keep them in minnow traps to carry with him fishing. To bait one's hook with a live minnow seemed at first as cruel to her as the thought of fishing with a baby. For the minnows themselves were in their flexed and almost transparent innocence, not having yet become aware of fear except as a dizzy reflection. She wished she could put them in a jar and keep them, but this was something they taught her early— that wild things were a part of their element and out of it likely to perish quickly. Still, there was always the hope that some winged or finned or furred thing might prove the exception.

It was strange that her dreams also contained a kind of geography, with trees and rivers, birds in the trees, fish in the rivers.

Until the day when she suddenly realized that it was, as she had often been told, all a dance. She gets up in the morning, dresses, moves from task to task as though she were a partner in the dance, as though she were following the lead of a strong and confident partner.

She remembers watching her father at some festivity—was it a Firemen's Ball? How gay he was, how strong, how confident. How he swung the ladies and flattered them and joked with them, until their faces flushed and strands of hair loosened from their elaborate coiffures.

Once the music stopped and he came up to her, his eldest daughter, and took her hand. Stiff as a piece of machinery she was when he tried to whirl her in his arms. Her feet became heavy as though she were walking through clay with enormous thick-soled boots. Her steps were stiff and pedantic; she tried to remember her dancing school lessons: one, two, three! Her heart felt like a lump of black coal in her breast. She could not relax to the music, be a tree in the wind, grass bending on the hill. In boarding school she was tall and wiry so in the girl's dances, the man's part had naturally fallen to her. She was stiff and aggressive and always knew better than anyone what to do. That is, with her head and her will she knew it. Her body was nimble but not graceful, obedient but not yielding.

"Let yourself go," her father would say to her. "Don't be stiff."

But within her, the haughty Cinderella sisters sneered, "How can you ever be anything but stiff?"

Ice, she thought, cold and glittering and stiff with icicles. And underneath the frozen, icy stream, who would ever hear the live, imprisoned water sing?

There was the afternoon that Quince murdered her doll. It was summer. Visitors had come to call on her mother. Quince had been brought in from playing, made to take off the boy's clothes her mother usually dressed her in, put into a starched dress of dotted swiss with a flowered sash, a flowered hair ribbon tied on her rebellious topknot. The ladies grimaced and beamed and exclaimed. One of them had brought her a doll, an unusually fine one with a stuffed body, china arms and legs and a hard china face painted with false rose dimpled cheeks, with curved and puckered lips slightly parted, showing little pearly white teeth. The hair of the doll was dark and artificially curly; the eyes were coldly blue, like marbles. When closed, under the waxen lids the lashes fanned the cheeks. Quince was told that the doll's name was Frances, a name she loathed.

She held the doll roughly by one arm and pouted.

"Say thank you to your Aunt Frances," her mother bade her. Why should she say thank you for a gift she did not want? Quince's memory stirs still with an impression of draped knees like walls against her; the smell of bread and butter on the tea tray; the silver teapot, resentment gnawing in her heart like an unpleasant small animal.

"You'd better go outside till you make up your mind to behave," her mother said coldly.

Banished she had gone to sit on a pile of sand near the steps. Dressed up as she was, she didn't know what to do next. The doll lay on her lap with its china face turned upward, simpering and cold and hard. Quince took a smudged spoon that her sister, Sophy, now deep in her nap, must have left there, and she began pouring sand between the painted and parting lips. The sand trickled and vanished like a snake into its hole. A fiendish joy welled up from the deep cistern of the child's heart. She aimed the pointed spoon between those rosy lips like a dagger. She fed the hard grinding sand in, while malice grew in her, an urge to punish, an urge to kill, to destroy this image of the feminine to which she was commanded to conform, this stereotype, with its fixed unreal smile, its unaltering prettiness.

The hot sun of the August heat beat down on her, but she ceased to feel it. She had become a maenad's child, aware of an ancient power to rend and kill. The doll's blue eyes stared up at the pale sky vacant of healing clouds. The china head grew heavy. Heavier, and lolled back over the little girl's lap. All at once, with a snap it split from lip to opposite temple, leaving two sharp jagged edges through which a drool of sand trailed slowly like blood back into the heap from which it had been spooned.

Quince and her sister, Sophy, who wanted the wild animals to run free.

Who cut the checkrein on Chili, the black stallion, and fidgeted when they were talked to by their unexpectedly gentle father, who explained to them that the checkrein was really a help to curb the wild thrashings of his head when he trotted elegantly between the shafts of the two-wheeled racing cart. They plotted, but did not quite dare to carry it out, to sneak out of bed and let the half-broken filly out of the corral to run wild in the night. On the other hand, their mother hated and feared everything wild and wanted everything to be tame and obedient—including her husband and children. Yet she sometimes told them what an adventurous little girl she had once been, dressing in bloomers, and riding her horse astride on her grandfather's ranch before it was considered correct—or even hygienic—to do so. How the children wished she would not bind her hair so primly on her graceful head, would let it flow free in beautiful strands like the gypsy girl in the painting. How was it the children had such wild spirits when both of the parents were usually so strict?

Sophy would one day be taken in hand by the elegant aunt who made her bind her astonishingly voluptuous breasts with tight brassieres. This was the period when women's figures were forced to conform to the demands of fashion which that year exalted the "boyish form." I suppose it was part of the will to enforce one's will everywhere upon nature, and upon women as the symbol of nature. Throughout her life, Sophy never forgave her aunt the sagging breasts she would carry to her grave.

Quince's experience in the night forest. Night and darkness and the unseen, through which she goes blindly feeling her way. Her primitive fears—the pinecone dropping slowly that made the hair rise on her head. Cat's eye in the dark. Screech of the barn owl and the cry of the seized mouse. This is your hour and the power of darkness. Groping through trees on a wet misty night, fog rising off the water. Sound of fish leaping. This is our primitive fear of darkness we carry with us from our long past.

Quince returns in mind to the time when she believed in metamorphosis. When everything could be a deity or a fairy in disguise. Magic. The power to change one's outer shape at will.

But the man she married liked a thing for its essential form, and so she slipped away from him at last. Can the magic world be assimilated to the human? The "irrational" to the modern world of science and industry? The powerful magic of science. Does magic have to be renounced in the end? Or is it a world that can live beside the other? Must Prospero at last destroy his books and bury his staff? Children dream of magic to help them escape from the reality of the all-powerful parent who thwarts and frustrates their wills. The fairy godmother ruled in that realm, all beautiful and all good—but the wicked witch is always beside her too. And the presence of the wicked stepmother. What evil wishes we have when we are young, which the fairy tales express for us! The wicked stepmother kills us, stews us and buries our bones under the tree. Who is it that will enable them to live again? There are magic figures running through our dreams: sinister women, villainous men.

Quince would later be shown the dream of the young woman who had to choose between the golden buckle and the veil with the icon of the butterfly painted on it. The butterfly: the soul. The "imago" of the Self. The buckle with its sharp and pointed tongue, in its way a kind of pin or brooch, like the one Oedipus blinded himself with: The buckle is a masculine warrior's ornament; the veil, feminine and flexible. Works upon the invisible. Works like a metaphor.

For a moment only, a moment on the dark porch at Three Mile Lake [Michigan], love woke and spoke in the heart of the child, Quince. Inside the house was lighted, a party was going on; she was supposed to be in bed. Lurking in the shadow, she saw her father come out of a lighted room and close the door behind him. He stood against the railing, looking out, perhaps, toward the silent lake—she cannot remember now. A whippoorwill called. Then her father looked down and saw her. He, for once, did not reprimand her (as her mother surely would have done). He listened beside her to the whippoorwill calling again and again, and even let her put her hand in his, standing there barefoot, still in her nightclothes. Hardly a word passed between them, but the child in some unconscious way became aware of the grown man's feelings, far too deep for her to understand in words. She was aware of the love of nature, of his longing for the free and outdoor life he had given up when he had returned to Detroit from the not-quite a decade in the west he had made himself a part of. How can a small child—she must have been no more than six—understand such feelings? To discover that her usually sociable and gregarious father loved to be alone in the night as she did—as a child did. A moment, seldom again, if ever, to be shared.

Thorns and roses, brambles. Thornbushes; the thorns and roses belong together, like the butterfly and the caterpillar (perhaps even like the butterfly and the sharp-tongued buckle). The sharpness of the thorn was known early to Quince, because she was one who went barefooted at a very early age: barefoot in the meadows and woods, stepping on thorns and prickers. The story of Androcles and the lion they acted out in school. The sharp needle with which her father took the splinter out of her finger. The beak of the hummingbird, the fang of the snake, the barb of the fishhook; the thorn of sleep; the hedge of thorns that surround Sleeping Beauty—she who has pricked her finger on a spindle. The animal horns that threatened above such moist mild eyes; the sharp points of the rockers on her mother's pink rocking chair she always fell over when she ran to see her mother, in bed and pampered in the mornings. She bruised her bare ankles every time. Did she also bruise her heart?

Sharp words, pricking the heart or stabbing it. Her own sharp tongue. The hypodermic needle with which the lion in her dream finally was slain. "Life is like sucking honey off the thorn."

The days when phonographs used to be played with needles, hard needles, soft needles. The softest of all were cactus thorns, giving the best sound, but too delicate and easily broken. Here is a different use of a sharp point: not to wound but to bring forth music. A transformation process. She sometimes dreamed of—or perhaps imagined—a record where everything that ever has been is recorded. Here the sharp point is a sensitive instrument, a delicate probe. In her dreams, it had feathers, downy soft as a bird's breast.

Looking back on Quince, I see that she herself grew as a kind of cactus plant, surrounded herself by sharp defensive prickers—protecting her heart's own scarlet flowers.

April 28, 1964

Found old notes on John Cowper Powys, remarking that "It is hard to worship Demeter in America." Does he complain about the American men, their competent grasp of the essentials of machinery, restless concentration on the industrial exploitation of nature because of this lack of development in relation to the feminine principle? The expression of Logos without Eros?

The women of America, longing for men who would understand their essential nature, men who would have a feeling for nature, who would help to husband the earth, not to mine and exploit her. How is a woman to live with men who are machine-minded, who are unrelated to their own animas, to the woman within, who would help them understand the seasonal rhythms of nature.

The remembrance of my father who blundered and cut down the wrong tree, the flowering apricot—in his blundering way hoping to please his wife, to do a job she had asked him to over and over. Now she is sick in bed, and in his sympathy he wants to please. But he has no feeling for the vegetative life. He does not understand trees; he does not know them, one from another. So he cuts its down. Then the woman flies into a rage. The tree is destroyed—an aged tree that had taken decades to develop it to its own gracious maturity. There is no way of replacing it, no way of atoning. The fault was due not to malice aforethought, but to unconsciousness, to failure to ask a simple question. The man's ego is insulted; he cannot bear to recognize that he has made a mistake and to ask forgiveness—not reconciliation becomes the important thing, but the frantic desire of the woman to punish the man, to avenge the injury he has done to her, to make him suffer as she suffers—the axe having splintered her own heart as it splintered the heartwood of the tree. It is the goddess who weeps and rages, the goddess who wept when the Sacred Groves were cut down in Palestine and has gone on weeping ever since. It is the man who defends his own ego. His manhood is threatened, his pride in himself, his longing to be rewarded for a good deed. In the woman he sees, perhaps, the Terrible Mother.

What a woman always looks for is a hero who will slay dragons for her. A Perseus.

My mother used to point out the constellations to me when I was a little girl and we first went to live in the Pajarito Canyon. The sword of Perseus that glittered in the northeast. I had storybooks that told me the legend of Perseus, who had cut off the Gorgon's head and rescued Andromeda from the dragon. But my father could hardly bear to kill anything, let alone cut off a dragon's head—or a Gorgon's. He went hunting bravely enough but came back most of the time empty-handed. "The deer just looked at me with those big beautiful eyes and I couldn't shoot it," he said. Once a hornet stung him on the back of the hand, and he cried out in panic as though utterly terrified. My mother caught him and soothed him and quieted down his pain—after sending us out of the house, a long way off, so we couldn't hear the cries of the frightened animal he had become.

My father's heroes were Teddy Roosevelt and Colonel Leonard Wood—neither of whom my mother could stand. Why? Neither is a woman's hero—my father has a copy of *The Winning of the West* in his library. He also had books by Bret Harte and Mark Twain and O. Henry and a worn copy of *In Darkest Africa* by [Sir Henry] Stanley. I never knew my mother to read those books. She preferred Zane Grey and James Oliver Curwood and Gene Stratton Porter, *Freckles, The Girl of the Limberlost;* later, Edgar Rice Burrough's *Tarzan.* She used to recite to us with great expression Kipling's *Ballad of East and West,* though this had no woman figure in it at all.

I think my mother unconsciously longed to have been such a man rather than a woman at all. She had been the only girl in a family of four brothers who spoiled her outrageously. But I think also teased her and left her behind when they went forth on boy adventures. She found she could win their admiration by being "as good as a boy." Perhaps that was why no one had ever killed a dragon for her. She was too good at killing them herself.

There is something in a woman that makes her desire to be part of nature. I feel it in the spring when grass turns green and fruit trees begin to open their buds. A longing to stand with hose in hand and water around the roots, or spray dry patches in the lawn. Or a longing to clear out tangles of brush from ditches and send the water flooding over the fields. A longing to plant trees.

But the pioneer women, and my mother was in a sense one of them, were unable to stay in a place long enough to gather fruit from any trees they planted. This uprootedness must have been hard on them. The men were hunters and nomads at heart. They had not the patience to stay and see things grow. Better to travel on in search of fields that would produce with less toil, in search of gold dust which had only to be washed out of the stream or dug from the earth, the possession of which would give a man freedom—freedom from bondage to the earth, from the necessity to produce his bread by the sweat of his own brow.

I think of the Donner party on its migration to California. They were possessed by the American dream. The dream of endlessly fertile land, of their own herds, the old Biblical dream of the land of milk and honey. None of the party seemed to be men who enjoyed adventure for its own sake. They made the long trek across the wilderness to get to golden California and took their ill-advised shortcut in the hopes of getting there most quickly. They knew nothing of what it meant to cross a wilderness. They had never seen, I imagine, mountains anywhere of the stature of the Sierra, or even of the Wasatch. They had never experienced a desert.

I know my father always had a kind of lust to own land. He's never driven through a landscape without noting a place where wood and water and pasture might make it possible to homestead. There was a settler in him. But more, the land enticed him with mirages, with rosy dreams of what a man might make of it. The undeveloped possibility always lured him—yet, once he acquired the property and began to live on it, his patience began to give out. The real effort of building and farming quelled his ardor. Easier to dream, by far, than to build—easier to dream of the unattainable beloved than to settle down with one woman—the woman who insisted on putting down her roots wherever one settled and then trying to chain the mobile man to her. It was the woman who longed to see the tree they'd planted come into blossom. The earth that refused to yield her produce unless a man toiled for it day and night against all the fury and uncertainty of the elements—injustices and irrationalities of weather.

To own land. It is funny how that changed the feeling one has. One will toil endlessly for one's own family, for one's own piece of earth. Even the Pueblo Indians, communist though they may be in most of their ways, must have each his own few acres of land, even though this is only an allotment from the tribal lands. It is the way each man must have his own woman. My wife. My husband. My beloved. The sense of ownership that can drive a man green with jealousy if his wife so much as looks kindly on another.

My comfort: my word.

Quince, of course, is not her family name. It is only a name I have given her, looking back from the adult world. I do not know exactly why I called her this. I remember when I was a child (or perhaps it is Quince herself who remembers) that I often longed to have a name of my very own, not one that had been chosen for me by my parents and expressing their own ideas of what I should be like. I wanted to give Quince a name that was not common or ancestral, that had overtones of poetry or mythology. The dictionary told me Quince meant Cydonian apple, from the town of Cydonia on the northern border of Crete. It belongs, like the apple, to the rose family and is a native of Persia and Turkestan. (I did not know, when I named her, that I might be putting her under the protection of Aphrodite who never was one of my favorite goddesses.)

My mother had a quince tree growing in her garden in Santa Fe that fascinated me. The branches of the tree were crooked and scraggly. The flowers and leaves were ornamental, but the fruit was a disappointment, hard greenish-yellow knobs that did not soften as they ripened. They could only be eaten after much cooking with quantities of sugar. My mother made them into jams and jellies that had a transparent greenish color and a flavor and delicate aroma like nothing else I have ever tasted. There was something faintly alchemical, too, in the sound of the word, a poetic resonance with quintessence, which suggested to me, perhaps, the distillation of a life.

My name, my given name, was Margaret. The diminutive by which I was always intimately known was Peggy. But why give the child a name by which they never intended to call her? Or to call her by when they were addressing her with wrath: "Margaret Hadley Pond, you bad, bad girl." "You know better than that, Margaret Hadley," as though Margaret were the obedient ladylike character they had intended her to be when they named her—and the name of the sinner when she fell from grace.

Peggy, on the other hand, was presumably the darling of their hearts; it was the playful name: Peggy, Pegeen, Pegasus, and sometimes even a lilting Margarita. Peggy was the pet name, the colt name, a name that when one came to a woman's estate, one might put off and become with greater dignity and deeper wisdom, Margaret.

Margaret, Margaret, sweet as the violet
Shy as the hermit thrush down in the dell,
Maker of poetry, never discover me,
No use to ask, for I never will tell.

A teacher had written that on a valentine when I was twelve or thirteen, the year I discovered I could write poetry as well as read it. What that valentine did for my shrinking ego. Whoever, in Quince's life before, had guessed the secret of my inner self, and compared it to such things as a violet or a hermit thrush? (Deep as I was then in Shelley's "Ode to a Skylark.") The teacher was a man with a deeply lined, sensitive face, and I think, looking backward, evidently a tender heart. He has composed and painted a valentine for each of the little girls in his classes, but mine, I thought, was quite the nicest of any. Could a man, one of those stern authorities, possibly feel that way about me? Not since I was less than five had I thought they could be anything but critical and demeaning.

Before that I had managed to be, for a certain amount of time at least, the apple of a fond father's heart and eye. "If only my father hadn't married a witch," Quince used to tell herself angrily.

November 5, 1964

The world of poetry was Quince's first delightful sound. First the laughter of the "Birdie with a yellow bill," and the ornery little shadow. Then, and she was still not very of old at that, perhaps seven at the most, the mystery that throbbed and echoed in her of the galloping man, "And nigh long in the dark and wet / a man goes riding by" and "Dark brown is the river, golden is the sand. . . . other little children will bring my boats to land."

In talking over historical developments in New Mexico, it boiled down to the relationship between man—various types of men—and nature. There have been the Indian warriors, and the Indian caciques or medicine men. In America, men like Cortez, Coronado, de Vargas, discoverers, explorers, conquistadors, whose goal was gold and glory. And in the background, religion. The religious cults of Central and South America, intricate, highly developed, and they say, cruel. But did the Aztecs make more sacrifices than we?

Quince knew this because the Littlebird plateau was a center of archaeological activity. Her parents' friendship with Van Morley [archeologist known for Mayan studies], who was already busy in Mexico, and who used to tell the fascinated children about the great stelas in Yucatan with dates carved on them. He could ask them for their birth dates and then translate them into Mayan hieroglyphs.

On a slab of rock where the trail went up to Tshirege, the stone serpent, and she, a child standing alone with the wordless wind blowing past, could feel still the ancient spell of its guardianship. No relation at all, the learned men said, drawing down their eyebrows and shaking their wistful heads—no relation at all to the famous Quetzalcoatl of Mexico who was both serpent-god and powerful hero, who vanished on a raft of serpents into the West, not suffering death in the body so that like our Elijah and his fiery chariot, men could live forever in expectation of his return. As for Awanyu, he had grown angry with mankind and thrown himself into the sky, where he moves in majestic processionals as the Milky Way.

February 3, 1965

Clusters of memory. How our memories do not rise consecutively, but in clusters around a certain, very often sensually stimulated, note. As a certain effect of light, of air on the cheeks, a birdcall, the scent of wild roses will bring up trains of related images. In autumn, we experience all our autumns.

I Ching, p. 30: The primal powers never come to a standstill, the cycle of becoming continues uninterrupted . . . . Between the two primal powers there arises again and again a state of tension, a potential that keeps the powers in motion and causes them to unite, whereby they are constantly regenerated. Tao brings this about without ever becoming manifest.

p. 32: The point of view of *The Book of Changes* is based on the principles of the organic world in which there is no entropy. Tao reveals itself differently to each individual according to his own nature.

p. 307: The Creative knows through the easy; the Receptive can do things through the simple. The nature of the Creative is movement; the nature of the Receptive is repose.

p. 316: Going back to the beginnings of things and knowing them to the end we come to know the lessons of birth and death.

p. 326: Tao, which manifests itself as kindness, corresponds with the light principle, and justice corresponds with the dark principle.

p. 29: The trigram *Keeping Still* (Ken=Mountain). Here the seed in the deep hidden stillness; the end of everything is joined to a new beginning.

Three
The Pattern of Ancient Crossing

Peggy and Fermor on her seventieth birthday, December 1, 1973, in the yard of Camino Rancheros in Santa Fe. Peggy is wearing the three-strand heishi necklace, a fiftieth anniversary present from the families of their three children. From the Kathleen Church Collection.

Lament

Ancient camels
crossing a puddle of hot rock
left indelible footprints.
Your footprints still startle me
into aching recollection.

The tools left hanging in your workshop:
the little knife you gave me
like the one you always carried
wherever you were,
in the car, on picnics,
to open whatever needed to be opened.
to dig out splinters,
to tighten screws
when the world seemed to be falling apart.

It is the workman in you that I weep for:
the squares and the levels,
saws all shapes and sizes,
nails for every imaginable place or purpose,
screwdrivers, nuts and bolts—
there was nothing you would not try
to make or mend.

You are gone now.
How often my own life seems past any mending.
(1975)

Sonnet XV.
For F. S. C. 1900-1975

I am thinking this morning of the beauty of the earth
as you and I both loved it, wondering
how my vision is still half yours—the broken surf
of morning over landforms; slant light; rolling thunder
at the edge of summer picnics; the high dancing

flight of the sandhill cranes, their cry that echoed
like water rippling over smooth stones, over the far
   expanse of
bright air. Within and all around us time flowed,
making, unmaking mountains; the crystal essence
still glitters in the sand grains of dry rivers.
Nothing seems lost—light's changes, wind-swept
   silence,
I gather pebbles feeling your quiet presence
companion me still in all we loved together.

(1978)

Lament and elegy—time-honored poetic forms Peggy Church used to express her feeling for the loss of her partner, Fermor, who died February 2, 1975. In the midst of the Mary Austin research and writing, during one of Church's most productive decades (four poetry collections), Ferm fell ill from a brain tumor. Peggy had renewed her interest in a series of literary seminars offered at St. John's College in Santa Fe, including studies of Pablo Neruda and readings by Robert Bly and John Holt. The illness and death of her husband are largely omitted from her commentary in the Pajarito Journals, but are embedded in Church's intense conversations with herself about how to write the Pajarito experience, interspersed attempts at historic accounts, her father's story, and a creation of the family's mythology set against the background of the American Southwest. The many approaches attempted during this decade of journal-keeping suggest Church's heightened sense of time's fleeing—an urgency to find some form for the Pajarito years.

What attracted Church to Austin as a subject was what she considered Austin's sacrifice of her feminine self to the ego-expressing claims she made for her work. Church was constantly thwarted in her research by Mary Austin's own inconsistencies, suggesting to Church, as some other critics of Austin maintained, that she imaginatively constructed the heroics of her life in the California desert and, as a self-declared folklorist, perhaps took liberties with other supposed facts. At one point, Church traveled to California to consult a vineyardist in an effort to verify a drought Austin had reported, but

Church could not substantiate. To her surprise, the vineyardist reconstructed the record of drought cycles from the record he had of
grape-growing, paralleling Austin's description and dates. Church
soon realized that the importance of this discovery was not the accu-
racy of dates, but what the drought signified in Austin's life— how
she initially felt in that strange environment, under hard circumstances. "What she felt was a drought in her soul," Church concluded. She discovered from these circumstances that reality was
more a matter of attitude than accumulated facts. "Innocently expecting to find the most accurate chronology in her own writing, I
might have taken a look at my own difficulty in recalling when various events happened. Or even how they happened—the tendency to
exaggerate or make metaphors of one's own experience." Another
time, referring to this experience, she noted: "I might have realized
this is how history gets written."

In these 1970s journals, history, lament, and elegy are inter-
twined. Church stalwartly tried to tease out all the existing sources to
contextualize her father's life, for instance, in the same ways she had
gone sleuthing for facts on Austin. She tracked down and collected
newspaper accounts, letters, financial ledgers, and photographs.
She also used the journals to compose longer narratives, vignettes,
thumbnail histories, some of which form the basis of talks she later
gave at the Los Alamos Historical Society or the School for American
Research. Despite the loss of her husband, perhaps to help counter it,
her work took on a renewed energy, as the journals reflect her con-
current reading of Colette, Rilke, and others.

Less interior, the Pajarito journals of this period function as
notebooks and workbooks for the writer. But at the same time,
Church exposed in the seemingly common everyday experiences of
the Pond children and the family history the sort of profound reality
that Marcel Proust regarded as the highest art:

> The grandeur of real art to discover, grasp again, and lay
> before us that reality from which we become more and
> more separated as the formal knowledge which we substi-
> tute for it grows in thickness and imperviousness—that
> reality which there is grave danger we might die without
> having known and yet which is simply our life.

No wonder it was a very simple encounter with Austin that Church most strongly remembered and that compelled her to keep working on the Austin biography. She had met Austin over a pot of soup in the 1930s shortly before Austin's death. In this domestic setting, Church says she felt most profoundly kin:

I had chosen the safe framework of marriage and maternity, a conventional woman's life, at least outwardly—she had chosen commitment to her career for the sake of which she would put away "childish things." I admired her and felt guilty before her—and yet felt what we most had in common was the fact of being women, with the mysterious, instinctive wisdom of the importance of the secret ingredients of the pepper-pot soup.

Though humorously put, Church later elaborated when she felt stymied and almost abandoned the biographical project: "We cleave to the woman to find the woman inside ourselves. . . . I must go on with the biography for the sake of the creative spirit."

By the end of the 1970s, Church had turned almost exclusively to the Pajarito Journals, not only writing in them sometimes daily, but also rereading, retyping, and reconsidering earlier entries. She would enter the decade of the 1980s and her own eighties still seeking to express what she felt a touchstone, "the pattern of ancient crossing."

(*Untitled*)

Poems ache
in the heart
the way stones do
in our abdominal organs;
stones that must travel a rough way
to excretion, tearing tissue,
sometimes no exit;
a mineral convexity
is wedged firm
in the constricted channel;
nothing issues
forth except now and then
a mute tear.

(1975)

Ashley Pond holding the infant Peggy in front of the house in Watrous, 1904. Courtesy Los Alamos Historical Museum Archives, Peggy Pond Church Collection.

Pond home in Watrous, ca. 1904. Courtesy Los Alamos Historical Museum Archives, Peggy Pond Church Collection.

Office in cabin on the Ramon Vigil Ranch, 1910s. Courtesy Los Alamos Historical Museum Archives, Peggy Pond Church Collection.

Ramon Vigil Ranch, 1910s. Courtesy Los Alamos Historical Museum Archives, Peggy Pond Church Collection.

Hazel, Ashley, and Peggy Pond, 1910s. Courtesy Los Alamos Historical Museum Archives, Peggy Pond Church Collection.

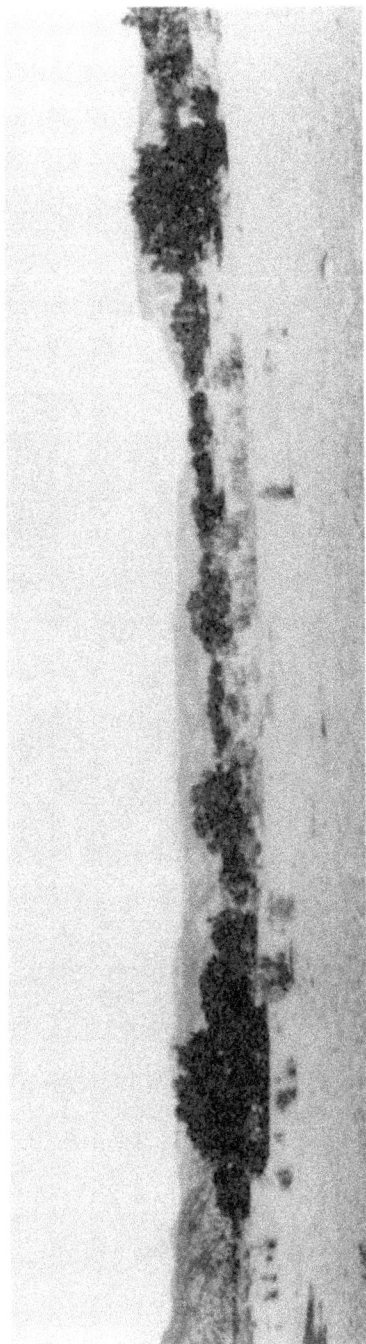

Buchanan Hill in background, Pajarito Plateau area, 1920s. Courtesy Los Alamos Historical Museum Archives, Peggy Pond Church Collection.

Pond family picnic, Pajarito Plateau, 1914 or 1915. From left to right: Hazel Pond, Peggy, Ashley, Dorothy, the governess Ellen Purdue, and Ashley III. Courtesy Los Alamos Historical Museum Archives, Peggy Pond Church Collection.

Living room, Ramon Vigil Ranch, 1910s. Courtesy Los Alamos Historical Museum Archives, Peggy Pond Church Collection.

Pajarito Plateau, 1920s. Courtesy Los Alamos Historical Museum Archives, Peggy Pond Church Collection.

Rito de los Frijoles, 1922. Courtesy Los Alamos Historical Museum Archives, Peggy Pond Church Collection.

Fermor and Peggy Pond Church, 1970. From the Kathleen Church collection.

Journals, 1970s

A recollection of [childhood] nights in Pullman berths on trains, curtained in; raising the still shade from time to time and peering out at the lights of a station or small town, lights in motion, and the deep blackness of the unknown behind it. Rattle and clack of the iron wheels on the rails. Being carried in the belly of a flexible dragon over a continent. The flat stretches of desert, looming layered cliffs, the pine forest after Flagstaff. At rest, yet being swiftly drawn forward, the space so small one felt cradled like an infant.

Or the acrobatics of climbing into the upper berth and undressing there, stowing one's items of clothing one by one in the green string hammock, the sleeping closed up as in a cocoon, and the same accented rolling rhythm of travel.

How familiar we grew with trains in our many transcontinental journeys. Waiting at Lamy to see the signal arm drop and the one-eyed monster appear slowly down the track, stopping at last with the white-coated genial porters stepping out. I smell the trains, coal dust and travelers' dust, and feel the prickle of the air on my bare arms and the steamy heat of the dining car corridor as we waited in the long jostling line. Hours of tedium, but a gay adventure. The continent unfolded itself, the track unwound like a ribbon or long line of music.

The continent was engraved within us, especially that part of it west of the Rocky Mountains. We knew its landmarks; the Continental Divide; the San Francisco peaks; the Mojave Desert. On the homeward trip from California, we gazed far off at what we thought to be the Enchanted Mesa (but it was really only another mesa whose name we did not know). Our mother told us stories. Blue sky, flung space, seen through the smoke-coated glass.

Later, how much more familiar that landscape would become in the long automobile journeys, back and forth over rough and dusty roads, distance becoming time to behold; cloudbursts, sandstorms, hours, sometimes, of monotony. Yet even the monotonous landscape unfolded sudden contours.

One grows old and times and places one has lived through are imprinted within us; memory is an unwinding scroll, physical memory, indentations of light, like the holes cut into computer cards. Time leaves its fossil print within us.

Yesterday we went to Garcia canyon to picnic under slits of cave dwellings, fragments of pottery, corrugated fragments of cooking pots, angular shards of bowls with black and white remnants of design.

That women should have dwelt here once, and in the midst of their hard, uncomfortable lives, made their pots and decorated them, caring for symmetry and beauty. The smoke-blackened ceilings of the caves, the coated floors—and I knew from childhood how cold a cave can be in bitter winter.

January 17, 1976

As I put the lid on the hot water pot this morning, came one of those flooding moments of awareness—the rounded circle within the surface of the water gleaming up; my knowledge of the nature of hot water—that it must be kept covered to prevent the heat escaping too fast. A lifetime of acquaintance with natural facts, and also, an experience of the mystery of shape, the magic of the circle, and underneath the plane surface, the dimension of depth. As running water from the tap is a holy act, so the putting of a lid onto a pot is also holy. The beautiful abstraction—the sense of wonder rising in me to meet the act.

Yesterday I kept being aware of so many different facets of myself— as though I were being aware of many separate persons who have lived my life, all from a slightly different aspect.

There is the person who grew up among the domestic animals, the dogs, the cats, the horses. And the wild animals—birds, fish, insects. The playful animals of childhood—chipmunks, rabbits, squirrels. And the fearsome ones—mountain lions, rattlesnakes, skunks, which were both attractive and repulsive.

There is the person who experienced life in relation to the family: father–mother; sister–brother; aunt–grandparents—the various male–female polarities.

And I also was aware of domestic servants. Black Bertha in my parents' home; and the various Indian girls and Spanish-Americans at Los Alamos: Tonita, Dolorita; Bessie; Ernestina, over whom I exerted my tyranny and of whom I used to dream.

I think of dear Lucia at Ranchos de Taos, illiterate but full of earth wisdom. And in Santa Fe, the years of Tina, whom I relied on but never loved. And beloved Recita, Cacique's daughter. And Maria.

Then in the afternoon, watching the documentary on Blake— those long years when I filled myself with Blake—from 1934 when Haniel first sent the lines about self-annihilation and eternal death, through 1956 when, during the nightmare nights of analysis, I slept with the collected poems under my pillow.

And then the "person" who became intensified with the life of nature, the rhythm of the seasons, the light and color of New Mexico landscapes. Loving it, wanting to be a part of it, wanting to know it, as one wished to know the body of a beloved in every intimate detail, down to the crystalline structure of the mineral grains, the chemistry of the clays, the relation between heights and depths that shape the rivers.

The smell of bat dung or rat nests in the cliff side; the presence of household fire, tame fire; tracks and trails.

January 18, 1976

Rereading my other journal entries about Poli and young Baba. My frequent "cruelty" to these dogs, the demon that ruled me, the wicked stepmother. But worse than that. Part of oneself, dominant and ferocious—a complex, irrational, uncontrollable self. This too was born within the infant? Born or acquired? She is still appalled when she remembers the untamable inner violence, called up whenever she failed to achieve obedience from those around her, whenever her will was thwarted. And this insoluble dilemma still haunts her:

the desire to love, yet the desire for power. Is this the effect of the animal world? The domestication of animals? The animal libido? The price of domestication? She dared not trust love?

February 6, 1976

Suddenly began thinking about my years at the Los Alamos Ranch School when I was, in part, so miserably unhappy that I made everyone else so. How I lamented to the psychiatrist in New Haven that I needed companionship—I needed to go to Santa Fe to see my friends. How I felt no companionship with Ferm—or anyone else. The male domination was poisonous to me, the absolute conformity of men to the strict regime that was devoted to forcing conformity among the boys. This was the atmosphere into which I was plunged after two years at Smith College where I had been extroverted and happy, with my own unformed soul and my animus notions of how a husband ought to be related to his wife; that he ought to companion her and help fulfill her intellectual needs. My fantasy, idolatry even, of other women whom I perceived to have this! How I kept running away (even as Mary Austin from her desert) to my friend Gay at Carmel, to feed my arid life upon her passionate life.

October 13, 1976

I think of the eastern slopes of the Sangre de Cristos tapering so suddenly off toward the plains. The difference is that over there [east of the Rockies] they have no element of mythology. No mountains, so far as I know, are sacred, no trails worn hip-deep in rock.

The history seems all surface. Beginning, so far as I yet know, with Coronado's journey across them in search of the Seven Cities of Cibola. And then the trials of mountain men, searching out beaver to enrich the great fur companies who employed them. Slaughter of the buffalo herds, decimation of Indian tribes; land-hungry men aggressively claiming title to river valleys and watercourses. Wagon trains creaking and straining, loaded with commodities; the tracks of the Santa Fe Trail fading that were once deeply rutted. Fort Barclay, Fort Union, built to protect the invading traders in commodity.

The cattlemen, the railroads, the mines, the lumber industries that raped the landscape. Who ever looked on the dawns with wonder and humility? The wild animals were prey or predator and no one said a prayer over the animal he killed.

How can one live without mythology?

Aggressive men with their herds of cattle. But no angels appeared to them to reveal the sacred places. No God spoke to them in the wilderness. One wonders who knew the names of the stars and the constellations that marked the seasons?

Here, at the edge of the Rio Grande Valley between the eastern and the western ranges, an ancient mythology has spread. The Tewa world is sacred; earth navels are renewed; rain and running water are numinous.

The Spanish brought their own mythology, built mission churches, carved and painted images of the holy family and their saints. The mysteries traveled with them, the Catholic mysteries of bread and wine and transubstantiation, rooted in pagan mysteries of man's ancient past. Their progress was attended by the favor of their warlike virgin—but a mother-divinity nonetheless.

On the eastern side of the mountains how lonely, how uprooted the women must have felt among the Protestant patriarchs, their own souls starving, as Mary Austin's starved, for any myth that related them to the feminine.

(Strange if my search for my own roots on the eastside of the mountains should bring me again to Mary Austin!)

Notes for Littlebird Trails over Pajarito

Before he started the school at Los Alamos, my father had tried to run a kind of glorified dude ranch in Pajarito Canyon for a group of Detroit automobile men whom he'd lured into buying the thirty-two-thousand-acre Ramon Vigil grant for a sort of recreation club. My father was an avid fisherman and so he was particularly good at luring!

I don't know how he first discovered the Pajarito Plateau. One year he'd been trying to develop a farm near Roswell; the next we children know, we found ourselves with our mother on the train that used to connect Santa Fe with Lamy Junction. After the flat plains around Roswell, and after the poppy-flooded fields of California where Mother had taken us that winter to go to school, we thought the granite hills on the way to Lamy were funny—just like pink hams stuck with cloves, or like Noah's ark scenery with trees dabbed on. I was going on eleven, my tow-headed sister was eight, and my blond and freckled brother not quite six. I, of course, thought myself immensely superior to both of them—except for the disadvantage of being the one who was always supposed to have "known better" when we got ourselves into scrapes.

When we got to Santa Fe, we stayed all night at a place known then as the DeVargas Hotel, so we could get an early start for the ranch the next day. The DeVargas was on the corner of Washington and Marcy Streets. It was really quite a fancy hotel, three stories high, and about the only thing I remember about it was the smooth and shiny pair of banisters which descended from the top floor without a post or impediment of any kind. They were the most wonderful banisters I ever slid down. I wonder now what on earth I could have been wearing? My mother usually dressed her daughters in khaki-colored middy blouse and bloomers for country life, but would she have let me wear bloomers in a hotel? And would I have dared slide down a banister in a dress? Probably not when my mother was looking, though I knew she herself had been quite a hoyden as a girl. She wore bloomers and rode astride long before it was the proper thing for any female. But now she was grown up. She was twenty-nine years old and really worked hard at being strict.

The DeVargas Hotel burned to the ground several years later when I happened, to my great disappointment, to be away at boarding school. It was after this fire that my father helped organize the Santa Fe Fire Department and was its chief for many years. He had a lifelong passion for putting out fires. The house he lived in during his last years in Santa Fe had a firepole in the closet near the head of his bed by which he could descend to the garage below, giving him a pretty good edge at being first, or at least among the first.

It was exciting to find out that we were going to live in a wild place called the Ramon Vigil grant ("Ramon Veehhel," not "Raymon Viggil," as we children smugly learned to correct our illiterate visitors from the east). Ramon Vigil was a relative newcomer who had bought the grant in 1851 from Antonio Sanchez. The latter was a descendent of Pedro Sanchez, to whom the grant had originally been made in 1742. This was when Gaspar de Mendoza was governor of New Mexico under the king of Spain—before the United States of America had been dreamed of—a fact about which we children could not have cared less at the time they were taking pains to drum it into us.

It was far more exciting to discover that the Pajarito Plateau on which the grant was situated—we always referred to it as "our ranch," even though it was no such thing—had been the home of Indians before the United States or the empire of Spain existed, even before Columbus discovered "America," which as far as we children had been told was where history began.

There were caves in the canyon wall just back of the corrals with pictographs carved in the smoke-blackened ceilings; fragments of pottery strewn all around like pieces of a picture puzzle; arrowheads to be found. I seemed to have a special knack for that—all colors and sizes, and sometimes bits of blue turquoise in the red ant hills near the ruined pueblos on the mesas. Life seemed to be a continual treasure hunt. We even hunted zealously for pots of gold at the end of the rainbows that often arched right down the base of the cliffs. "Right over there—just behind that big rock—just behind that clump of sagebrush"; so near we could never quite give up hoping.

Because my sister and I had been stuck in a convent in Los Angeles during the spring that the Pajarito adventure was beginning, most of what I know about details comes out of newspapers. According to *The Santa Fe New Mexican* for March 24, 1914:

"The Detroit men now negotiating the purchase of the Ramon Vigil Grant are at work on tentative plans for a recreation settlement, consisting of a rambling, picturesque club house and surrounding bungalows about twelve miles from Buckman over in the cliff dwellers country."

The "fine clubhouse" was remodeled from a disused barn. When my mother first saw it, her heart really sank. It had no floor; windows and doors were missing, and cattle wandered in and out, along with squirrels and mice and all the other creatures that liked to adapt man's abandoned dwellings to their own use.

If there ever was a fastidiously tidy woman, it was my mother, and her fifteen years of married life certainly put all her tidy as well as her decorative instincts to the test. The first house my father had taken his very young bride to—she was only seventeen when they were married—was washed away in the real New Mexico flood of 1904. This was in Shoemaker Canyon a few miles from Watrous, which is seventy-five miles away from Las Vegas, where my father was getting ready to open his first school. All our clothes and possessions were lost. Navajo rugs were plowed out of fields for years afterward, and a huge commercial size icebox has never yet been found. My father took his wife and ten-month-old daughter, which happened to be me, back to his family home in Detroit, where he made a valiant, but half-hearted effort to become a businessman. We had a really elaborate house somewhere out in the country with a real lake almost in the backyard, but by then my father's severe case of New Mexico-itis had become chronic. Around 1910, after his father died and left him with an independent income, he got hooked on the idea of a farm near Roswell.

I never understood just why the building he put up was a garage with a concrete floor. A little tarpaper-covered lean-to was built on one side for a kitchen, and another lean-to served as a sleeping porch. The sleeping porch had no screens, and I remember we had a pet lamb [that] turned all at once, it seemed, into a sheep and had to be eaten.

Mother took heirlooms from the ancestral home in Detroit and placed them attractively around the garage to make a combination dining–living room, but I know she always hated the place. When it grew terribly hot, we children were allowed to take our naps on the cool floor under the dining room table. After her Roswell experience, even the Pajarito packrats could have seemed possible to Mother.

But she was nothing if not game in those days; I think her greatest talent was really for creating homes, and I must say that my father provided her with some rare opportunities. I remember when I was very little that she even took a course in architectural drawing, and she always claimed to have taught one of Santa Fe's leading architects about the importance of certain practical details such as closets! With the help of another architect, the barn [on the Vigil grant] was ingeniously turned into a two-story house with white frames around the windows, a sort of porch at one side with a white railing and white-painted posts, and an elegant portico at one side with a balcony on the top upheld by white pillars.

The barn had what we called a "tin" roof; the sides were covered with sheets of galvanized iron, painted, as I remember them, barn-red, but the white pillars of the porch and the portico and the white-painted trellises somehow gave the building an air of unsuspected grace. My mother was a gifted gardener. She planted spirea around the porch; roses grew on trellises around the window; nasturtiums flourished in window boxes outside the second story windows. Somehow or other she managed a flower garden, for wherever we lived I remember vases of delphinium and baby's breath all about the house.

She had been promised, I am sure, plenty of house and garden help. A Spanish-American family or two lived on the place. They wrangled horses, kept them shod, milked cows, did laundry, and pitched-in in the kitchen. *The Santa Fe New Mexican* refers to "Korean gardeners, Japanese chef, and a Filipino assistant," but I have no memory of them specifically.

When I first saw the mesas where the present Los Alamos now stands, I was on a pack trip from Pajarito Canyon where my parents were living. We were going to Puyé. I was about eleven or twelve, and it was the first time I'd been on a real grown-up expedition. It was a long day ride, the longest I had been on. I don't know who was along besides my parents and Vay Morley and a humorous old guide named Ruggles.

I was given a little bay horse to ride named Peanuts that I'd never seen before. Peanuts embarrassed me terribly, bucking me off before we'd even started. I had just put the saddle on and cinched it up and mounted full of pride, hoping the adults were noticing how well I knew the ropes. And the next thing I knew, Peanuts had doubled up in the middle and was lurching and spinning like a cross between a top and a firecracker. I'd fallen off horses millions of times, usually from being run away with. But the minute Peanuts started to spin, I realized there was a whale of a difference between falling off a galloping horse and being bucked off. There is a double-jointed kind of stiff-leggedness to the motion that seems absolutely calculated to separate each vertebra from its neighbor, and it didn't take more that two or three spins to convince me that I wanted off of there but quick! The next thing I knew I was on the ground in kind of a random pile of my own arms and legs, and Peanuts was continuing the rodeo performance off in another direction. I wasn't half as scared that I might have broken my neck as I was that I wouldn't be allowed to go on the trip after all. So I got back on and even managed to sit sort of convincingly, despite being sore, on the horse. My father didn't condemn my horsemanship, as I was afraid he might. When he and Charles Ruggles caught Peanuts they found a burr or something and decided that had been the trouble. My real error had been in forgetting to lead him about a bit the way I'd been taught to do before I mounted, but I was forgiven, Peanuts was resaddled, and after that gave no more trouble.

We started up a trail that went back of our barn on to the mesa north of the canyon. The upper part of the trail was steep and rocky. There was a place where we had to get off the horses and lead them, scrambling up ahead of them so they wouldn't jump on us in their own scramble. On top of the mesa, there was an old wagon road. The ruts cut deeply through the bare tuff. I suppose they had been made by wagons hauling lumber to Buckman in the early days. There was a place about five miles west called MacDougall's farm. Past there we were really in thick pine forest, with here and there a little clearing and the tumbledown shacks of a "bean ranch," [and] sometimes a few cattle straying about. We crossed Los Alamos Canyon on another remnant of road about where the bridge is now. There was a ranch on the mesa called the Brook farm. Our trail went just west of the fence, at the base of the mountains, following the old forest service telephone line. I remember the cleared fields, the little muddy pond, a few old cottonwood trees, and that long and splendid view to the east of the Sangre de Cristos.

We crossed Pueblo Canyon, and right up the other side, and were on what we know now as Barranca Mesa, again a few cleared fields and bean ranches, lots of oak brush, as I remember, and a great silence when we sat down for a while to rest. Later, when I first went to Los Alamos to live, I tried several times to find the "telephone trail" between Pueblo Canyon and Guaje, and missed it.

Guaje was the steepest of all the canyons, and I love it because of its quick-splashing stream. In most of the other canyons, the stream beds were dry, or else the water was very evasive, sinking underground, and coming up only here and there under the roots of some big tree.

It was late evening when we finally got to the canyon that borders the Puyé mesa on the south and made our camp. Having got that far, my memory fades out—except for a recollection of the wild tales that Ruggles, the guide, kept telling us about creatures called the "whim-wham," the "whanky-doodle," and the "side hill hodag." What the first two were escapes me, but the idea of the side hill hodag was really delicious—the creature whose legs are considerably shorter on the one side than the other, so it has to live on hillsides, and can easily be caught if you frighten it and make it turn around and go the other way! Stories like that are easy to believe when the moon is making black shadows on the ground under Puyé and owls are making hollow noises full of magic.

October 27, 1976

The land puts dreams into the minds of men; my father's love of the beauty of New Mexico was deep; his dream of making it possible for young boys to experience the outdoor ranching life which seemed more vital to him than learning from books. His similarity to Waite Phillips's dream when he gave Philmont to the Boy Scouts [Philmont Scout Ranch near Cimarron, New Mexico].

I have seen the environment in which I spent my prenatal months, as well as the ensuing first ten months of my life—that land in Mora County which my father owned before the flood ruined him. This must have been the disappointment of his life—to have owned this beautiful land and had his dreams destroyed by natural disaster. I have seen this land, and it has felt oddly familiar to me. Why do the Indians always have such an attachment to the land in which their ancestors lie buried? What do they project? What do I?

November 11, 1976

Dreamed I am in a very small group, apparently a poetry seminar, led by a blondish young man. He gives me some sort of wry encouragement. I tend, rather ostentatiously, to depreciate myself a little, to behave as though I did not know my worth. But I enjoy the class and begin writing something.

All of sudden, the bank of earth in front of where I am sitting (for the class seems to be held out-of-doors) begins caving in. An enormous hole opens up just in front of me, showing the instability of the earth underneath. But I seem to be in no special danger; the cave-in does not reach as far as where I am sitting.

I move back a little and continue my writing. Then a pretty blond woman begins reading aloud to someone else in a strong voice. I then begin to make a fuss, saying, "I guess I'll have to leave the class. There is simply too much noise for me to concentrate on my poetry writing." We move upstairs—a room with a large sunny balcony around. The "teacher" smilingly, but authoritatively, deals with me, saying he understands my problem. Had there not been a terrible flood shortly after I was born? He implies this must have been trau-matic—that I carried the unconscious memories of that night of terror. The darkness, the sound of rushing water, the terror of my mother and my nurse.

And I realized this must be so. That was why the earth opened into a black hole ahead of me—and why I was so insecure in many ways.

And I related in my interpretation of this dream to Lear in the tempest. His rising madness. My own fear of libido rushing from the depths. And perhaps this fear must be brought out of its depths, ex-perienced and recognized.

December 3, 1976

Water . . . But I spread out too far, for my first intent was to make of the Pajarito country the microcosm. We had everything there but an ocean. We knew of only one river, the Rio Grande, which bordered our happy wilderness, its grandiloquent name ap-propriate only in early summer and then becoming pure exaggera-tion. There were only, in the whole plateau, only two or three perennial streams. Others flowed a little way and then sank into the sand and vanished. We knew they did not die, for sometimes they ap-peared again, mysteriously, a little further away, bubbling out over a ledge of lava, or under the roots of a tree so that we knew the water had been there all the time, flowing secretly in an unseen channel

—minor editions in our minds of "Alph, the sacred river" flowing through its caverns leisurely down to a sunless sea.

We children made the most of the little water we had. We dammed it and built villages beside it; we made all kinds of boats, very miniature, and sailed them upon it. We diverted it to water secret gardens. We learned shivering respect for the muddy torrents that poured down our tame brook after summer rains and the hurried muscular energy of the water in spring when all the water seemed obsessed with haste to get back to the nearest ocean after its winter's captivity in the mountain snowfields.

Water was a deity we could understand; [on] its presence almost everything that lived depended. When the summer rains delayed, we watched the country dry up and felt in our flesh the torment of cracked earth, bristling dry grass, stunted flowers, old trees that became no more than withered branches. Only under the north-facing edges of stones could anything try to grow. Lichens persisted, tough and adaptable and crusty, capable of endurance as a camel. But no wild life we knew fed on the lichens.

The mountain looked cool and blue, but the few clouds that rose above it were tenuous and sterile, hardly able to cast more than the wannest of shadows over the fevered land. The sun traveled across the sky golden and burning. Leaves lost their exultant springtime look and hung harsh and without motion. Pine needles boiled with the antiseptic fragrance of turpentine. Most of the birds disappeared, though hawks and buzzards were more conspicuous than ever.

Watrous flood . . . Re-reading the newspaper accounts of the Watrous flood last night. Strange how my father, who so feared fire and fought it all his life, should have almost been ruined, almost annihilated by flood.

A young man in his 32nd year (a little more than halfway through his life), his young wife, barely eighteen; his first child, a daughter, still an infant in arms. The flood arises swiftly in the dark of night. In the small hours of morning, two-thirty A.M., the great Dane dog awakens her master; the water is flowing over the bedroom floor.

(But this is according to the story handed down much later to me. I do not see how it can be quite true, for he was living then in the two-story brick house, and the bedrooms were, presumably, on the second floor. The brick house is standing to this day.)

The family, in their night clothes, with not even time to put on their shoes. They wade, a young nurse, the mother carrying her baby, the father supporting them, to a barn on the hillside. The water has spread out like the Mississippi from wall to wall of the valley.

The shivering women are piled deep into the hay; they laugh at their plight, make jokes (humor, humans' greatest weapon against terror) until daylight. The father can then hitch up the team of horses and drive by a circuitous route to the little town of Watrous, which has become a kind of refugee camp.

In the little hotel, a mother and father are thought to be dying. Two of their children were drowned, and the exhausted parents were found clinging to a pile of tables in the house that was soon swept to fragments.

So, ten months old, without consciousness, the infant is exposed to mortal danger and rescued from it. She is held safe in her father and mother's arms: the episode apparently left no scars. Nothing in the psyche dreams of flood nor flinches at the sound of rushing water.

"The most exciting event of my life," she often laments, "and I can remember nothing of it."

December 4, 1976

The primitive and heroic world into which I came at birth. My mother said the bag of water broke, and hers was a dry labor (like mine with my third child). She was only four months past her eighteenth birthday.

Then, only two months after her nineteenth birthday, she faced an ordeal as strenuous as the birth. Waked in the night, time only to seize a "dressing gown" and her baby, to face the raging waist-deep waters, to be carried through them by her sturdy husband. A party of three men, two women, an infant and a small black dog, huddled wet in the cold hay all night in that barn on higher ground against the hillside. How many horses were in the barn? And in the morning, it must have been a team of horses hitched to the wagon to carry five persons and the infant to town, perhaps a two-hour rough journey, with the young women huddled in the hay, the men with Navaho blankets hugged around their bodies.

Spent three hours in the state library yesterday going over the flood newspaper, and realizing again what a miracle that we escaped.

Also the extent of the storm which covered a twenty-four-hundred-mile area from Flagstaff to Kansas City, and how far south I am not sure. Its center was in the Pecos high country just west of Las Vegas, so that all the streams that ran from those mountains were swollen with rain; the great leashed power and energy of water frantically working to return to the ocean from which it came.

This "land of little rain," these thousands of "dry" gullies which carve the land all around us, millenniums of erosion, mountains being torn down cliff by cliff, grain by grain, to be engulfed by inland oceans and then uplifted to form limitless plains. The heaving and buckling forces within the earth—the vents opened through which the molten lavas flow.

Lately—almost within the last decade—we have learned of the "convection plumes" within earth's mantle, upon which the pasty slabs of the continents are carried, seemingly rigid bodies slowly spiraling, circling the globe.

Just below Watrous is a sudden rent, a slit in the horizontal monotony of the plains. The Mora River, which has been sluggishly meandering almost invisibly through the land of low relief, suddenly straightens and carves itself in an east-west valley between two ridges of sandstone which it traverses for perhaps five to seven miles before turning southward through Cherry Valley and the unseen escarpment of the Canadian River, the Red, which entrenches itself in an east-west course.

There are forces on the face of the earth and within the earth struggling with each other. Cataclysmic forces. The violence of water seems to come from the sky, the heaped clouds, the lightning, the downpour of water. The water rushes into channels it has formed drop by drop and trickle by trickle. Water which is our life. Which can be our death.

February 22, 1978

I think of those years of deep winter on the plateau. Snow used to heal the country of the presence of human beings. I used to imagine the silence of the Valle Grande before the automobile road went into it. And the former inhabitants must have huddled near to one another for warmth, cherished their stores of corn in the covered pits, hunted the deer with urgent prayer. How brilliantly the stars burned over the white silent mesas, making the sky seem even more immense and black.

Familiar stars. They must be part of my Pajarito story.

We did not have television or even radio, but we had the living drama of nature. Sky drama, the progress of the seasons, from that long drawn-out first autumn, the deep winter, the release of moisture in the spring, making cascades and waterfalls down the cliff faces, the earth rich, black, soaked as a sponge on the north-facing slopes and in the protected crevices and seams.

How I lived in the fairy gardens of the mosses, with the rounded spore cups like miniature forests above the carpet of green and the ferns that grew valiantly under the overhanging edges of small rocks, the fertile smell of decaying loam.

I do not remember the progressions of the flowers. Usually, on the mesas, sudden, very small composites, daisylike, growing in solitary daring in the first full sun, protected from wind by their low-growing form. I do not remember pasque flowers then, only much later, on another part of the plateau, but we found violets, purple and white along the stream. Blue clematis bloomed, hanging from still unleafed shrubs. Toward autumn the dainty-flowered clematis called virgin's bower tangled itself.

December 8, 1978

For three summers and a winter, Pajarito became our marvelous playground. I remember the first afternoon when we sprang out of the car as though spring had released us—like jumping jacks. We ran instantly to the corral and barns without even bothering to pay attention to the metal-sided, red-painted "house" which would be our new home. It was late afternoon, and a swarthy whiskered man named Felipe was milking a smooth-sided Jersey cow. He smiled at us. He offered to let us try our hands at milking. I remember the feel of the teat, soft as a doeskin glove. To squeeze it looked so easy, but the cow, in silent stubborn laughter, withheld her milk. Felipe drew us each a mug full, warm and frothy, in it all the essence of a sun-filled field. Looking back I think now that it was one of those magic drinks of fairy tale which gains the wanderer admittance into that world or enables him to understand the language of birds. Perhaps, it held secretly the ingredients of a love potion. I fell instantly in love with the canyon world; my sister developed a life-long attachment to horses.

January 11, 1979

Tired and toxic this morning—the uncooperative inner stress—of feeling the burden of finishing the research on the Pajarito Plateau, the Ramon Vigil Ranch, my father's life. I want to do it, but I cannot seem to make the time. The conflict rends me and causes stress. I fall out of Tao. I am divided, too, about the focus of the story. Am I too eager to "pick nits" and correct history? The impossible child who is always right? Shades of Mary Austin who made a career of telling everyone where to get off?

We used to speak of it often as "The Pajarito"; the Ramon Vigil; the Ramon Vigil Ranch. Officially, at least by 1916, it was "The Pajarito Club." I suspect my father intended to make something like Vermejo Park [a privately owned recreation area for businessmen near Raton, New Mexico]. The only evidence I have is the photograph which shows him on horseback outside the entrance to the Vermejo.

In those days there was plenty of hunting on the plateau: deer, mountain lion, wild turkey. Fishing, however, was practically nonexistent. Instead, there were expeditions among the canyon and mesa ruins, horseback rides in a setting of marvelous wild beauty. It was a man's life. Teddy Roosevelt perhaps established this pattern. Maybe it was the escape from the industrial revolution. When did the move begin? Has anyone written on it?

I think of writing an essay about my experience on the plateau. Doug Schwartz asked me to write something for *Discovery*.

I can still remember the first time I saw it—the drive out from Santa Fe, hot and in the brilliant sunshine of mid-June. Did we ride in the "touring car" with its top down? Over the eroded gravelly hills, along the side of the Caja del Rio mesas, then the long downgrade into Buckman, the dingy relic of a one-time village—really only a loading place then for lumber and cattle.

From Santa Fe, the plateau is a place of mystery, an archetype of a lost world. Those tongue-shaped mesas, the blank-faced escarpment. My mind filled with illustrations of books, of fairy tales, I could not help comparing it to a kind of fortified defense, fortified like a medieval castle with steep walls and a moat around it—the river in a slow curve at the base of the escarpment. Like an adventure from fairy tales where the hero-youth ascends into a giant's realm, performs the ordeal of crossing a magic river, scales an impossible height, penetrates a towering fortification and arrives in a secret land, guarded perhaps by dragons.

The plateau, seen from the eastside of the river, seems enchanted—like something remembered in a dream.

At Los Alamos, I had a horse of my own from the beginning and a beautiful worn and supple old western saddle that had belonged to my great-grandfather when he ranched in Colfax and Mora counties. The saddle had been passed on to my mother, who would never officially give up title to it, though she let me ride it for more than twenty years—in fact, until we left Los Alamos and my riding days were over. The saddle which I doted on as though it were part of myself is now in the possession of my brother's family, but his children, like mine, turned out to be skiers, not horseback riders, and so are the grandchildren.

Of course, my father had made us all learn to ride without a saddle and wouldn't give me one for years. That was when I was about eight years old, and he had given me an ornery white horse named Sam that dumped me off almost every day. "You ought to know better than that how to ride," he scornfully told me. But one day his team of mules ran away. There was no horse he could chase them on but Sam. He hadn't the time to saddle up but leaped on bareback—and Sam ran away with him, he who had been one of Roosevelt's very own Rough Riders! The next day he went off to town and bought me my first saddle. Sam, no doubt glad to be properly clad for once, never ran away again with either of us.

In Pajarito Canyon, we still rode bareback most of the time. We either scrambled up by grasping the horse's mane, putting one foot on the bump at her knee as though it were a step (you had to be barefooted, as we always were, to do this); or else, if we were lazy and there was no need to show off in front of guest-ranch visitors, we would lead the horse beside the stump of a cut tree and climb up before she moved aside.

The mare, Daisy, I first had at Los Alamos, was a stubborn creature who liked to lead me on a cockeyed chase with ears laid back and an occasional flippant show of her heels, round and round the hay bins in the corral before she'd condescend to let me catch her. It seemed that half my afternoon riding time was spent stalking her, with the bridle in my left hand, held coyly behind my back (of course, I knew she knew it was there all the time), and my right hand enticingly cupped in the hope she'd think I carried a palmful of oats. I don't remember whether she was the kind who opened her mouth obligingly when she knew the game was up or whether I had to poke the bit hard between her clenched teeth, like a little boy who will not eat his spinach. With her temperament, I'm rather sure it was the latter.

Daisy was a good trail horse, though, and I never had to worry when I was out with her alone. My rides were usually alone, for my husband was kept busy with the boys—on whom the presence of women was supposed to be a debilitating influence. It might remind them of their mothers from whom Mr. Connell, the director, was stubbornly certain they must be firmly weaned. To tell the truth, I've always liked best to be alone on a horse, among the cliffs and pine trees or on the side of a mountain; the listening is always so much better, not to mention the difficult art of keeping still.

I carried a lunch in one of a pair of saddlebags and always a slicker tied on behind. How well I remember the brim of my Stetson filled with the rain running in dribbles over the end of my nose. The enticing smell of wet horse and saddle leather is something I don't know how to explain to my grandchildren, except that it goes perfectly with the smell of coffee boiling over a campfire and the smell of wet pine needles or of moldy logs among spruce trees. At least I'm sure that aluminum and canvas backpacks are nothing like it.

Once in a while I'd go fishing if I came to a live stream like Guaje, but the fish, if any I managed to catch, were always too small. They should have been put back, except I never could get them neatly off the hook. The only time I caught a really good one I'd forgotten to bring any grease for the pan, and I'm afraid I burned him to a crumpled cinder.

When my sister and I were children on the Pajarito, we were crazy about horses. She had a black, roly-poly horse named Black Beauty, of course, and I, a spindly sorrel mare named Dolly—but not by me. If I could have had my choice, I would have ridden a wild stallion with a name like Aldeberan or Bayard or Grani. Dolly was chased by a mountain lion that first summer and got a great gash on her shoulder from crashing into a barbed wire fence. I couldn't ride her for weeks but led her about to graze and tended her wound myself, rubbing some marvelous black ointment that my father called "jam" and used for all his animals and children. In the process, Dolly and I grew fond of one another, and I grew even fonder when Dolly produced a colt with all the liveliness its mother lacked, a ruffled scrap of a mane, and an expressive twitch of a curly tail.

My father had a wonderful black horse named Seal who would never stand still for him to mount, so he used to run at a gallop alongside the galloping horse and vault on for all the world like a circus rider or a mythical hero. We used to play at circus riding too, using one of the wagon horses if we could, because they were more docile and had the broadest backs, but for them to stand for a few seconds was all we could hope for. The ground, we decided, was a lot harder to fall on than circus sawdust could have been.

Not satisfied with our live horses, we also made imitation steeds out of scraps of lumber from a disused sawmill. We hammered on triangular bits of board for heads, and made flowing manes and tails of string, frayed rope, or even sometimes real horsehair snitched from the barn or the fences. We each thus acquired a whole string of horses to which we gave the most elaborate literary names. With these we played continuing games of horse thief. My mother used to recite Kipling's *Ballad of East and West,* and we dramatized the theft of the Colonel's mare, which was the Colonel's pride, over and over again. Each of us had our favorite steed and our favorite hiding places among the rocks or abandoned shacks. The aim of the game, of course, was to steal one another's favorite horse and add it to our own string.

Pajarito Canyon was really a terrific playground. I grow sad when I think of my grandchildren growing up in development houses, scooting their mechanical toys around on pavements and sidewalks, and being chauffeured by careful mothers wherever they go, absorbing adventure ready-made from TV, with little opportunity to create their own.

It seems to me I played with my brother and sister relatively seldom, partly because, being the eldest, I was so bossy. I do think I was the most imaginative at making up games, not to mention that my games seemed always to get us in trouble with parental authority. I did enjoy being by myself among rocks and trees and animals and wonders of the skies and seasons.

Though we lived in a canyon, the night sky was magnificent: the canyon walls made a kind of channel up which the stars marched. I still have a book called *The Friendly Stars* out of which my mother taught me the names of the constellations and of the special stars that glowed in them. Though I took a year of astronomy at college and learned to identify the separate stars by the letters of the Greek alphabet, the ones I remember best are those my mother taught me—Vega, Altair, and Deneb—the Lyre, the Swan, the square of Pegasus, the sword of Perseus, and Cassiopeia's mysteriously upside down chair. I still watch Vega in the Lyre, shining down above the Santa Fe Opera in summer with an aching sense of sustained recognition.

The smell of the barns, the stalls, the straw soaked with strong smelling urine, mixed with steamy manure. The grainy smell of oats, the sweetish, still slightly moist smell of hay. The sparrows always pecking and scratching about. The hen's eggs found warm in hay piles or mangers or feed boxes. She remembers the smell of disinfectant used around horses—creosote—and the strong-smelling jellies used to cover open wounds made by the rubbing of too-tight saddle girths. How the horses, unsaddled, would roll as soon as they could in the corral. The animal so grotesque when it lies down, the thin neck stretched on the mounded sides heavy and ungraceful. The flies will not let it rest. It rolls completely over and then gets up again.

She remembers the care with which her father trained the children to care for the horses. How to catch one's horse, creeping up quietly so it will not run away, holding the bridle with one hand behind one's back. She kept the horse backing up so as not to leap past her. Memory of not flinching, showing no fear, whether, even as a small child, you can prove yourself master.

She remembers how he taught them to watch the horses for saddle sores, sometimes along their backs, but most often under the tender belly. Sometimes the skin would be rubbed raw and a round sore appeared, which had to be dusted with a disinfectant powder. If the sore was very bad, she couldn't ride for a few days. She was taught that the best thing was to properly girt the horse in the first place. If sores developed, the inference was that she had been careless; the penalty, no riding for a few days.

Always the emphasis was on caring for and responsibility toward the animal. It was not just a plaything. A kind of initiation was required before one was found worthy of a horse, and in the association one's sense of reality was developed. Daydreaming and fantasy had to be curbed.

She learned the horse had to be physically cared for and also disciplined. It must be taught to give up its wild freedom and learn to respond to bit and bridle. And this was best done through winning the animal's trust, slowly, patiently. There were many who believed that the animal must first be "mastered," must have its rebellious spirit "broken" and indeed the procedure was usually referred to as "breaking." The rider, the trainer, would by brute strength enforce his will, would allow the frantic animal to exhaust its strength until it learned the futility of rebellion. She remembers how she and her sister had read in *Black Beauty* that the checkrein was cruel. The conflict with her father's practical teachings.

Growing up among animals! Do autobiographies mention them? The dogs, Princess, Arco, Rags, Boy and Boris; the German Shepherds, Theda, Draga, Buddy. Then we marry and have our own, Ponce, Buffy, Jaime, Eloise, Beau. At last Poli-kota, the white butterfly (in Hopi), and Baba-the-Turk. As much or more a part of our lives as our own siblings.

February 2, 1979

Four years ago this morning my dear companion died. Whom I married [more] from my love [of the] Pajarito Plateau than for any other reason, so we could live there. And then lived on it for eighteen years, plus the two in Pajarito Canyon which began it all.

From what point of view shall I tell mystery? My own, I suppose, would give it most reality. But where to begin? With the old woman remembering? The old woman exploring the almost obliterated trails of memory?

How the plateau became a part of my inner geography. With the child, ten years old, scornful of dolls, pagan instinct, having cut her teeth on myths of the Greeks, on the poets whose geography is timeless and universal.

February 22, 1979

It started snowing about six o'clock last night, and by midnight about four or five inches had fallen, the most at any one time this winter. This morning, after a restless night, I woke late to a white world, a gray heavy sky, and still low barometer. It is utterly still. Nothing moves. The paper delivery truck did not make it up the driveway. The world has become a still picture or like the suddenly immobilized world of Sleeping Beauty.

February 25, 1979

I must first, of course, write that sketch of the Pajarito which Doug Schwartz [Church's friend and representative in Santa Fe] suggested. How the hearts of children responded to it—at least my sister's and mine did. And this child, at least, in that delicious condition of prepuberty, her body still flat as a boy's—the wonderful irresponsibility of childhood, playing at life, while the adults lived and contended with it and left their auras of rage or despair hovering about like birds of ill omen to confound us.

To be thrust suddenly into the midst of a prehistoric world! The talus on the south-facing slope back of the barn covered with scattered shards, angular broken pieces of pottery, each with a tantalizing fragment of design, like the unsorted pieces of a giant picture puzzle, or like the words in a dictionary torn from their alphabetical order and flung piecemeal by some explosive wind, or like letters from an undeciphered alphabet spilled all out of order, untranslatable.

We children picked up the pieces and filled our pockets with them, at home filled shoeboxes, and when these overflowed, filled the half-bushel wooden boxes that fruit came packed in.

Winter on the Pajarito (sketch): Overnight the sleek horses grew fuzzy coats. Suddenly we were able to take out our sleds, on which we mostly just pulled one another around, for to our disappointment the canyon was not adapted for sledding. Its lower slopes were too rocky, the upper walls upright as walls of great buildings; on the south-facing side, the snow melted off too fast. On the north-facing side, the slopes were still too deep and encumbered with shrubs and trees. The road that went up it in a long diagonal was soon rutted. After some experimental efforts, we sighed and put our sleds away.

Even our horses were a disappointment. They stumbled and lurched; their hooves quickly became clotted with snowballs which we had to dig out over and over again with sharp sticks.

There was so little to do to keep us out from underfoot. Luckily, my father had imported a governess that first summer who stayed with us all year. I wonder whether it was mother who paid her salary out of her cemetery inheritance? Her name was Ellen Purdue. She was rather plain, but not forbidding. We always called her dutifully, "Miss Purdue." It was a French name, she said, that meant "lost," which sounded mysterious, even a little pathetic. No doubt we heard Daddy play upon the name, for he was adept at wordplay and filled our days with unforgivable puns and mockery.

In the summer months, Miss Purdue walked and picnicked with us. She started out immediately having us make a collection of wildflowers. We gathered them and pressed each one between the pages of a book and then mounted them carefully on sheets of drawing paper which were later bound with strips of gummed paper called *passé-partout* (I can see how my French vocabulary was increasing).

In winter my father fitted up one of the rehabilitated sawmill shacks into a one-room schoolhouse. Was the outside painted red or am I unable to eradicate the image of the "little red school house"? The three children in the carpenter's family and we three reluctant scholars.

I remember very little about our Pajarito school days [with their governess]. My mind was subject to daydreaming or else to making a relentless nuisance of myself. One afternoon I got the giggles and was sent out of the room until I could control myself. I made off as fast as I could to a rim of the tributary canyon and there hid myself among the rocks, looking back defiantly at the prison house I had escaped from, hatching plans to run away—and then wouldn't they be sorry? Sorry, perhaps, when the frustrated rebel returned and had to be severely dealt with and probably given a spanking.

What I learned at Pajarito has lasted my all my life, but it didn't come out of the dull-covered textbooks—especially out of the Wentworth *Arithmetics*, nor the geographies with their drawings of seaports or oil rigs (yes, even in those days)—and their dreary statistics. Arithmetic always defeated me and still does. But I remember one day Miss Purdue sent me out to measure the fenced field and, multiplying one side by another, to find out how many square feet there were. This was an accomplishment—a bit of knowledge I worked out for myself. What could I have learned from laboriously measuring the shadow of a tree and somehow calculating its height? Whatever it was gave me another thrill in which school became not only a tedious recitation of dull facts having nothing at all to do with myself, but a course of learning "how to." A source of discovering for oneself. And I was excited, now and then, as though I myself had sailed out and discovered America.

February 26, 1979

While doing the research I must not forget the protagonist of the story, the Pajarito Plateau, that particular section of it known as the Ramon Vigil grant, that section of earth, formed of fiery molten ash, ash spread like a river of fire down the slopes of a volcanic mountain. How soon after the earth cooled did life take root and begin to grow? Microscopic organisms; the volcanic ash is porous, barely consolidated; leaching begins with the first rains.

March 2, 1979

This "history" of mine will be worthless if I cannot put feeling into it. I go back to my father. I think he must have been born a man of feeling—but in his days, the masculine values were emphasized—the "manly" virtues. This meant suppressing the woman in himself. And so he went on to suppress the woman in his children, the rippling faces of feminine.

My mother—how did she become such an Amazon? She, too, taught to live up to the masculine code of duty. She doted on the story of the Spartan boy who let the fox gnaw his vitals rather than speak up before summoned to. How does a child learn anything about her feminine nature? Why does she project it onto Nature? I suppose my mother was really a better man than my father was.

I do not know whether the three children in my memory are real or whether I have made them up as I went along. The physical world they lived in affected them all so differently.

How differently the plateau has been looked on by all who knew it. By the Indians who found its canyons shelter from the cold; its mesas a fortress against enemies who were aware of the great tensions that move between earth and sky and believed they could influence those energies for their own.

To the man who put up his sawmill and reduced the great red-barked trees to lumber and sawdust.

To the men who used it for grazing ground and a safe bedding place.

To the men who herded their meager flocks of sheep and goats.

To the men who hoped to use it for their playground, an escape into nature from the raucous industrial city in which they were making their fortunes.

To the woman, the wife of the ranch foreman, who died there in the cold November flu epidemic.

To the children who played their own traditional games and invented their own mythology, almost entirely oblivious to the grown-up world.

Last, but unfortunately not least, to the military minds who came seeking a site for secret research into the development and production of a fearful nuclear weapon which many fear may in the end lead to the extinction of all living species on our planet. I cannot make myself agree, personally, with this conclusion. I don't have that much faith in the omnipotence of the human race.

March 6, 1979

How to put the child's personal story among the arid facts?

The area of land, so large, so beautiful. The way the cliffs caught the sun on their huge, upright plane surfaces—the modulations of color from almost chalky white through rich cream to salmon pink. The colors came in bands, the strong, cliff-forming layer at the top, smooth as though some kind of varnish had been poured over it; the softer layers underneath, winter, gritty, with knobs of pumice, tiny fragments of obsidian; the sloping shelf between the layers where soil had accumulated, where stiff and bristly desert-type shrubbery grew, blades of yucca, defiant yellow senecios with gray leaves; now and then a piñon or even a young pine managed to establish itself. (But here I am drifting to my adult view!)

The flowers—because of Miss Purdue, stories my mother told of girlhood visits to her grandfather at Watrous on the other side of the mountains—became companions. So did some of the birds. The mourning dove whose soft call flowed in a low triplet through the summer air, the bluebirds I built a cumbersome house for out of a big wooden egg crate, a shingle nailed over the front and a round hole in the center of the doorway. Someone nailed it for me in the big yellow pine tree that stood halfway between the house and the barn, and miraculously, a pair of brilliant bluebirds actually nested there and raised a brood of young. The big piñon jays cut the air with cries like scissors. The vultures we called buzzards soared and floated on the currents of warm air that rose from the heated canyon walls, making slow circular patterns and sudden slanting drops. In the late autumn, the juncos, the first harbingers of winter.

To set forth the conflicts and tensions that were part of the experience. The male and female conflict; the adventurous life of the men, always going forth on horseback to explore, to hunt; the night "Cinto," the Filipino houseboy, ran "amok"; the morning of the mountain lion; the insidious presence of rattlesnakes. When we found them, we used to run to tell our mother who would neatly shoot their heads off with her little pearl-handled revolver.

The mating of the mare with the stallion which we were not allowed to watch, though we climbed the cliffs in back of the barn and tried to see from far off. The mare trailing a long membrane, a mysterious afterbirth from the secret place beneath her tail; my father's secrecy about all this sort of thing.

The death of my sister's pony, Black Beauty—my sister's heart broke and hardly in all these years has been mended.

The evening our little brother sat down on a crochet hook left in some work thrown down carelessly on a chair. The parents had driven to Santa Fe to spend the day. The little boy screamed as much in terror as in pain. I, stunned by his cries, ran away somewhere behind the barn where I could not hear them and never learned how the crochet hook, like a barbed arrow, was extracted. Years later my sister remembered that, of course, Daddy, with his surgical knowledge and his experience with the wounds of horses and of dogs, had cut it out.

March 9, 1979

I do not remember at Pajarito being assaulted by the wind as later on in the Los Alamos area. We lived in a canyon sheltered on every direction but the east.

The presence of water: the live little stream that flowed with an easy sound across the stones, or after a cloudburst, ran furious with red water. Most of the time we could run across it barefoot, with the water no higher than our ankles.

"To me the important thing is to lay bare and bring to light something that no human eye but mine has gazed upon." Colette

March 10, 1979

All of my mother's love was given to her garden. I think of her as queen of tulips, of iris, of delphinium, of hedge roses, of lilac, of mock orange, of snapdragon. She planned her garden borders as an artist plans the composition and color of a painting, as a musician plans harmonious sound. Her herbaceous border modulated from one season to the next—with the exception of July, she always said ruefully. July, when all the spring blossom was finished and the flowers of midsummer not yet opened. Now I think of it, there may have been a submerged poet in her, for she relished the sound of the official Latin names of her plants, introduced her iris each one by name of royal or aristocratic dame. I loved to hear her say "Rosa Spinississima" of the binary Scotch rose that grew along one side of her garage. She ruled her garden as though it were the precinct of a goddess. If oblivious child or boisterous dog ran through it, her voice changed to that of a clawed animal, one of her own cats, perhaps, bristling in defense of its progeny.

March 11, 1979

From Colette, quoted in *Earthly Paradise:* "My father . . . turned his mind to politics. . . . But just as his boundless generosity ruined us all, so his childish confidence blinded us . . . fiery tempered and afflicted with philanthropic views. . . . I shall conquer people by educating them; I shall instruct young people and children in the sacred names of natural history, physics, and elementary chemistry."

In many ways how like my father who longed to be a warrior, yet lacking military fields of battle, waged tempestuous wars against the state of society, for reform of the educational system which attended to the mind rather than to the growing body.

Colette here makes a list of the tools of her writing trade. I am reminded of the tools of my mother's trade: her sewing table, her tidy workbasket of Indian straw, the needles always neat in their cushion, the flannel strawberry stuffed with emery in which the needles were plunged up in an effort to sharpen them like swords. Emery, I learn, is a coarse variety of corundum, a word which derives from *kuravinda* (the Sanskrit for ruby). I remember the embroidery scissors in the ingenious shape of a stork, his bill the blades, his long legs the handles; the old silver-studded thimble, engraved with the name "Mary," which was her grandmother's name; the Victorian sewing table with its drawers sectioned to hold neat arrays of spools of every color thread, always kept neatly wound without revealing loose ends; the treadle sewing machine, later adapted to run with the aid of a little motor, the spool of thread that bobbed up and down in a kind of frenzy. Did the sewing machine mean the emancipation or the enslavement of women?

I know that I have never been able to establish a rapport with my machine.

March 16, 1979

I sit here on my "day" bed waiting for Mary Reisley to bring the information about the location of my father's farm in Roswell, miraculously discovered through her sister. I try to understand what bound them together. As for Ferm and me, it was the love of music and the New Mexico landscape and its weathers. My father married a gay young beauty who had been, in a tangential way, bred to ranch life, the life which was for my father an escape from his inherited background. Yet mother also inherited the dislike the Hadley women had for ranch life. She did not actually like the out-of-doors, except for swimming. Both my parents were excellent swimmers.

My mother's house was her palace, and after my father died she made her castle smaller and smaller. Toward the end she was haunted by a dream in which she was confronted by a room with four bare walls, and nothing in the room but a little potty right in the center. I suppose this potty was her last and only throne.

March 26, 1979

We coveted each other's imaginary horses. Horses were our status symbols, our source of pride, accessories to our germinating egos. I wandered by rocky pools and dreamed of the great winged horse, Pegasus.

Among the real horses with which we were surrounded, the stallion "Chili" was the only one approaching the imaginary ideal.

How strong he was; how his great muscles rippled under the glossy black coat that seemed to give off miniature rainbows from each separate hair; how his nostrils flared; how delicately and yet high he stepped when harnessed to the two-wheeled training cart. He was seldom ridden and very seldom harnessed. He had the standing among us of a kind of god, a heroic character who might have come out of the *Iliad*. He was the archetypal horse. Male vigor emanated from him, a barely tamable energy at which we wondered and were half-afraid.

Reading in *The Wild Horse* in America the myth of the "beautiful stallion," citing Zane Grey's *Wildfire*, which I dimly remember because we too dreamed this myth in our first years in New Mexico. Also it has come into literature through Robin Jeffers' *Roan Stallion* and Lawrence's *St. Mawr*. And before that the fragment in the book of Job. This was a living archetype, the horse more significant, the image more appealing than the bull, an embodiment of a wild, fierce energy which was yet capable of being mastered and directed. The stallion was one of the manifestations of a god—like the great animals in Job. It awakened something in the unconscious, or was the embodiment of something in the unconscious—a pure masculine energy. The visionary wild stallion, like the visionary Antony whom Cleopatra describes to Dolabella. Or was it like the god of battles and vindication upon whom the Jews called in their psalms? It was a Yang animal to be sure. And it was merciless. Its strength and energy were purely phallic, for a gelded horse lost the undesirable part of the energy.

Animal energy like the explosion of energy in nature, rainfall, flood, fire. I suppose one feels the rain as something sexual, the gathering tension of cloud, the sudden rush of air, the release of tension when the rain begins. The Indians dancing their desire into the earth, believing that their rituals controlled the rain.

The instinct for stealing horses that we knew in our "stick horse" games. (Oh, Hermes, god of thieves, who began by stealing cattle!) Because the horse was power and because to steal is a most ancient human trait. Think of Prometheus! Think of Eve and the forbidden apple! The fairy tales are full of it. The hero often has to commit a theft, and often the Princess herself has to be stolen. Think of packrats stealing! Which came first, the stealing or the trading?

Even adultery is a form of stealing. To steal a mare is, of course, to steal fertility. As stallions steal bands of other horses by defeating or running off the leader.

Sin begins with theft. The forbidden apple. Prometheus and fire. The Trojan War started by a theft. Jessica stealing jewels and gold from Shylock. Stealing is to take something from another's possession without paying for it. Remember Augustine's terrible guilt at the theft of pears.

On the other hand, the terrible determination to possess and to defend one's own.

April 4, 1979

I do not know how early I became aware that I was unable to give love, at least not in any outgoing way. I do not ever remember feeling love toward either of my parents—though I yearned to love my father, love meaning a kind of union of similar feeling, that which was hidden deep within us.

Indeed, how does a child love its parents? I do not know.

I remember the night on the sleeping porch at Wabanaki, where it occurred to me that I was different from the other boarding girls I slept among. I was never homesick, in that I never felt the longing for my mother, which they apparently did, one of them to the actual point of sickness.

Nor do I think my mother loved her daughters. Somehow I could never seem to express or explain to myself the relationship that existed between us. Mother kept us fed and clothed and warmed as any dutiful bird its nestlings. What we learned of maternal love was learned among the domestic animals we were surrounded with—the cats and their kittens; the bitches and their waddling puppies; the hens with their baby chicks that followed her and were warned by her cluckings and scurried to shelter under her engulfing feathers; the colts—each close to its dam, even grazing in the same field—it never ventured far away as though it were tethered by some invisible field of force. I depended on my efficient mother. I trusted her, I admired her justice, but I did not know what it was to love her, to want to embrace her, to long for her in absence.

Mother had a gift for creating around us the physical attributes of a secure and attractive home. She had an instinct for arrangement and decoration. And though she never dwelt in one place for more than a year or so, she made each new surrounding seem familiar.

Most of our furniture was inherited from my father's home: heavy mahogany tables of all shapes; an oak dining table with expanding leaves and a set of oak chairs with seats upholstered in red velour that is part of my earliest memory in my grandfather's ostentatious Detroit home. It remains as a symbol of the Victorian patriarchal role which the males of the family used to play, the father who ruled his household like an anointed authority, whose word was law. Once seated among us at that table, he assumed the mantle of his own father—or rather, perhaps, the archetypal father. He criticized our appearance as soon as we sat down, as though we were passing military inspection. Was our hair combed? Were our fingernails clean? If company were present, he admonished us—or was it my mother who did so?—that "children should be seen not heard." If we had personalities of our own, we were not allowed to demonstrate them. In his best moods, he joked with us, but we could not always be certain that he was teasing us. His humor was sometimes a two-edged sword, ambiguous, and often with a barb that sank into our buried feelings, so long to be cherished.

April 5, 1979

I keep thinking of my mother and how sometimes the human soul can secrete a kind of venom. Someone once said of Mary Austin that "the milk of human kindness had curdled in her," and wondered what had happened. What transformation—chemical?—takes place?

April 12, 1979

I think of my fear of lawless men, of lawless youth. The image of the bull from which I fled into conformity. My sister who also used to dream of the bull that threatened me, her sister. She, however, grew up to be far less afraid of the Dionysian energy than I.

Margaret N's suspicion that my mother's illness and retreat from life in her last years grew out of some unconscious guilt in relation to my father. Had she led the bull about by a ring in his nose? And did I follow her pattern?

My father, tamer of horses, rider of stallions—how did he wheedle my mother to return to him with the promise of living on the Ramon Vigil grant, that wilderness? What did he say when he went to Los Angeles to fetch her home? I think how he wooed her the first time on a ranch in mountain country. Now, ten years later, he offers her a kingdom on another ranch—a kingdom that only existed in his imagination.

Two days after this entry, I dreamed of the lamp which used horse manure as its fuel. I thought how these memories have formed a kind of compost and still contain energy.

April 13, 1979

I remember suddenly, when we lived in Santa Fe, how the dressmaker used to come in and fit us for going-away clothes. Though mother was far more adept at sewing than any dressmaker.

On the ranch, though, she dressed us in khaki middy blouses and bloomers. Where did the store-bought clothes come from? From the catalogue, I suppose, mainstay of farm and ranch people. Sometimes she ordered from New York shops, from Altman's or Bonwit Teller. I remember an elegant little "pongee" suit, with a fully pleated skirt and a straight cut blouse in which I am photographed dreamily reading a fairy tale book. Mother, in the Pajarito photographs, wears skirts to her ankles. I remember her gay promise to me that when I was sixteen I might wear my skirts to my shoe tops. Alas, by the time I was sixteen, World War I had come and gone, and women's clothes would never be the same.

May 25, 1979

If I write it to tell the story of my father, it is biography; if the story of the piece of land known as the Ramon Vigil grant, it is history. If I write the story of the poet who tells the story, it is autobiography.

It is personal ecology, a life in its setting: earth, sky and light; winds and stars and waters; the flowering of plants, birds, animals large and small, feeding, or feeding on each other.

Man, the most terrible predator of all, filled with lust (a word which originally meant "pleasure, delight, appetite; a desire to gratify the senses, bodily appetite.") "Energy is pure delight."

No, I cannot fit my father into this category of predator. He loved that landscape, the light on its cliffs, the fructifying snows and rains that blessed the years he lived there—the grass. He came into that wilderness with almost a Biblical eye; he envisioned it as the land of milk and honey, with teeming flocks and herds—dairy cattle to supply his table with the whipped cream he loved, as a child loves frosting.

Her father's fixation on starting a school for boys; the masculine ideal. Yes, that first Los Alamos folder says it all. She tries to be the boy that could have gone to school. She becomes a tomboy. Riding her horse before she is five. The photo taken of the child in the little soldier coat and cocked hat (odd that her mother dressed the little boy in Russian blouses that made him look as girlish as his sister; she despairs because the little sister looks so feminine). Her mother is pretty and feminine to look at, but the photographs most like her are the ones in which she plays the part of a debonair boy in some theatrical. The mother is, or before she became a mother, Rosalind.

May 26, 1979

A long talk last night with Dotty about our months (was it eighteen altogether?) on the Pajarito. She repeats the thought that is was such a special, marvelous, beautiful place. Apparently, it has inhabited her memories as it does mine. And now we talk about it together as if we had lived in paradise. Perhaps we did.

I am thinking, too, about my grandfather who made a big fortune. How did he manage to keep it? My father wrote his partners that he (Ashley Pond, Sr.) was always "rotten at managing his own affairs, but completely scrupulous at managing the affairs of others." How can a man be so divided? How did Grandfather Pond so manage as to hand on a large fortune intact (divided between son and daughter) and to write such a will that his son was unable to have access to the funds from the entire estate? There was always the income from the buildings that were not allowed to be sold during the lifetime of the direct heirs. And the stock in the Woodlawn cemetery which he left to my mother directly, "for the education of her children."

Agatha Christie: "One cannot ever go back to the place which exists in memory. You would not see it with the same eyes—even supposing that it should improperly remain much the same. Never go back to a place where you have been happy. Until you do it remains alive to you. If you go back, it will be destroyed."

June 6, 1979

I think the David James letter may be the backbone of my story. Chapin's resume of the partner's relationship with Pond, accusing Pond of "improvidence." But what real proof of improvidence was there, when they never really gave Pond a chance?

Would the [Fred] Harvey Company have been willing to develop the place at their own expense? Hopefully somewhat on the order of the facilities at the Grand Canyon?

Daddy always claimed that the view from the Plateau east across the Rio Grande Valley was many times more beautiful than the Grand Canyon. (True in some ways; hyperbole in others.)

June 15, 1979

Burch Ault suggested that I must tell the Pajarito story in poetry.

Perhaps I can start with the poetry of the first summer there. When it seemed, for the child, the temple of a god. Those powers that move between earth and sky. Emphasized in my mind, the companionship of water. Those canyons formed and carved for centuries of time by running water. Those rents in the solid plateau. How could the mild little stream at the bottom of the canyon have done all this? Yet after a summer storm, we could watch the fingers of the rain at work, the movement, and stir of sand and sediment as the mountain, the cliff, furnishes water with the tools for its own destruction.

Energy is mass times the square of the speed of light. Gravity furnishes the motive power. We were exposed to the power of gravity all day long. The steep cliffs we climbed, the rocks we sometimes fell from. The great tension between height and depth. Perhaps this was the way the god appeared to us most plainly.

... *gravity* ... "in physics—gravitation—the force by which every mass or particle of matter attracts and is attracted by every other mass or particle. Force that tends to draw all bodies in the earth's sphere toward the center of the earth."

June 16, 1979

In John Steward Collis's chapter on communication, he does not remark especially on communication that transcends time, that allows us to associate with thinkers and poets and artists of the past—to live with them in memory [*Living with a Stranger: A Discourse on the Human Body*, 1979].

Perhaps this was one of the fascinations of the Pajarito—that awareness that came to this child of memory engraved in the rocks. The memory of a vanished people who left traces of their lives which made them seem, however strangely, like our own. The patterns they had cut in the dwelling places; the designs, now broken into scattered fragments of the clay pots in which they stored their food, carried their water. The handhold and footholds by which they ascended their steep cliffs. The deep trails worn in the tuff that marked their comings and goings across the wide plateau. Makes me aware of how we, too, will be gone someday from this place.

June 20, 1979

Still reading Collis's *Living with a Stranger*. Now his chapter on "Reproduction" speaks of potency. "Surely the power, the force of life, lies in the genitalia. I am sure that any man who displays great energy, who puts out great vital force and accomplishes mighty things in any field of life, has great sexual strength, whether that vitality is elevated, curbed, botched, or diverted."

I think of the strangeness of castration, the fact that we were so mysteriously surrounded by it at the ranch; the difference between the great stallion and the gelded horses, the bull, the steers. The docility of the mares. Yet this is not true, exactly, of mares. They too are filled with fierce energy of which no one can deprive them.

June 22, 1979

My father's interest in livestock was not just for the hope of making a profit, but because he loved the animals themselves. He loved being an "animal husbandman." One of the fascinations of life on the Pajarito was that we lived among the domestic animals my father acquired and cared for. He could not resist buying sleek cattle and elegant horseflesh. A part of his dream of starting a school for boys was that they should have experience of living among animals and caring for them—the symbiosis between mankind and animal kind, each needing the other. The responsibility of the human for a living creature.

June 23, 1979

Now I must begin to write the Pajarito story in earnest. The material is all in—all but a few stubbornly missing links. My father is out of the Club. The grant is about to be sold to the Bond brothers who plan to use it for grazing.

June 26, 1979

Reading the sheaf of 1917 letters yesterday. I felt a pang when Chapin's friend James said no particular attention need to be paid to Ashley Pond who was "good and honest enough but as a business man a joke." And those letters between Joy and Chapin referring to the time when they were trying "to get rid of Ashley." Finally they bought him out—but were still plagued by his insistence that he stay on as manager.

And the last letter from my father to Chapin, ironically urging him to invest in mining stocks. I thought of all that worthless gilt-edged paper now stored at my brother's. Not one mining venture paid off.

June 27, 1979

And I return to my passionate effort to make a myth of the Pajarito—a myth that relates the human to the nonhuman, the world of rocks, trees, animals, stars.

June 30, 1979

And mostly the story of water; the presence or absence of it. The law of falling water, the downward gradient toward the imbedded river so that the canyons slit the plateau like the ribs of a fan. Water in its manifestations—snow and ice—splitting the rock surfaces so that more water could enter and pry apart the impervious, slowly soluble rock.

July 13, 1979

On the way to Taos this morning, I stopped awhile by my father's swimming bridge, and the lighthouse flash of memory picked out another buried time. (Time dried and tied in bundles like the bundles of *cota* which I gathered and dried to make a tea. When I pour boiling water over the dry brittle twigs they soften and release their still lively essence.)

The bridge, the rocks, the strong sinuous flow of the river suddenly brought me face to face with my father's last years.

The only drive I remember taking with him alone—the day that gave birth to my poem, "Foretaste." On that day my father took me to Pilar [Taos County, New Mexico]. It was May 1929. I was a young woman, not yet twenty-six, feeling this surge of poetry in me as the landscape unrolled before us. My father may have been as ill at ease with me as I was with him. I longed to share the rapture with him as I felt the wrinkled and colored world flow past. For I knew that his passion for the wide beauty of the land was like my own. In 1929, I had been married five years. He had two grandchildren.

Once I wrote a poem called "Caprice" in which I told how "all day long with an old bent pin / I fished for the minnows that tumble in." It was written to remember a day when my father took me with him fishing on the Pecos River. While he ardently fished, I dreamed upon the rocks. I loved to watch the fish, but I was not patient enough to work at catching them. Yet the poem is dated February 1923, and I was away at Smith College at the time. Perhaps I wrote it out of a summer memory.

July 25, 1979

I have been reading a little in Rilke's letters—the year 1914. For at this time I was an eleven-year-old in the Pajarito Canyon. Yesterday I sat down to see if I could really express what the book is about. I read through the Littlebird notes from 1964, when I invented my alter ego, the child Quince.

But my father keeps concerning me as "the great child." How in his public life he was so out-giving, but in the private household a kind of tyrant sometimes.

The Pajarito letters show him filled with enthusiasms, possessed by a demon—wedded to the land, obsessed with its beauty, trying to make Ramon Vigil his little kingdom. And indeed it was, as in the fairy tales in which the hero ascends as by a magic beanstalk, or falls as into a well (Neruda's *poso*—by which he meant, of course, the kingdom of man's nature). I fall into my father's nature "as into a well," hoping to emerge with a branch of truth. To enter another's life is to enter a world, a kingdom, a special geography.

My father reminds me of General Beale on the Tejon ranch who, as Mary Austin expressed it, "married the land in his heart." General Beale, too, was betrayed by a flesh-and-blood woman.

Women typically seek community, conversation, society. Mary Austin, too, betrayed her land. Yet many of her books are about men and their relationship to the land. She would have understood only too well a man like my father. He had that feckless nature she attributes to her husband—a man in love with the land and its possibilities. *Starry Adventure*, p. 401: " . . . the way you felt about the future of New Mexico, the brooding sense of it, something the land purposed within itself, using men, not used by them."

December 10, 1979

Peace of the predawn morning, my most beloved time. Since earliest childhood, where my memories begin at Three Mile Lake [Michigan]. I, the wanderer, escaping from my naps out the low nursery window into the quiet and wordless world of nature: the stir and life of the lake, the minnows clustering in their pale schools at the edge, the fish leaping far out and then falling back; the perfect rings of water widening, spreading; the almost iridescent surface of the water; the kingfishers diving in their gaudy dress; the smell of apples in late autumn, fallen and rotting under the trees; the barnyard and the pasture, soggy and swamplike, where cowslips grew, the marsh marigold among the liquid copies whose odor was at once attractive and repulsive; the gold of the flower so brilliant against the dark soil, the petals waxy and glowing.

I would have loved to touch one, but never quite dared wade through the slimy ooze. The image has never quite faded from my mind, that brilliant gold, the light feeding itself on filth and darkness. Perhaps all my life since I have longed to reach out and snatch the golden flower, that rapacious instinct that is part of the human soul.

And I remember with wonder and awe that my husband, when his life was being destroyed by a brain tumor, subjected to one of the multitudinous invasive tests to try and locate it, had a vision of columns flowing, pulsing light, buds of gold opening into flowers.

December 12, 1979

So it is not true that women cannot have a passion for landscape. It is only certain women who do not. And my mother was one of them. Perhaps Roy Chapin's wife and Harry Joy's wife were others, and General Beale's who made him forsake his rolling hills and flocks and herds and the memories of his long solitary journeys on horseback across the United States for Washington society existence.

But how to account for my own passion for that piece of land? Did I absorb it through certain invisible emanations from my father? My sister and I both reveled in the poetry of Henry Herbert Knibbs which celebrates the West as we felt it. Or did we feel it because we had read it first in his poems?

December 14, 1979

From *The Eye of the Story* by Eudora Welty: "Another reader might see the novel as a prism suspended by a thread and turning on it. Set in motion, forward and backward, at the delicate control of the author it turns its faces to us and the present moment moves into time past or time future. In so doing it constructs a pattern out of its own fractured light, reflections and shadows; they glance, crisscross, pass through and modulate one another."

My mind hovers around the Pajarito story and how to write it. The detective work I have done—the fascination with it. Uncovering a land's past everyone has forgotten. Picking up clues out of memory and then verifying them in reality.

December 15, 1979

I remember at Pajarito when I first fell in love with dawn. The rising of the sun, the coming of the day. How I used to love to go out before daybreak in my bare feet and my khaki middy blouse and bloomers, tiptoeing down the steep stairs that descended between our parents' room and mine. My parents would have flayed me alive if I stepped on a creaking board and waked them—then out to the fenced pasture where the horses stood quietly, not yet starting to graze, as they would begin to do at first light.

The pale predawn sky arousing a resonance with all my life's dawn hours. Usually the dawn on camping trips, waking in a sleeping bag and peering cautiously out into the chill shadowed morning, or the dawns after sleepless nights of illness—the silence of the wordless world.

I dip the spoon of honey into my tea. The fragrance rises. I think how the bees distill different fragrances from different flowers. I think of Rilke's notion of the "bees of the invisible," again—how he says it is the poet's duty to store up the perishing world in the invisible—the "angel within." How out of touch I have been with the angel for so long.

And the pueblos have a well-elaborated conception of symbolization of the middle or center of the cosmos—the *sipapu*, the earth-navel.

Four
Pajarito Cycles:
The Cycles of Selves

Peggy Pond Church on her eightieth birthday. Photo by Cynthia Farah, author's collection.

Construction

I saw in my dream last night
a lean dog dragging squared lumber up a hillside:
two-by-fours made of redwood, one shorter than the
    other,
cut by a careful carpenter who knew in his mind's eye
exactly the angle they should fit together.
The dog had a nonchalant look as though thieving were
    his hobby
whether or not it had any useful purpose;
just indulging his instinct made him happy.
I watched him lug the lumber
into a shed-like machine shop and hide it under
the rusted wreck of an old car
the way a dog in the wild will drag part of his kill
back to his den and worry it at his leisure.

When I woke I found myself thinking of the poet,
    Neruda,
who works on a poem, he says, like a carpenter.
First he chooses the wood for its fragrance and its color,
its smoothness and its resonance with deep forests.
Next he saws into the board until the sparks fly;
from the sections he makes his verses.
The poem begins to take shape like the hull of a stout
    ship
exultant to ride soon on the moon-shaped waters.

I too feel
that poetry and construction have much in common.
For a lifetime I have been dragging home stray boards
that I hoped my poems or my house might someday
    have a use for;
scraps left over from finished houses;
beachcombed remnants of old wrecks,
a few smoothed pieces of fine wood
that a cabinet maker couldn't find a use for;
the growth of the tree in its grain still sings

like fragments of torn music.
There is a longing in the wood to find its meaning
again in being part of something
before its essence returns to earth
or before fire
gives it back once more to air.

Remember when we were children the smell of
    shavings,
the curls from a planed board,
the smoothed board
balanced over a log to make a see-saw?
The notched board we loosely hung to complete our
    rope swing?
Remember the stilts we made from the sawmill
    discards,
the stick horses we galloped on,
even the random chips that became boats
knife-carved to race on our flowing summer water?

We gathered the scraps of whatever cast off around us
to furnish our own bare space,
half imitation, half fluent imagination.
How could we let anything lie that held promise of
    becoming?
How could our hands deny the urge for making
that possesses all human kind?
A dog can twitch in his dream and
run after rabbits till he wakes.
Only we humans
can make houses or poetry or music
out of the stuff poets say all dreams are made on.
                    (1980)

With the celebration of her eightieth birthday in 1983, Church enjoyed the attention of several writers, friends, and fans whose articles, visits, and letters reminded her of how respected and beloved she was among New Mexico artists and writers. Twice in magazine interviews, she alluded both to her first poem and the way her poetry initially got written when she was eleven years old. Tapping her fingers to a rhythm matching the Rito de Frijoles, the fickle creek in Frijoles Canyon where she played as a child, she managed the line "Oh bird so blue, will you tell me true." Rising in her later years at five or five-thirty A.M. to work on poems and journals for two to four hours each day, Church remained the disciplined poet whose love of music, training as an amateur pianist, and sensitive ear listened for the words and phrases for poems even as she had felt them in the landscape of her childhood. In her poem, "For a Mountain Burial," published in *Birds of Daybreak* (1985), she returned to the transformative quality of her bird imagery, concluding: "May all ghosts take the form of birds / and begin singing / among the birds of daybreak." But she also revealed that to make this happen, she might journey up into the mountains to sit and wait for a word needed to complete a poem. Despite the growing chemical sensitivities and the slowly developing eye problem she later would learn was inoperable and would lead to blindness, she remained physically fit, an inveterate hiker, the rhythm of her step, like the tapping fingers, opening to the poem's voice and sound.

And like a dog in another poem, "Perhaps in Our Old Age" (1982), she wanted to continue to ". . . unearth our childhood / like a bone hidden and long forgotten / by an old dog, and gnaw the marrow of it / and bring the taste back again." Poetry took precedence over finishing the Mary Austin biography or writing her father's story; she usually finished two to four poems a year. But she continued the Pajarito Journals, making them more the place where she practiced the integration of childhood memories, sometimes recalled in dreams, with the ceremony of writing—ever the musician, the "construction" artist, gathering the "fragments of torn music."

As for homemaking, also referred to as an essence of human construction, for Church these latter years contained another move, an effort to recenter oneself at the retirement center, El Castillo, just off the Santa Fe Plaza. She began to write to May Sarton again in 1983, reigniting the two women's exchange of letters which had begun in the 1940s, the two discussing moves, aging, what it means to be "old" poets. Church becomes increasingly occupied with her unfinished and unpublished work, with its organization, and the future of her files, journals, poems, and letters. In her March 14, 1984 letter, she describes aging as "a river sweeping forward," and notes another dream in which she swims a river with her father. As she attempts to build a new habitation around her with the move from her home in 1985, she copies a page of her journal to Sarton in her letter of February 2, 1985: "Strange how the past continues an existence of its own, even in the crowded overflow of today." She notes the changes in Santa Fe as an example and says: "Parts of our past we never quite outgrow." Feeling herself more alone, without companions with whom to discuss poetry, she admits the journals are becoming even more important sources of conversation, as if she could create almost another character with whom to talk. She writes to Sarton:

> The island of order in all the disorder! Survivor of shipwreck searches the wreckage, constructs and furnishes his new dwelling place out of what the sea has cast up, out of the pieces of driftwood and old bottles. The instinct for order. The bird constructing its nest. We weave our habitations around ourselves. All along in the midst of my indecision and chaos the merging pattern was clear. Like the order in which poetry emerges. I think of Wallace Stevens, "The Idea of Order at Key West," that all my images should turn to navigation.

Sarton's response was a buoy for Church, for the other poet had just read Church's final published volume of poems, *Birds of Daybreak,* and responded with a deep ecstasy:

> Dearest of poets, this is an upside down letter. I was going to answer at long last your letter of April 14th yesterday, but got interrupted, and now I am glad I didn't because the poems came in the mail. I read them yesterday and again this morning at five with tears of relief streaming down my cheeks. I have felt so far from poetry, imprisoned by the endless correspondence and no escape ever,

but reading you was to feel the source well up with over-whelming force. There is no poem here that did not reach me at the deepest level, and what comes through—long pause while I think—is perhaps more than anything that you are rare in the depth of your root in that landscape, that vertical landscape which goes deep into the past; so must the Delphic oracle have spoken beyond the merely personal with which we are overwhelmed in all the "con-fessional" self-enclosed poetry I see most of the time. And it is also the grandeur of an old woman and what she has come to know. I really cannot praise this book enough, and you will, I fear, think I am too effusive . . . don't.

Each woman's letter thus became a lifeline for the other, so that Church's effort to work diligently on new and unpublished poetry, contemplating a final volume which would function as a kind of au-tobiography, continued its resonance with the themes and images of the private journals and the human connection of two poets' ex-change. Church wrote to Sarton: "I cherish you for sharing your poet's heart."

The Pajarito Journals stop in 1983, so pressed did Church feel to get her poetry written in what she knew were her last years. She even told an acquaintance that she consciously turned to the poetry again, leaving the unpublished manuscripts and the journals: "Somebody else can take care of these other things." But the journals, though ending almost two years before Church's death, illustrate nevertheless the poet's ever trying to construct in some meaningful and lasting way, "the growth of a tree" which in its discovered "grain still sings." Even as she left the last volume of poems and did a final reading in Taos in 1985, two months before her death, we perhaps get the greatest sense of Peggy's character in these final journals. The solitude and privacy she needed for writing are celebrated here; the shyness that she sometimes assuaged through the published poems and nonfiction and the readings speaks intimately here as well.

Church once said about Haniel Long's poetry and his life as a poet, the "finding" of one's life is a heady experience that one desper-ately wants to share. "It is as though one held in one's hand the mus-tard seed that might become the greatest of all trees and longs to summon all the birds of the air to shelter it." Friend and correspondent Lawrence Clark Powell, a follower of Peggy's published work, remarked of her final published poems: "I am reminded, when I read these poems, of picking up a river rock—perhaps that river rock—smooth in the hand, part of what the river itself does to time. In the cooling air, one still feels the rock retaining the noon time heat." With the journals, as with her poems, formations that they are of a landscape felt and seen—birds, bread, stones—we hold in one hand the warm remnant of a mountain. In her final journal entries, in their themes and refrains, Church comments on the cycle of selves, just as in a later poem, she examines Black Mesa from different perspectives and metaphorically:

Black Mesa: Dreams and Variations

1.
In a twilight of rain
the mesa gathered her robes around her,
veils of mauve and blown smoke,
colors of dark cloud lined with a buried sunset.

The mountain, the Black Mesa,
loomed suddenly before us like a ghost ship,
a figment of clouds and torn sails
gone aground out of time,
cast up out of a never-existing ocean.
No seacoast welcomed her,
only the bare hills and a desert river.
What resonance of waters,
what urge in clouds and in stone to take form
in a reflecting eye had seized us
to be its collaborators?
The Black Mesa
waked an old legend in us, tales of a black ship
or a ship with black sails we could only half-remember,
an alien dream projected from a past world.
through our rapt eyes
on the curtain of rain and darkness.

2.
On this afternoon of vision
they were dancing the Turtle Dance at San Ildefonso
in a medley
of shells and green boughs.
Left alone
for an hour on the other side of the river,
closed in by a slow rain,
I slept in the labyrinth of myself.
I went down through the vertical corridors of heaped
    time
with their indelible graffiti
their coiled and unascended music
down to the melt of the world and the unformed crystal
    essence
that would someday blossom and reflect light.
I listened at the root of Black Mesa
like an attached child
that hears only its own and its mother's heartbeat.

3.
The mesa,
alert to sound of the drums and of strung shells,
of ascending male voices,
guarded her mystery
in cinders and slow crystals,
in a mantel of river stones,
in the sloped debris of worn hills,
in facets of retained light.

Monuments to earth's fire,
the melt of her inwardness:
unnamed gods came surging
forth from the womb's dark.
Taking light in their hands as they rose
they wove it like a vestment
over hills wrinkled with time,
over stones long abandoned by their rivers.

4.
Landmarked center of a universe,
terrestrial axis,
still body at the center of time's motion,
I have watched morning and evening revolve around
    you,
heard the seasonal birds fly over,
handled the washed stones,
looked down on you from the stretched rim of
    mountains
at the valley's either side.
Always you drew my wandering gaze toward you
from whatever height I leaned on.
From each direction I saw the light drain downward
seeking to fill your dark well.
You are a lodestone,
compact essence of extinct fire,
a hand reaching
out of earth's whirling depth to seize light
and make yourself its darker habitation.

5.
Black Mesa,
hard core from which a landscape
has been eaten away by rainfall and a river.
Washed gravels at rest above earth's tilt
lie level as instruments among the torn hills,
anatomy of an island or an altar.
Oceans of light wash round her.
The Black Mesa devours light
like a collapsed star,
drawing it down into the dark shaft
from which her substance fountained.
Leaning columns of black rock
intrude shadow
like bars of upright music.
Only the pale grass at the surface shines
softly in winter,
a platform raised for the feet of holy dancers.

6.
The river levels the land around the mesa.
Sleek as an animal, muscular as serpents,
it is bearing our world away.
The river's aim is only to flow onward;
the mesa's to remain.
Among the stars and seasons
she keeps her fixed place.
Though the earth moves beneath her,
though the mountains perish,
she is rooted too deep to tremble.
She has been through this all before.
She will still be here when the hills crumble
and are heaped along a no longer living
river.
When the drums fall silent
who will they be who someday come to dream her
into themselves again?

                                        (1985)

Peggy Pond, with mother Hazel, Three Mile Lake, 1908. Courtesy Los Alamos
Historical Museum Archives, Peggy Pond Church Collection.

Peggy Pond Church reveling in her first canoe ride, Cochiti Lake, near Santa Fe, 1984 or 1985. Courtesy Kathleen Church collection.

Peggy Pond Church at Otowi Bridge, 1980s. Photo by Greg Sorber. Author's collection.

Peggy Pond Church on picnic in Jemez Mountains with Peter Miller, Edith Warner's goddaughter, and Peter's husband Earle, 1980s. Courtesy Kathleen Church Collection.

Journals, 1980s

April 3, 1981

But what I want to do now is get busy on Pajarito—the story of my father and his partners, which is also the story of a time. And woven into it is the story of the child, the child who found herself seized by the poetry of the place.

That first year—for the child it began in June 1914; but for my father, the Pajarito began to exist in 1913.

Perhaps the story should begin with the coming of the railroad into the Rio Grande Valley. The surveyor, the civil engineer who went up on the plateau surveying for the railroad, to see how much marketable timber there was. When the trees are cut down, the gods begin to withdraw.

And weave into it somehow the necessity of water—the need for rainfall. The preciousness of water. How little there really was and how ancient inhabitants had treated water as a god. Water—how much of it there must once have been to carve those steep canyons, to grind up and roll away the loosened rock. My first spring on the Pajarito, when the snow melted, and the stream woke from its thin and icy sleep. The spring of 1915.

1914–1915: the little microcosm of climate. My father came in a wet year. Everything looked so promising. Then the problem of finding a source from which running water could be pumped into the buildings.

April 4, 1981

So much of me is bound up with the Pajarito experience. How can I harmonize the subjective and the autobiographical with the objective and biographical? My autobiography. How nature is woven into it. And mythology. The stars as companions, the books of legend. And poetry. Against that background of cave dwellings and Stone Age artifacts, I had begun to read Greek myths—myths of an already "sophisticated" people, with a literary background. The pueblo and cave dwellers were still hunters and gatherers, in the earliest stages of agriculture. I had to somehow assimilate myself into their world, revising my mythology.

August 11, 1981

So depressed yesterday after taking Kate onto the [Pajarito] Plateau and to Frijoles Canyon. Never, never go back to Paradise. The remnants of forested mesas, the ugly masses of the technical installations, the traffic, everybody speeding, nobody stopping or staying. No place on earth to be alone in the presence of the gods. No place sadder than a land whose gods have deserted it. One must learn to have a high place within oneself.

August 21, 1981

I consider my revulsion to the Pajarito Plateau which I used to love so. The gods who once were sought in the life-giving rain have been driven forth (or faded in the rock face); the gods of man's arrogance, his hubris, those monumental laboratories, have replaced them. The search for means of dealing death having replaced the prayers for life.

There is nothing reverential in the presence of death. Something like the mass death that Neruda imagined at Machu Picchu. Nothing to make one think of death as transformation; something that brings to me only abhorrence of what life has become.

September 7, 1981

The *Brand Book for the Territory of New Mexico*, issued July 1, 1900, registers only a horse brand to Ashley Pond of Catskill, New Mexico, on the left hip. Catskill was at that time a rapidly declining lumber town on the Maxwell land grant. It had been in existence for about ten years. By 1900, the timber had about run out. The fifteen miles of branch railroad from Trinidad, Colorado that served it was becoming too dangerous and too expensive to maintain. The line was abandoned and the tracks removed in 1902. Today there is nothing left of Catskill but ten magnificently Assyrian-looking beehive charcoal ovens, a thinned forest, and one of the most magically luminous views of the eastside of the Sangre de Cristo mountains that I have ever seen.

The general manager of the Denver, Texas, and Fort Worth Railroad named the town site because he said it reminded him of the scenery in his home state—which must have taken a stretch for the homesick imagination.

How my father happened to pick just that spot for the beginning of his western adventures I do not know—I cannot even bring myself to imagine. What connection could there possibly been between Detroit, already that bustling industrial city, and Catskill, a denuded lumber town? My father, a graduate of Yale, a rich man's cherished son and those rough-looking lumberjacks pictured in the early pages of his album?

He had a cowboy working for him at Catskill named Albert Horton, whom he had picked up when he arrived at Raton sometime in 1899. Apparently, he did not immediately go in for cattle, for he would have had to register a separate brand for them.

There is a snapshot of this formerly citified young man intently reading in front of a smoldering log fire, seated on a chair that looks handmade of wood that has scarcely been peeled. He has on a pair of moccasin-type shoes with one of the strings loose and trailing out far behind. His pants may have been khaki—it was before the days of blue jeans—a bulky well-worn sweater engulfs his upper half, and a bandana, that badge of western attire, is knotted around his neck. It must be cold, I think, for he is wearing a rumpled hat with its brim turned up in back. His face is clean-shaven as are the faces of the young men who appear with him in other photos of the same rude and dilapidated interior. I am impressed with how extremely young they all appear to be. One of his companions is wistfully playing a guitar and, except for the clean-shaven face, might have been a contemporary of our hippies of a year or two ago.

When he is pictured with older men, as in one scene around a cowboy "dutch oven," they are even more slouchily attired, and all sport neat mustaches above their upper lips. The neatest looking fellow of them all wears what looks almost like a turtleneck sweater with a sheriff's star impressively pinned on it. The sweater has gathered a lot of burrs. The whole crew of six (my father included) looks as though it had been off for some days on a merry chase.

In 1901 my father went to Watrous, taking Albert Horton with him. It seems odd that I never heard him mention Catskill. The name was only a rumor to me when in the course of my research, I happened to discover in the *Brand Book* the "Lazy A," registered to Ashley Pond, Catskill. I realize now he rarely spoke of his past. He much preferred to let his mind dwell on the future which, for him, was filled always with rosy dreams, visions, wonderful intentions and opportunities that had a way of fading out like desert mirages the closer he approached. I wonder if he ignored the past partly because it contained too many ruins of projects that came to nothing?

My father had grown up as the cherished son of an eminent Detroit lawyer whose first-born son had died when only a little boy. Ashley Pond, Sr. had married late and was forty-five years older than his son. He was a brilliant yet inarticulate man who found it difficult to express affection. He was said to be as nearly unerring a reasoner as a man can be. He achieved leadership in his profession by sheer weight of legal learning and an integrity that made him respected by colleagues and opponents alike. Upon his death, a Detroit paper commented: "His was a generous gift."

This must have made him a rather hard person to live up to, though, especially for a son—my father—who was born with a warm and outgoing nature, tempestuous and to the end of his days, completely incapable of that kind of logic.

In academic studies his grades were adequate but unimpressive. At the age of sixteen in his New England prep school, his rank was 6 in 22; his exam 4 in 19. He spent a lot of time in the school infirmary with prolonged stages of bronchitis which was due, he always believed, to the harsh climate. I sometimes wonder if his illnesses didn't give him an unconscious alibi for never being quite able to live up to his father's expectations?

As an athlete, he did far better. He became a runner and in his college days competed at an international meet at Oxford—competed, but did not win. A newspaper item from that period, July 1894, is significant: "Seated in front of the Lake St. Clair fishing and shooting club yesterday afternoon, Ashley Pond Jr. talked entertainingly, yet regretfully, of the Yale team's trip to England. He takes his failure to win any of the events in which he participated very much to heart, and says he wants to spend a few days at the old club so he can meet with his friends in installments and not have the question, 'Why didn't you win?' come to him in a saengerfest chorus."

The approval of friends always meant a great deal to him, perhaps because he was never really certain of his father's affection. The ship on which he returned from the meet in England arrived a day late. His father's first words, no doubt to be taken humorously, must have stabbed the defeated athlete's heart: "Well, your boat is about as fast as your Yale sprinters." It wasn't until long after he was dead that I began to suspect that he had always been a frustrated hero, not that he lacked courage, but that fate seemed to have different plans for him and managed, over and over, to deny him the chance to slay real dragons and realize promised kingdoms.

After graduation from Yale, Ashley Pond, Jr. enrolled in New York City's College of Physicians and Surgeons to study medicine. While there, he had been an enthusiastic member of Squadron A, the crack cavalry regiment of New York City's National Guard. After only a few months, he was forced to resign due to another siege of respiratory trouble. He recovered his health barely in time to enlist in the Rough Riders. A telegram to his father from Tampa, Florida, dated July 25, 1898, reads: "Health fine, work, weather, flies awful. Send interesting newspaper." So much for the would-be hero's dreams of glory and thrilling cavalry dashes for he also missed serving in the Rough Riders—only trained.

October 30, 1981

So we come back to Jesus' marvelous parables of the Kingdom: "The Kingdom of God is as though a man should sow seed and should sleep and wake night and day. . . . the seed groweth of itself he knoweth not how . . . ." The secret energy of life is within the seed. It grows in response to night and day, to heat and cold. It becomes a tree in which all the birds of the heaven can lodge. It is the yeast which leavens; it is perhaps the wind which "bloweth where it listeth"—invisible as the wind, but manifest in the clouds, the leaves, the grass, which its music moves.

As a child at Three Mile Lake, watching the ripples and the spreading circle on the water. Watching the contact (the interface) between the unseen and the seen; watching the blowing grass on the hillside beyond "the stone wall where huckleberries grew." "Who has seen the wind? Neither you nor I, but when the leaves hang trembling / the wind is passing by"—marvelous simple poem that used to haunt me, and Stevenson's "dark brown is the river . . ." and on and on to Bryant's "Thanatopsis" which I loved and learned, though I cannot now remember a line of it.

December 16, 1981

How to reconcile the opposition between "fact" and the inner autobiographical element? The history, the child's experience, the father's story? The relation between the land—unconscious nature—and the human beings who have lived upon it; between the numinous quality of the natural forces and man's use (and abuse) of the land, its eventual rapacious destruction?

Indians recognizing, establishing the gods there; pastoral people grazing their animals and cutting wood; "capitalists" trying to make a profit, who knew nothing of prayer and disregarded the ancestral spirits: recreationists, archaeologists, government bureaucracy.

Underneath, the theme of the beauty of the world, nature going about her own business: the primacy of water.

My father's memory somehow lives in mine. I remember how, in the months after he died, I had the curious fantasy of swimming like a fish through the channels of his brain, among his most personal and archetypal dreams.

The cycles of the year. In old age the woman has seen so many cycles. She was born in winter—perhaps I became sentient through my mother's senses in that broad canyon of the Mora River. Did my mother walk by that autumn stream, growing heavy, pining for her girlhood? Else why would I, who never saw my birthplace until grown, feel that landscape so familiar, as through imprinted on my own field of memory?

The off and on years of California residence made me uneasy, for the yearly cycle was not so marked. Two seasons only—and flowers blooming continuously all year long. Trees perpetually in leaf.

Roswell assaulted me with summer heat—the small apples ripening, the melons; then the blasts of winter, when I rode my horse, Sam, among the singing telephone poles on the bare pebbly hills.

Not until the Pajarito did I experience the year's cycle. Perhaps the experience of the former inhabitants, long vanished, vibrated still within the cliffs, the rocks, the shards of pottery. Lives gone, life gone, but ever present. Man's spirit leaves its fossil imprint in the things he made, like the extinct camel tracks in the hardened volcanic ash. So perhaps the Pajarito story begins to blend with my once-projected almanac. The cycles of the year in New Mexico.

Pajarito which I came to in full summer—the prevalence of wildflowers, our governess who made me notice the wildflowers and their differences, and then the first long-drawn-out autumn, the dry rustling of the oak brush, the grass turning pale and feathery, the return of the slate-colored juncos, the sudden blast of winter stars, bright-armed Orion and Sirius, breathing hot on his track.

Snow falling and the tracks of field mice from clump to clump of grass, half-buried in white drifts. The cycle of the year I witness the waxing and waning of life. Its repeated disappearance and return.

The cycle of change—the law of opposites—the dance of the opposites of life and death.

January 11, 1982

Longing to get going on the autobiographical Pajarito story. Last night watching the "Flame Trees of Thika" [featured on PBS's "Masterpiece Theater"]—shots of the little girl and the kingfisher. Was this the same bird I marveled at at Three Mile Lake?

Kingfisher: (King's Fisher) any of a large number of Coraciiformes birds (family *Alcedinidae*). Usually bright colored and having a large crested head, a strong beak, and a short tail.

Halcyon: *Gr. alkyon, kingfisher; akin to Latin Alcedo, influence by Gr. hals, and kyon,*conceiving, from popular belief that the bird hatched its young dying. The halcyon days of the solstice. 1. In ancient legend, a bird believed to have been the kingfisher, which was supposed to have a peaceful, calming influence on the sea, at the time of winter solstice.

The edge of Three Mile Lake—knew only the part of it a few yards below our house, but it was for a few years almost my universe. A usually placid expanse of quiet water inhabited by fish, water-striders, and leeches, the fishing ground of men and birds.

She begins (the child I was, whom I now watch from afar as though she were another being) about five years old when her memories begin to cluster together and make islands. Tiny minnows swarm in the shallow water, always a swarm of them. The kingfisher dives beautifully and comes up, holding something squirming in his bill. Brilliant feathers, beauty in motion, not to her the "king's fisher," but the king of birds. But now, almost seventy-five years later, her thoughts begin to play with the former idea, and she sees the bird, the king's fisher, as something like the Emperor's Nightingale, a story that later entered her life.

In the fairy tales the birds have special powers, as all animals do. It takes magic to understand their language; they do not, as a rule, speak directly to a human being but can be overheard discussing his fate among themselves. The interesting thing is that the kingfisher is still alive with her to this day.

Rilke (*Duino Elegies*, Appendix 4): (Letter, November 13, 1925, to his Polish translator on the meaning of the elegies): " . . . for our task is to stamp this provisional, perishing earth into ourselves so deeply, so painfully and passionately that its being may rise again invisibly. We are the bees of the invisible. The earth has no other refuge but to become invisible in us."

April 7, 1982

Trying to center myself all day. After lunch I sat down at the desk, looked at the Pajarito notes on "Weather in New Mexico." Next

I looked up the program for the Jungian conference and see the subject of Al Ortiz's talk on the 30th: "Ritual Drama and Pueblo Indian Cosmology." I look up his chapter in *Perspectives on the Pueblos*. It is called "Ritual Drama and the Pueblo Indian World View."

"A world view provides a people with a structure of reality; it defines, classifies, and orders the 'really real' in the universe, in their world and in their society. . . . If world view provides an intellectually satisfying picture of reality, religion provides both an intellectually and emotionally satisfying picture of and orientation toward that reality" (136).

"A world view . . . a system of symbols by means of which a people impose meaning and order on their world" (137).

So the child in Pajarito Canyon encountered the Tewa world view little by little, in shards and rock drawings, in exposure to the dance rituals, in the conversation of archaeologists with her parents.

She brought to it her own embryonic world view, inherited from classic Greece, from fairy tales and literary background (at ten and a half she already had a considerable literary background!). In the Catholic schools her parents began sending her to at an early age, she absorbed Bible stories—not as fascinating as fairy tales (she realizes now being too patriarchal), but with a certain familiar structure.

In her secular schools, there were fragments of another form of ritual—a way of ordering the year: the making of Valentines, April Fool's Day, the gathering of flowers for May baskets, dances round a maypole. Then a big jump through the unschooled summer to Halloween, and soon Thanksgiving (a patriotic day), and finally Christmas, the sacred story mixed with the secular, the pagan Christmas tree, another feast of lights.

So she comes to the Pajarito and finds herself set down among stern rocks in a landscape that does not fit what has become of her interior geography at all—the patriotic songs she had learned with such relish ("thy rocks and rills / thy woods and templed hills"). Did this mean the hills had temples in them? She supposed so, but it did not sound somehow like the America she knew. And "beautiful for spacious skies, for amber waves of grain; for purple mountains majesties above the fruited plain"—something to dream of, but here the "purple mountain majesties" towered over bare unvegetated hills; the waves of grain were represented by meager Indian corn patches, or square fields of green alfalfa; the fruited plain was a stretch of dusty sand spread by a mud-colored and sometimes furious river that nothing grew beside but desert willow and cottonwood in a thin discontinuous band.

The draped and neatly coifed and wreathed Greek gods and goddesses could not feel at home here; the leprechauns would not transplant out of Ireland; the Norse gods certainly could not abide so much unmitigated light. There was no church, large or small, in which the holy family could feel comfortable.

May 10, 1982

Thoughts and dreams again about my father. How he relates not only to my childhood but to my womanhood. For it is I who am still fixed (at least in my dreams) in the traditional bonds, despite the childhood mythos. Those long years at Los Alamos Ranch School when I existed in a kind of prison, dominated by an authoritative, dictatorial animus. Dominated by the dream image of my father and his attachment to the land and landscape.

The man who took Father out to see the Pajarito around the 23rd of October 1913, Captain Fritz Muller, a colorful character, tall and soldierly, who as a United States cavalry man, had taken part in all the Apache Indian campaigns, including the capture of that much-maligned warrior, Geronimo. What must have aroused my father's admiration even more was to discover that Captain Muller, at the time of the Spanish-American War, had been a member of Roosevelt's Rough Riders and had actually been present at the battle in Santiago de Cuba. My father, who had enlisted in the Rough Riders, had been forced to wait out the war in a camp near Tampa, Florida, with nothing more exciting to do than drill in the muggy heat and keep his equipment polished and horse ready. To top it off, young Ashley, only twenty-six, contracted typhoid there and spent the duration of his service in the Savannah hospital. No wonder Captain Muller, representing the United States Bank and Trust Co. at Santa Fe, easily persuaded Father that he was getting the thirty-two thousand-acre Ramon Vigil at a bargain—$80,000, about $2.50 an acre. Actually, the bank, needing to sell on account of various debts and mortgages of former would-be purchasers, had authorized Muller to ask only $56,000. Apparently, Muller, as director of the bank, failed to inform them of the price he was really getting, planning to pocket the difference.

December 27, 1982

Dream. Of my father, but can remember nothing, only his genial presence in his baggy outdoor clothes. The outdoorsman I must have projected onto him, a version of the "ghostly lover." Its influence on my marriage that still lingers in the shadows.

The marriages our psyches force us into. Oedipus, forced by fate to kill his father and marry his mother, and endure the consequences. We are born into myth as into our biological life. The fixation on the father as the powerful one to all of us who have been more or less brought up in the Christian religion. (I grope for insight.)

Perhaps my dream last night means the disappearance of these "father figures" who have haunted my life. In marrying my husband, perhaps I hoped to marry my inner father and tried to make him fit the picture.

Perhaps my father was a Dionysian character, a man of the forest of the irrational. Indeed his lust for the land and his tempers were irrational. A primitive, a master of animals. Why is it that women are attracted to this kind of being? Perhaps the hero of the "wild west," perhaps a kind of centaur.

How can I depersonalize my myth? Having written the releasing poem for Patty, how can I now write a releasing poem for myself? But why in my old age am I suddenly faced with this problem?

This wild energy not content with daily domesticity. This man who was an embodiment of fire, but who could not deal with his own fiery nature, and so became a fireman and fought it on the outside.

The father in last summer's dream who forced his daughters to burn the documents, one of the most mysterious dreams I have ever had—and their own transformation by the fire.

This element represented by the father because he is our first experience of man-kind, man-kin.

How did his own passionate nature affect me? Was he imprinted on me rather than my mother, who, I think, tended to shun her infants at birth? Man, the first nurse?

But how about his own real life? What was his essential inner struggle? How can I exorcise the ghost by writing his story?

On the other hand, there is the enigma of how women turn into monsters and devour men, become tyrants. The female will, the determination to own, to possess. A man is driven to possess a woman, and then to fight her off from poisoning him and binding him in the threads of her maternity.

December 31, 1982

Pajarito was many worlds. The world of those who tried to possess it, but possession only—even my father, following the Spanish, the *pastores*, the Texas ranchers, the lumber barons, the Ramon Vigil Land and Lumber Company. And I myself, who never "owned" it, but discovered it as part of a sacred world. Those worlds that live within us—or that we make there.

"Times and places, mountains and seas and houses and cities; all these are only the lived experience of those who inhabit" (Kathleen Raine's *Farewell Happy Fields*).

My Pajarito world was like no other. It was, perhaps, an artifact which I myself constructed.

Some Approaches—to My Canyon Summer

We came out from Santa Fe over sandy hills here and there with scrawny juniper trees and interrupted by sandy arroyos. Most of the time the road seemed just two rough tracks; sometimes the two tracks turned into ruts so hard and deep that my father, to avoid scraping the car's bottom, had to straddle the ruts and go along with two wheels in the middle of the road and two wheels along the edge of it at one side. Once he had to get out and shovel away a part of the ridge and fill the rut with branches broken off the bushes he called juniper "trees." The wheels and tires of automobiles in those days were very narrow. When he came to one especially sandy arroyo my father got out two long strips of canvas which he always carried with him and spread them across the sand in front of the wheels and then drove over them. While he was doing that we children got out and walked around. The ground was very hot and dry. The juniper trees made a little shade, but it didn't seem very cool.

Over in the west, where we were going, there were a lot of clouds like big white cauliflowers that got bigger all the time. The mountains underneath them were blue and shiny. One minute they looked very far away like the farthest edge of ocean, and the next moment it would feel as if we could reach out and touch them. When my father said that was where we had to go, we got pretty discouraged because how can you get anywhere in a country which seems to jump right around while you were looking at it? You couldn't even see the road most of the time because it was always disappearing over the top of a little hill and turning somewhere behind the trees. Half the time, it seemed to us as though we were going right back where we had started from. We kept coming to wide sandy places that looked like rivers, but they never had any water in them. The sand was harder to get across than the water would have been. Sometimes the car's wheels would just spin around until they dug a hole in the sand; then Father would have to get out again and dig. We'd all get branches and pull up weeds to put under the wheels until they could move again.

When we were sure we were never going to get anywhere, the road suddenly grew steeper. We looked down and saw a kind of winding crack at the bottom of it with green frills along the edge. My father told us that was the Rio Grande, and we were going to cross it on what turned out to be a very rickety wooden bridge. We would go up the other side and then soon be home.

The trouble was that the water was so deep this particular June that some of it was running over the top of the bridge, and you couldn't tell whether the bridge had any bottom to it because you could only see the railings in the middle. Father said the river wasn't usually like that; in fact, people were usually very scornful when they first saw it and said, "Do you mean to say you call that little trickle a river?"

The hill on the other side looked a little like perfectly flat country that had been turned up on edge. The road just went up to the bottom of the flatness and disappeared. All we could see were some jagged lines that looked like they'd been drawn on a blackboard.

It took the car a whole hour to climb that hill. Twice we had to stop because the water in the radiator began to boil. We'd have to wait until the rumbling noise stopped and it was safe to take the radiator cap off so water could be added.

The sun had already gone down behind the mountains by the time we got to the top. Far below us was a kind of purple world, sort of blurred and mysterious, as in a dream. The river we had crossed was a tiny silver thread. Far back on the other side of the world were the mountains beyond Santa Fe where we had started and which seemed like years ago. They were like the color of Valentines, blood-red, only like real live blood, not just something out of a painting. The color was running off the edge of them, up into the sky where it seemed to melt into nothing.

I remember I built myself a kind of dugout once on the north-facing side of the canyon. I constructed a kind of stove of pieces of tin and a stovepipe that went up through a hole to the surface of the ground. The trouble was the stove almost completely filled the hole. The chimney worked and I was proud of my construction, but very quickly found I couldn't stay in a hideaway that squeezed me tight against the only source of heat.

Evenings I remember we used to gather around the piano with Miss Purdue, our governess, playing and singing songs like "My Bonnie Lies Over the Ocean." I spent as much time as I could in winter reading books, down under the sofa in a sunny corner of the living/dining room. Andrew Lang's red, blue, green, and pink fairy tale books were my meat and drink, and my sister's too, for I still have a set of books in which she colored all the beautiful maidens' hair in indelible crayola gold. The apparent discrimination between the amicable fair-haired maidens and the dark-haired witches or their wicked daughters disturbed me as much as the apparent preference for boys rather than girls in the adult world. Besides, my sister and brother were both towheads while my hair was just plain brown.

When we got up plays based on our readings, I usually played the witch's part by choice. There was something more interesting in being the clever bad one, rather than the persecuted good one who could only get along by the help of the fairy godmother or a magic wand!

When spring came and the snow melted, the canyons filled with the mysteries of running water. It poured in rivulets off the dry rocks and filled the rock hollows with miniature lakes. The earth in the side canyons ran too full to be stepped over, too cold to be waded through, so we turned lathes and poles from the sawmill into vaulting poles instead of our stick horses and swung across. Or we nailed the triangular blocks of wood to the lower part of our poles and wobbled about on stilts.

The traces of Indian life were all about us. We picked up pottery shards by the tons, learned to find arrowheads in the talus at the base of the caves and on the ruined mounds of the dwellings on the mesas. It was exciting to now and then find blue heads in the red anthills. The ants seemed to me to have a kind of aesthetic taste in the way they covered their dwellings with tiny glittering quartz crystals or fragments of colored stone that were foreign to this geological area—even bits of turquoise.

And then there were the mesa tops themselves. You could see east and north and south for miles in all directions, ridges of blue mountains, rims of steeper canyons, the great depression of the Rio Grande, bare and windswept as though an ancient sea had been rolled back. What a sense of encompassing life it gave me—and still gives me: a sense of mystery, of forces not of man's making.

January 30, 1983

I take another look at Kathleen Raine's *Farewell Happy Fields*, the beginning of her autobiography. But I have a feeling that Pajarito is perhaps all I need to do of mine. There childhood flourished and ended. When we left Pajarito, it was my own "Farewell to Happy Fields." For at the end of that last summer, a male colt kicked me hard in the pubic area (for which I had never been taught a name). Pulling down my bloomers to inspect the rising bruise, I discovered three rough and curled black hairs had grown on my naked skin.

I can look at the Pajarito as such a unitary world. Becoming aware of the vanishing of the former inhabitants—their leaving. The cycle of the year that had contained them when they themselves had been the center of a sacred world.

October 19, 1983

Suddenly occurs to me as I brood on the Pajarito experience that the contact between the life of the present day pueblos and the prehistoric ruins was the thing to be aware of. The continuity of the tradition, the opportunity to be aware of the life still going on little changed, as it had once been lived on the plateau.

Although the "prehistory" was not so long ago and had existed at the same time as the history—recorded history in the rest of the world—not a thousand years ago, only half a millenium.

And the geologic history of the world I lived in was not so old either. But it was the geologic history that had determined the environment which the prehistory was lived.

October 23, 1983

Yesterday, walking out to pick up the paper, the full moon flooded the world with its light.

I recalled the nights at Los Alamos Ranch School and those years that seemed filled with the presence of the moon. The moon that seemed to be the mistress of shadow; shadow of ponderosa pines on white snow. Because the ground was white, the shadows seemed blacker. In the coldest months of winter, the snow crystals gleamed and sparkled. If there was anything I loved most, it was the world covered in untrodden snow as though it was virginal—or the silence of snow falling at night among the pines—the almost soundless rustle.

New Mexico has been called the Land of Sunshine. But has anyone pointed out that it is also the land of moonlight?

A few words for a talk to the Southwest Archaeological group on December lst: The effect of the ruins, the artifacts, the petroglyphs on me as a child, the emotional or feeling impact; the communication.

We are all in a way seekers for the eternal, something that exists outside of time. Perhaps archaeologists unconsciously are seeking a spirit that persists among the fragments—a reality that transcends our daily lives.

To Bandelier and walked about a mile down the canyon, picnic by the stream—yellow narrow cottonwood leaves, alder. Then walked to the open "mini-meadow" and rested against a grassy hollow close to a pure, almost transparently yellow, box elder; the sun riding just above the southern cliff giving the effect of late afternoon. How evening comes early in an east-facing canyon and winter too. How the horizons narrow and directions become vertical. Above–below measure an axial world. The climate of the canyon so different from the mesas, stretching the mind in different directions. Different ways.

The violence that formed the canyons is so evident. The platform of basalt which overwhelmed the bed of the original stream. Then the eruptions of fiery flowing ash which smothered it; cones and craters where fire and the underlying water met and altered shape and substance.

For a while, as I lay under the golden tree on the peaceful autumn afternoon, I almost forgot that just north of Frijoles Canyon was where the atomic bomb was born—which still may destroy the whole world in a violence man perpetrated on himself.

But as I reflected on the violent transformations in the sun from which the earth itself emanated and which was responsible for the color in the leaves, the violence of water which had carved the canyon, the blasts of lightning which had shattered some of the tallest trees, I thought it is not after all so strange. Perhaps it is only nature.

It is impossible to think of the atomic blast that may be putting an end to us. But the trees cannot imagine the lightning poised to strike them. Peace is an abnormal condition.

October 24, 1983

My soul was thrown into torment by yesterday afternoon in Frijoles Canyon. The stream, the leaves existed mindlessly, unaware of anything that existed beyond the narrow borders of the canyon. And the canyon walls were made of petrified fire.

Irony that the atomic bomb could have been developed on these mesas. How can I write peacefully anymore of Pajarito?

All afternoon I was aware of the bizarre juxtaposition. And aware of fate that uses mankind for its own ends. Ends that are destructive and violent. I was aware all afternoon of apocalypse. That at

185

any completely unforeseeable moment the terrible weapons will be unleashed. The volcano of time could erupt.

Miserable all morning about the Pajarito Plateau. About the destruction of my childhood paradise, the ordered world of the pre-historic Tewa. My idolatry of that land—and Edith and Tilano's—as a sacred world.

"What we do anywhere matters, but especially here. It matters very much. Mesas and mountains, rivers and trees, winds and rains are as sensitive to the actions and thought of humans as we are to their forces. They take into themselves what we give off and give it out again" [Edith in *The House at Otowi Bridge*, 18].

But is the plateau center of anyone's sacred world any longer? It has become the center of destructive forces which threaten to destroy the whole earth as we have known it. Giant machines with an evil eye have spread themselves over the mesas.

What is there we feel that is so special in those places once held to be sacred?

What is there special about Chaco Canyon in the midst of its wasteland? Or El Morro? Or Frijoles Canyon? What is it that speaks to our sensibilities that is different from any mountain top that has never been revered? Even the Grand Canyon, even the shores of the pounding ocean do not move us in the same way.

It has been seventy years since I went as a child to live in Pajarito Canyon. It was only for one continuous year and two con-tinuous summers, but I have never forgotten that earliest experience in what David Noble, in his article in *Discovery* on El Morro, calls "the natural and mythical world." It felt to me that the vanished in-habitants had left only a few days ago, as though their sleeping places were still warm. I felt close to them because I was sharing the same physical environment and the same seasons. Clouds and rain and the zigzag lines of lightning meant something special to them, as they do to me through my year-long visual experience with those energies. The designs on the fragment of pottery, the drawings on the cliff faces were like a language a child can read. Voiceless communication thundered all around me.

October 25, 1983

I keep thinking of Sunday afternoon's happiness mixed with despair. Frijoles Canyon: walking down the trail, first high above the upper falls. The color, and above all, the fragrance of autumn, not the odor of leaves settling into decay but the fresh sweet odor like opening leaves and blossoms in spring. The fragrance could have had no purpose in nature, either to attract or to warn predators. It was sweet and sensual and exhilarating.

Item: the word, "glad," comes from the same root as gold— *ghel*— meaning "to shine," "to emit or reflect light." This is the miracle of yellow leaves in autumn—that they reflect the golden light, even after the sun goes down.

The yellow leaves against the wall of black basalt; the detached leaves that floated on the dark water—the obsidian-colored water. The obsidian mirror of the Aztecs. The cottonwood trees and the box elders shining upward out of shadow. The sudden accent of red leaves; Virginia creeper that twined its way up a straight-trunked pine tree, at last thirty feet in its upward climb. Everything ascending with all its strength into the light, this mighty struggle against gravity. This transubstantiation of sunlight into light.

In this bright moment at the very edge of winter. Fingers of cold reaching out of every shadow. The sun's withdrawal. A few birds linger. No insects. Not the whirr of a single grasshopper.

The high rim of the canyon turns the sky into brighter blue, a celestial blue.

Rock is becoming grass, is becoming tree. The sun, is it a phallic mystery, a thrust of light?

October 30, 1983

Another beautiful afternoon in Frijoles Canyon with Hugh and Kathleen [her youngest son and his wife]. Thinking how the prehistoric inhabitants knew nothing of what we know about the canyon. The geologic history, its place in time, its fierce, volcanic origin.

The stream, the Rito, the Being who inhabits the place—and has created the canyon and itself.

Choked off long ago by the flooding basalt from the east. Finds its way out. Was there some kind of lake here above the silt where the falls break through? The crater, spitting steam and cinders.

Nature takes over to heal the wounds. Lichens begin taking the solid rock apart. Again and again between flows and ash falls the world recreates itself and is destroyed again.

We find and follow the trails of prehistoric people. We cannot follow the trail of the human psyche; it leaves no trace.

I was a child once on Pajarito, and the child returns again when I walk in Frijoles Canyon, in the canyon vegetation, the contained moist world, the familiar flora. Scrub oak making dense thickets—I remember the thicket in the pasture in Pajarito where the birds pecked and scurried, a hiding place you could creep into, a central is-land, and be safe and alone. You identified with the animal life—the chipmunks that hung around the lumber piles, the deer tracks on the north-facing slopes, the bluebirds you lured into your boxes, and the field mice.

Did field mice and squirrels threaten the stores of the prehis-toric peoples? Did they have an unending battle with thieving ro-dents and jays?

The caves high above the talus slope on the south-facing side of Los Alamos Canyon. As a child you imagined the long, steep climb to water. Did women carry jars on their heads all the way up? Did a population or a family live there? Before the great communities of Otowi and Tsankawi were built? Los Alamos, Pajarito, Water Canyon—were they running streams so long ago?

I ceased to live on the plateau almost thirty years ago—when I was forty, which is half my present age. The eighteen years at LARS [Los Alamos Ranch School] plus the two at Pajarito make twenty—a fourth of my chronological existence.

You escape from your family, your parents, your siblings. When they are wandering about the Tshirege ruins, you find a secret ledge on a low cliffside, an angle of rock that looks over the low talus and the brushy spread of the canyon, the thickets of willows that wit-ness the presence of an underground flow of water, perhaps a spring. You are transported in imagination back to those long-ago times. Or perhaps the ghosts of the former cliff dwellers come back to inhabit you, and speak within you.

October 31, 1983

The ghost of the Tewa woman looking for the fragments of her broken pots. The vessels she made and owned. Herself a vessel that contained new life.

What you wondered about: the grains of turquoise in the anthills. The Awanyu at Tshirege. The buzzards that circled above Tsankawi. The kivas, so secret, at San Ildefonso, now open to the sky, the sun, the wind, to every prying eye. The trails worn in the rock; the hand and foot holds. The masked figures on the rock faces. The repeated symbols of the little bird.

The shrines. The dance floor at Tsankawi. Why were the great Pueblos placed in high positions? Charlie Steen says, "A long, critical look at the locations of the ruins on the Pajarito Plateau fails to reveal any real defensive position."

What I never thought about: the exhaustion of firewood supplies.

The habit the Samaritans had of changing their dwelling sites. They themselves lived among ruins.

Charlie Steen describes "shrines"—cavelike rooms, small, isolated, with blackened interiors. "These must have been quiet retreats for individuals."

But do I not know that the Tewa retreated for individual prayers. Still, Edith followed a Tewa custom when she went by herself to the riverbank to pray. Edith used to go alone to tend her shrine. Peter Miller [Edith's goddaughter] makes her personal shrines, her places of offering.

There seems to be an instinct that calls us to pray alone upon some high place. Perhaps the cacique retreated for his periods of prayer—which nevertheless were for the benefits of the community.

Notes for "The Seeds of Wonder"

It was a world to fill a child with wonder. The cities whose ruins were our playground had mysterious names—Tshirege, Tsankawi,

Navawi'i, Tyúonyi, Puyé. At Tsankawi, the narrow trail had been worn more than ankle deep across the rock. At Tshirege, the Plumed Serpent marked the place where the trail went up from the broad canyon bottom. Looking up from the canyon, the sky seemed to rest upon the cliff's edge; the blue of heaven against the sharp, horizontal lines of rosy rock. Going up was to climb into the sky and there to stand with the world spread out at one's feet. These grassy mounds had once been a people's home. Children had been born here, had grown to men and women, had wondered about the world they lived in, had worshipped.

How could they help but worship? In every direction mountains stood against the sky like visible gods whose colored mantles were forever changing. The sun rose majestically above the rugged peaks in the east, journeyed across the great blue dome each day, and vanished at evening behind the curing slopes of the western peaks. Summer and winter the path of the sun moved south to north in unfailing sequence. At night the heaven was enormously alive with stars, not scattered at random but moving in annually repeated patterns from horizon to horizon.

To stand upon Tshirege is to be aware of the world—still—in the process of creation. Eastward, a great weather-born basin of eroded hills netted with dry arroyos; banners of rain moved across them in summertime. Floods rise and surge and as suddenly subside. The rainbow's glowing arch sometimes spans half the sky. Northward the rims of canyons rise one above the other like colored waves. To the south the canyon walls are green. With their backs toward the sun, moisture stays on them longer. Snows linger later in spring. Oak brush and fir find a foothold; the fragrant syringa and mountain mahogany create wild gardens. West is the guardian rim of the Jemez Mountains; beyond this rim, the great basin called the Valle Grande where a stream meanders and cattle pasture on wide, tree-margined meadows. To the vanished inhabitants of Tshirege, this valley was a fertile hunting ground. What tradition told them about it no one knows. Geologists say it is the crater of a gigantic volcano which long ago, in a series of eruptions, belched out the fine volcanic dust which formed the wide fan of the plateau.

To a child's mind this too was a source of wonder, awareness of the fury and violence of subterranean fire, of the ages of time to create from a wasteland of ash this great landscape of forested mesa and steep verdant canyon. Lava flows at the eastern boundary of the plateau were iron red and in places charcoal black. Steeply from their edge, one looked down into the gorge where the great river flows—the Rio Grande, a gleaming thread of water far below in the tumbled waste of rock. Sinuous it seemed, from this height, like a great snake, winding its way through the center of the world. Impossible that it should not be regarded as a deity, embodying all the power and mystery of water, life-giver to the earth, both fierce and tender, like all creative powers.

How to describe the silence that hung in those days over Tshirege? On a summer day, the land seemed to lie scarcely breathing. Small creatures scuttled inaudible among the rocks, dust-colored lizards, lumbering horned toads. Ants were busy in their hills. Overhead a buzzard or an eagle soared. A wild turkey would call out and then be still. Yet to a child, this solitude was never loneliness. The surge of life was there, life in its myriad forms of earth and air. The piñon glistened as though light were a fluid substance. Over the mountains white clouds billowed like enormous swiftly blossoming flowers. Around the ruined dwellings, fragments of pottery were scattered, still as brightly colored as the day they came from the fire that hardened them. Sometimes an arrowhead gleamed in sudden symmetry among fragments of flint from a faraway mountain quarry. A hollowed-out metate might have been used only yesterday in grinding daily bread. It is this continuity in our living that seems so marvelous. Body and bone and brain—made of the same substance as ourselves. As we project ourselves into their past, we feel the spirit's immortality.

What the child felt on the ruins of Tshirege was put in words by the poet of Israel long ago:

Before the mountains were brought forth
or ever thou hadst formed the earth and the world,
from everlasting to everlasting, thou art God.

At Tshirege the roofless kivas lie naked to the sky. Carefully hewn out of the rocky earth like ancient cisterns, they are filled now with wild growth, with flowering shrubs. Hidden among grass and leaves in the circular floor is the *sipapu*, the mysterious entrance from the underworld, no bigger than a snake's hole. The hewn stone blocks that formed the upper walls have long since fallen away; the long sky-pointing ladders that led through the roof openings have crumbled into moldy earth.

Yet to stand upon the edge of an ancient kiva is to be filled again with wonder. This was once a place of worship. Strange they should go down into the earth to form their prayers. The wondering child knew nothing then of the symbolic meaning of the kiva, the tradition of man's emergence from four worlds. Much later she would read about these myths in Bandelier's *Delight Makers;* still later in the work of Al Ortiz.

In the present day pueblos, the child had listened to the sound of the drum hidden deep in the earth, muffled like a fetal heartbeat. She had seen the dancers come forth from the kivas with their branches of evergreen, with symbols of cloud and rain woven into the borders of their garments. The air had been alive with the accent of bells and shells at knee and ankle, with the rattle of shaken gourds, with the sound of male voices in a rising and falling chant, with the rhythm of strong bare feet upon the naked earth. The child had seen men woven magically with the powers of earth and sky and had felt herself, her own small breathing self, woven into this pattern, until again, as in the silence upon deserted Tshirege, mortality merged with an ever-living Spirit.

One day after the dance, she had watched the men go to the edge of the strong-flowing Rio Grande. Singly or in groups of two or three, they entered the water, wading out into the current until it flowed over their thighs, splashing it in handfuls over their bodies. The branches they have carried in the dance all day were cast upon the water, and the river carried the green away into the gathering darkness. Once a man stood silently upon the bank with head lifted in an attitude of prayer, a recognized gesture of the heart toward the mystery of life, the oneness of life that had filled him when he merged with his fellows in the dance, the life that shone in the ascending arc of the blue mountain, that sang in the movement of the flowing water, that thrust forward now at the tip of the budding branches, that echoed in the laughter of the two children playing beside him.

For prayer and worship seem native to the human heart and by whatever names a man calls the spirit that has formed him, it is all one. Of earth and air, of water and of fire, each human life is woven. The colors are blended in hues in the rainbow, but all light comes from the same source. Out of the darkness of unknowing, out of the lifeless depths of earth, out of the burning mountain, forth from the seed, the egg, the womb, life has emerged and is continually emerging, bearing within itself the forming spirit. In the mystery of the sprouting corn, the Indian beholds the symbol of his life. Plants feed upon the earth and sun, flower and fruit, in blind obedience. Animals live and feed as innocently upon the plants and upon one another. Only man, it seems, may be aware that life in the stone, in the plant, in the animal, is somehow akin to the life in his own person.

"So is the kingdom of God, it is written as if a man should cast seed upon the earth; and should sleep and rise night and day and the seed should spring up and grow, he knows not how. The earth bears fruit of herself; first the blade, then the ear, then the full corn in the ear. But when the fruit is ripe, straightway he puts forth the sickle because the harvest is come." [Mark 4: 26-29]

There are no better words to describe what the child felt, standing upon Tshirege so many years ago, and now, no longer the child, the woman still feels, watching the gesturing hands of the Koshare at Santo Domingo. In the mystery of the sprouting grain man has everywhere beheld the symbol of his life. Out of the kivas of Tshirege, San Ildefonso, he too emerges to the light and transforms it into the substance of his flesh and blood and spirit.

On the top of Tsacoma [Chicoma] Mountain, there is an ancient shrine, a few piled rocks, a hollow in the earth. From each of the Rio Grande pueblos, a trail once led, perhaps still leads, up the slanting surface of the mountain. Each man approached the shrine by the trail of his own people, but the destination was the same for each, no matter what tradition ordained him. And there, as in every sacred place, each man placed in the earth the tokens of his prayer, small painted, feathered sticks, and went his way.

So it is that from wherever we set out to climb the sacred mountain, by whatever route we travel, we find ourselves at last before the same eternal and nameless presence.

Afterword

Women, Place, and (Auto)biography

After Peggy's death, a memorial service was held at St. John's College in Santa Fe so that family, friends, and fans of her writing could honor her in the tradition of the Society of Friends service. On this occasion, the connection of her life and her work was celebrated, signaling her readers' recognition that Church's poetics resound in the translucence of geography and self—of the poet and the world's body. Even as Church had written in the Pajarito Journals of a "time buried in oneself," she had explored in her poetic imagery a relationship of bones and stones, the connection of the interior world of the writer—history, memory, family psychology, myth—with the correlating geologic evidence of the physical landscape.[1] At her memorial service, poems were recited by lovers of her work, many of them suggesting Church was aware that the part of her that would remain would be her writing. In one poem, she wrote: "Our eyes have netted this land with lines of beauty. / Whatever once stirred in us will go on singing." Church believed in the wholeness of natural energies, which included humans and their environments. In one of the poems recalled, the poet finds a weathered and whitened bone that she thinks of as "wordless metaphor" in the shape of a butterfly. Of Edith Warner, she had written, she "sings herself into the green corn growing."[2] The residual self she means as both physical body and the body of her work, so that the act of dying, like the act of writing, is born in memory. She noted that

> . . . the important things have been the epiphanies, things seen rather than things done. I have never forgotten—I must have been between five and six—a brilliant cowslip growing at the center of a bog in cow pasture, my longing to approach it, barefoot as I was, but not daring for fear

195

I'd be sucked down into the bog. But the cowslip is still there inside.[3]

Memory, like the sustained image of the cowslip, is ultimately the reconciliation through creative acts, such as poetry and journal-keeping, of the inner and outer selves. Bones incandescent, Church would have said, exist not only in the private, inner, subconscious world, but in the bodying out of the poem, that is, the manifestation of the inner self in the act of writing. At the root of her own creative cycles, "the cycles of selves," then, is her journal-keeping. Though each poem did not necessarily come from the recordings or rumina-tions of the journals, still Church used the journals to ground ideas and language to which she returned as she worked on various writing projects.

As a young woman in her twenties, just beginning to write and publish her first serious poems, she wrote to Mary Austin that writ-ing was a kind of spiritual exercise, not unlike the spiritual exhilara-tion of hiking or swimming, yet it remained essentially private, unheralded:

> My dearest ambitions are fulfilled in any experience which comes through the avenue of the mind or the sense. . . . A paralyzing shyness and reticence has always made it diffi-cult for me to go forth and seek such (outside) experience, and so I sit and wait for it to arrive. So far the best of it has always come from the inside and has seemed too personal to be written down except in the private journal I always keep at my elbow.[4]

The journals thus functioned as sustained yet changing "conversa-tions" Church conducted through time—a dialogue with herself which was both spiritual exercise and meditative waiting.

The Pajarito Journals, divided originally into "Pajarito—Sub-jective" and "Littlebird"—in two large bound loose-leaf notebooks—focus on the primacy of her childhood years on the plateau in north-ern New Mexico. In these, the initial childhood wonder ironically transmutes through the decades to the festering psychic wound Peggy felt because of her removal from the Pajarito Plateau in 1941. What was at first utter joy thus is connected to a profound sense of loss, establishing one of the major themes in the journals: Church's reflections on the process of soul-making—testings and insights in an individual's life journey. In her graceful and evocative "After-word" for Haniel Long's long poem, *The Interlinear of Cabeza De Vaca,* Church gives us clues to her beliefs about the connection be-tween life patterns and the maturation of a spiritual self. Citing the example of John Keats, who struggled with the vagaries of the deep-est self, and Haniel Long, her mentor and lifelong friend, who, through his poetic projections of the trials of Cabeza de Vaca, passed through a "vale of soul-making," Church identified the provings of the heart as ultimately located in the place of the self. She writes of Long's *Cabeza:*

> Without straying in any important detail from the historical account, Long makes the matter-of-fact Span-ish soldier's journey an adventure of inner transforma-tion, an adventure in the invisible realm of the human soul. "What can describe a happening in the shadows of the soul?" his Cabeza de Vaca wonders at the beginning of the interlinear. What Haniel saw in the rugged Spanish soldier was, I am convinced, a reflection of his own inner journey. He was a poet who took the soul seriously in the same way Keats did . . . and once wrote: "I began by seeing how man was formed by circumstances—and what are circumstances?—but the touchstones of his heart?—and what are touchstones?—but the provings of his heart?— and what are the provings of the heart but fortifiers or alterers of his own nature?—and what is his altered nature but his Soul?"[5]

For Church, Nature and one's nature—the soul—are inti-mately bound. She seeks to break the binary conception of the physi-cal and spiritual worlds by demonstrating their connection. She also shows the act of recreating another person's life to be the writer's act of self-actualization. Like Long, she had projected into the nonfic-tion biographical treatments of both Edith Warner (*The House at Otowi Bridge*) and Mary Austin (*Wind's Trail*) the corresponding issues of her own life. But unlike Long, she also wrote privately in her journals, as an act of autobiography, using the elements of an older history—that of the Pajarito Plateau—to suggest the arche-typal in the immediate and directly experienced. Thus, the Pajarito Journals may be viewed as structures like the poet's inner skeleton—her psychological and spiritual infrastructure—from which emerge her public work, her poems.

Church's journals, as internal proving ground, exemplify something of her scholarship and creative interest in the connection between the woman writer, the environment, and the cultural diver-sity of a place such as New Mexico.[6] But these journals represent a range of issues and aesthetic explorations that supercede what com-monly is called regional writing. The journals may also be appreciated as examples of narrative forms and subjects considered a kind of women's autobiography. Church addresses the current issues in this scholarly area: self-imposed silences even in this most private form of writing, the struggle to speak with authority, her relationships with her parents, the private challenge to public or social convention, es-pecially in the inner debate about behavior related to gender. In Church's inner debate about autobiography—journal writing—she further grappled with the traditions of autobiographical writing: the chronological and the thematic. Within the personal, intellec-tual, and artistic growth that these journals reveal are other signifi-cant themes: the pristine female childhood lived against the back-ground of her idealistic father and practical mother, the psychic strain of the dispossession of her childhood place by World War II, and the specter of the development of atomic weapons of destruction at the site of her deepest peaceful experiences.[7]

Further, Church's journals coincide with the growing body of women's nature writing, which connects aesthetically, psychologi-cally, and spiritually with the more political ecofeminism, as well as the larger more established genre of western women's creative re-sponses to landscape.[8] In her simple childhood act of gathering Anasazi pottery shards on the plateau, Church enacted a habit of landscape that sent her puzzling about both ancient and contempo-rary mysteries. For her, the act of gathering was not simply romantic or nostalgic. She analyzed the complexity of her own life as com-pared to or influenced by others. She was often self-effacing, war-ring against whatever caused psychic and physical atomization. For this reason, the journals contribute to a larger arena of criticism: the psychological. Soul-making for Church was tied to questioning conventional notions of masculinity and femininity and how each is valued. For this reason, she spends considerable time in examining the effect of her parents' lives on her own. She embraces Carl Jung's principles of the animus and anima as projected aspects of male and female attributes in the makeup of personality. This helped her reconcile her attempts to understand the male/female attributes of her parents, even as she often questioned their behaviors.[9] Her belief in Jung's theory of the collective unconscious and of universal archetypes further influenced her self-analysis through examination of her dreams. She also adapted Jung's archetypal principles to the profound connection she felt with the "place of the bird people."[10]

Church claimed she never intended to write her own story; yet in the many forms in which she expressed the Pajarito story of her childhood, clearly her journals, diaries, and letters constitute an autobiographical desire.[11] For this reason, in considering how Church voiced her life story it is helpful to review her work against some of the recent scholarship on women's autobiography.

Estelle Jelinek points out in her study of women's autobiography, for example, that some women have not chosen the formal structure of autobiography believing their lives less interesting or dynamic, less heroic or public, than those of men who become the subjects of autobiography. Whereas both men and women have kept journals, letters, and diaries, which may form a foundation for autobiography, until fairly recently, women have been less likely to take the step toward formal publication. Evidence indicates that women have believed in the significance of these documents, yet may have internalized the general privileging of men's activities, thoughts, actions historically over their own. The pervasive conventional way in which women's experiences may be described—heartbreak, anger, loneliness, humility, confusion, self-abnegation—is not that of men whose stories tend to heroism and the exceptional. In fact, men's personal histories are nearly always augmented by their perceived successes in larger political or at least public history. Women's, by contrast, as much more personal, often are not related to career but to people, to the private or interpersonal rather than the public.[12]

Even in terms of avoiding deeply personal issues of self or emotional revelation, women and men detach themselves from such inner arenas in different stylistic or structural ways in their writing. Historically, women tend toward varieties of understatement. In a straightforward, more objective rather than glowing narrative, they may write obliquely, elliptically, camouflaging their feelings. Often their style may be abstract, intellectual, ironic, or mocking. This penchant is enhanced by the way in which lives are organized in the retelling. The issue of how organization defines true autobiography has been wed to the view of the coherent whole, a linear narrative, as mainly men's lives of accomplishment and success are connected to a traditional view of history. Such unity speaks to a belief in control and the primacy of a theme, a characteristic of personality, or a concentration on a period of time during which these men lived.

But in addition to their usual nonlinear style, women autobiographers admit to irregularity rather than orderliness as informing the self. Portraits of women are more disconnected, fragmentary, organized in self-sustaining units rather than chapters. Multidimensionality marks this pattern of diffusion and diversity and has generally been devalued, even as have the so-called subforms of memoir and reminiscence. For this reason, in her study *Writing a Woman's Life*, Carolyn Heilbrun comments on the necessity of women's working through the sanctioned yet masculine and therefore unsuited forms of autobiography as they redefine themselves and the form: "The woman's life must pass through the veil of predetermined ideas about the patterns of men's lives and often even if addressed autobiographically, the subject must struggle, behind the masks she adopts in response to conventional expectation or for the purpose of telling some truth safely."[13]

Certainly such feminist readings may only serve as a critical background against which to read Church's reticence in writing standard autobiography. For, if Church had no need to tell her story safely, still she seems most comfortable working through other lives to tell her own story. The inner debate in the Pajarito journals about how to tell her father's story—his romanticism yet sometimes stern or exacting parenthood, her own yearning to communicate to her father how she shared his love of the plateau, and thus create a bond with him—suggests Church's search for a suitable perspective through the male story. That she seems male identified, however, is also too simple a reading of her explorations of the exhilaration of adventure, individuality, and freedom. Whereas she sees an aspect of her story in recalling and retelling her father's life, and in reviewing the way in which Haniel Long projected his own spiritual journey into the poem about Cabeza de Vaca, Church also works through the auto-biographical by interpreting the lives of two other women. Biogra-phy, then, becomes the means for (auto)biography. Church chose to tell these lives by privileging letters, diaries, and journals and other such nonlinear methods of reflection and narration—the very forms some feminist critics argue have been devalued or overlooked. As Church sought a way to tell her own story, she voiced the lives of Warner and Austin, keeping her own autobiographical journals as she worked with the journals, letters, and manuscript collections of these other women. Certainly though neither Warner nor even Aus-tin conformed in their lives or work to male-identified ways of know-ing or creating, at least as we read them in the public sphere of formal autobiography, Church clearly found their lives heroic, adventure-some, and full of challenges and struggles. In speculating about these women, Church examined herself.

During the years in which she sought to gather and reconstruct her own personal journals, letters, and diary notes, she retold her Pajarito story in several ways, experimenting with voice, persona, or-ganization, and genres. The character of Quince, a child narrator, tells one part of the story. The Littlebird journal entries likewise emphasize the experience of the child, and though objective, persist in this focused point of view, much like a third-person, limited nar-ration in fiction. In addition to the two large Pajarito Journals, Church also kept a New Mexico almanac of animals, plants, and natu-ral facts that influenced her knowledge and perspectives on the pla-teau. These notes kept her observation keen and constant.[14]

Like her journals and other private writings, Church's biogra-phies of Warner and Austin allowed for the unconventional. *The House at Otowi Bridge* was called a memoir by its publisher and re-viewers. Church notes clearly in the preface that while her primary intent was to explore the deeper core of Edith and Tilano's lives and their relationship to place, to the Pueblo Indians, and to the nuclear scientists at Los Alamos, her telling was also to make sense of her own life, to gather those threads together.[15] Told in a poetic language, using the power of image, symbol, and metaphor, the book inte-grates the biographer's friendship with Edith Warner, with observa-tions of and reflections about her, and through the use of Edith's own letters and journals. The resulting narrative reads like a novel, recalling what one critic of women's autobiography calls the fictions of female development. The power of Warner's story seems to have tasked Church with the expression of a woman's life which calls for the shift from male-centered or articulated categories to female ones. In this case, Warner is prophetic, yet humble. In turn, the spiritual quest figure in women's autobiographical writing is doubly realized in the character of Edith Warner and the spiritual journey of her biographer.

Warner was a modest spiritual guide for Church, who most of all longed for harmony in her young married life, during which time she struggled with the conflicts between her talents and the needs of a growing family. But Church's biography of Mary Austin derived from a youthful fascination with this strong and gifted woman, coupled with her repugnance at Austin's ego and craving for recognition. Whereas the poetically described life emerged as much from Warner's own life and writings as from Church's inclinations as biographer, the metaphorical meaning of Austin's life took time for Church to see and understand. In fact, some would argue she artificially superimposed her own perspective on Jungian criticism of Austin, implying in the biography that Austin was possessed of her talents to the point of losing her tenderness and the noticing eye that enabled her to be a "tongue for the wilderness."[16] It was this act of trying to interpret the ambiguities and contrarieties of Austin's personality and life that made Church understand that writing a life was not fact nor chronology but instead the making of metaphors of experience. Church's own dilemma and occasional blocks with the Austin material were eased when she realized she could trust her own instinctive self when searching for the many Marys. Austin had despised her "Siamese-twin self," by which she described her artist and publicist sides. She likewise wrote about the challenge of the creative woman to reconcile the private and public selves. Church was finally forced by Austin's own symbolic and allusive, oblique and elliptical, references to relinquish the standard (male) autobiographical form. Journey, search, discovery, and progress became redefined as the adventure of inner knowing not dictated by linear, chronological, or heroic modes. She was able to conclude about not only Austin, but also herself: "I might have gotten some kind of lesson from my own experience of the way history gets written."[17]

By writing (auto)biography, Church purged the shyness, the sense that the world might not value her or other women's lives; she experimented with how such women's stories could be told meaningfully. Through Warner and Austin, she tested her own life's questions about male and female roles, family, women's creativity, and most of all the meaning of nature or place. There is a direct connection between Church's nature journals, her biographical readings of other women, and the communal, corresponding, and centering feeling she had in her natural world. She wrote perceptively of how the pueblo dancers, particularly the women in their lines, held that world together. This description of San Ildefonso life, in which both Warner and Church participated as sensitive observers, was not unlike Warner's description of what she considered to be spiritual equilibrium—absolute centeredness—in the lines of cranes knitting the sky. "Death could be like that," she said.[18] Church echoed Austin's own description of successful nature writing: "beauty in the wild yearning to be made human." Church's early poem, "I Shall Take Root Here Like the Pine," suggests this idea of the oneness with nature:

Perhaps I shall take root here like the pine,
I have been still so long even the trees
Think I am one of them. That fragrant fir
Confidingly sets free her hidden birds.
The brown-clad oaks let fall their leaves in showers,
And unashamed reveal their twisted forms,
Their bare unshapeliness. There is no sound
Save for the lulling of the lazy wind,
The buzz of flashing, iridescent flies,
The soft, sharp rustle of the blowing leaves.

I have no thoughts at all. The smallest pool
Of clear, unrippled water is aware
As much as I of wind and sky and leaves;
The way the shadows move, keeping the trees
Always between them and the seeking sun;
Of birds in cloud-high flight invisible
Save for that glint of sunlight under wing
Or silver throat.

Almost I am a part
Of the mute age-old cliffs and silent hills.
Perhaps I shall take root here like the pines—
I have been still so long.[19]

Writing nature for Church was another way of writing her own
nature. Bound to this activity was honor and awe, passion, and
love, but most of all the awareness that her woman's life grew and
changed like cliffs, stones, and pines. She recognized Austin's attempt to change negative or dismissive attitudes about women's nature by closely observing and then reinscribing the culture of
Southwest deserts and their people. Such reassessments in Austin's
nonfiction writing linked the lives of women desert dwellers with
the subtle, yet resilient and infinitely creative desert environment.
Austin thus revised the notions of nativeness and nature, of women
who were of the environment, not merely in it.[20] Austin and
Church both sought to redeem their own femaleness by writing
about natural places, each emphasizing the locus of childhood.
Austin's "A Friend in the Wood," and Church's Quince and Littlebird sections in the Pajarito Journals express both women's almost
mystical source of identity.[21] For Church, the detailing, and later
analyzing, rewriting, reorganizing, and editing of the self in nature
was a way of coming to terms with, but also of reconstructing her
identity.

Sacred Places and the Nature of Desire

Throughout the period of her journal-keeping, Church returns
in the Pajarito entries to the theme of the formulation of the child's
identity in regard to her mother and father and the kinship she feels
with the environment of her childhood. Church identifies the father
as dreamer, the mother as more realistic, so that the very success of
the family often came from her mother's own stubborn responses to
homesteading experiences she would have preferred to avoid—for
example, no electricity or running water and few neighbors in the
Valle Grande northwest of Santa Fe beginning in 1914. Church describes her mother as both liberated and imprisoned by the invention
of the sewing machine, a symbol of her domesticity, and throughout
identifies with the dream of her father. She writes:

For me the Ramon Vigil was the earthly paradise that children often experience in pre-adolescent years. It was my unlimited playground and focus of imagination and adventure. It was the place where I projected and visualized myth and poetry, where I first became aware of the stretches of time before historic time and of the life of nature in which before them was the world of geologic time. ... We lived at the base of a volcano whose fires had so recently grown cold that some of the ash was barely solidified into stone. So we became aware more easily than those who live in sedimentary regions that we exist on a rather fragile crust through which unknown forces have once poured and may perhaps pour again. The earth was not to us entirely a benign mother, but a place of uncertainty and strangeness. A chaos existed beneath our feet that broke forth occasionally in our dreams. ... I was ten and a half when I first saw the Pajarito and experienced what it was like to live within the boundaries of a once sacred world.[22]

These two strains—earth as fragile yet mighty mother, a terrain bounded only by its own sacrality—are the "threads of consequence" which Church later retraced as she repeated in various forms her earliest childhood imprints. These strains became a resonating voice in her work: "I remember at Pajarito when I first fell in love with dawn. ... [ellipses mine] How I used to love to go out before daybreak in my bare feet and my khaki middy blouse and bloomers, tiptoeing down the steep stairs between our parents' room and mine. ... [ellipses mine] the pale predawn sky arousing a resonance with all my life's dawn hours. ... [ellipses mine] the silence of the wordless world" (p. 156).

The journals are of consequence to the moments of Church's life as she wrote and rewrote them. One of the factors of her return to the journals in the 1960–1980s period was her critical work on Mary Austin, whom Church felt had "betrayed the land," not only because of her ego-centered interpretations or because she abandoned that primal experience for the visible community of writers in Los Angeles, Carmel, New York, and finally Santa Fe, but also because "her many books are about men and their relation to the land," rather than about women.[24] Bound in Church's childhood experiences, rather, are the sources of the feminine landscape—and consequently the implied description of the woman writer as explorer. Church became the spokeswoman for "buried time":

> I dip the spoon of honey into my tea. The fragrance rises. I think how the bees distill different fragrances from different flowers. I think of Rilke's notion of the "bees of the invisible," again—how he says it is the poet's duty to store up the perishing world in the invisible—the "angel within." How out of touch I have been with the angel for so long (p. 156).

This constant quest in the nature journals is that of the writer who can distill from the sensed moment metaphorical and metaphysical realities. It also is a search for appropriate language, the translation of direct experience into a corresponding vocabulary. One of the most interesting observations in these journals is Church's thought that Tewa sacred places can be anglo-experienced. Much of the journals' content shows her search not simply for identity or meaning but for a native rather than an outlander's vocabulary. In the human timeline of the journals, Church moves from the language of English myth and fairy tale to enunciation of indigenous or regional plants and animals, a lived language facilitated in part by a governess who helped educate the Pond sisters in local lore. Church writes:

> To be thrust suddenly into the midst of a prehistoric world! The talus on the south-facing slope back of the barn covered with scattered shards, angular broken pieces of pottery, each with a tantalizing fragment of design, like the unsorted pieces of a giant picture puzzle, or like the words in a dictionary torn from their alphabetical order and flung piecemeal by some explosive wind, or like letters from an undeciphered alphabet spilled all out of order, untranslatable (p. 138).

Connecting the language of direct experience to that of the literary or imaginative became a matter of reading the landscape, admitting to a wordless wonder that perpetuated the search. These journals form a woman's quest, therefore—a journeying forth in writing that ranges from initial experience to memory to dream to creative response. At the same time that she realized what it meant for a Native woman potter to continue to fashion pottery whose designs speak to the immutable cycles of life, even in hard, drought times, Church learned to honor her own making and marking as well. She recognized in the society of women this perpetual motion, which is at once nurturing, healing and sacred. She remarked:

> Yesterday we went to Garcia canyon to picnic under slits of cave dwellings, fragments of pottery, corrugated fragments of cooking pots, angular shards of bowls with black and white remnants of design.
> That women should have dwelt here once, and in the midst of their hard, uncomfortable lives, made their pots and decorated them, caring for symmetry and beauty. The smoke-blackened ceilings of the caves, the coated floors—I knew from childhood how cold a cave can be in bitter winter (p. 116).

Though the journals express throughout the deepest wonder, Church does not romanticize either her experiences or those of the land and people. When she says she realized she chose Nature in place of her rejecting and cold mother, she remarks: "The father's real insensitivity to feminine values. The mother struggling to grow her careful gardens, who said later that she never did anything for love, only because she felt it her duty. The child, rejected by the mother, or born, perhaps, motherless, goes to nature. Nature cares for her in a curious, detached way, showing no special favors, taking her in as one among her many children."[28] Fire, drought, windstorms, bee stings—"beauty and staunchness of trees"—but always the threat of danger. This is the bosom of the mother earth Church details, connecting it to the vulnerability of flesh and even its indignities.

For although her language is full of sexually charged words so that "desire" prompts remembering, conserving, and procreating as part of the act of writing, still she associates the ravages of nature with the human "prying fingers in the secret places." In a litany of woman-experienced indignities, she chronicles her connection to the victim: "The humiliation of childbirth; the propped positions, the opened knees, the doctor standing opposite, the obstetrician. The bloody rags and napkins. Alien tongue prodding within the mouth, wet lips, the belly wet. That animality of the body could be tolerated, but all her training had been against it. One's body is one's own. . . . [ellipses mine] And all the poetry she reads mystifying her by the constant reference to the other, the *thou,* the *you* " (9/27/60). Thus reflecting on the psychologically-theorized issues of woman as victim, and the literary/social corollary of woman as other, she comes to understand her feeling of separateness as a hallmark of the westernized, industrialized world by citing professional archaeologist Jacquetta Hawkes, who writes, "In urban, literate surroundings, self-consciousness becomes a sharp knife, cutting man away from his matrix."[25] But in her remembering of the Pajarito as natural world, Church ultimately sees sexuality as different from victimization. When, as she remembers in the journals, her colt at one point kicks her, she reaches down to the pain to discover for the first time pubic hairs.

The Pajarito experience, then, becomes the key to many cycles: the cycles of childhood, puberty, adulthood, the maturing self. In 1982, only four years before her death, Church wrote she believed that unity to be represented by "the Pajarito people . . . at the center of their cycle."[26] Her renewed attempts to understand the Pajarito experience begun in childhood are bound up in the repeated but varied recognition of the cycles of her life, of that "pattern of ancient crossing." The many worlds, the many selves, the many journals may be seen as a part of a larger pattern, at once rooted in the senses and revitalized as "an artifact I myself constructed."[27]

Part of this lifelong quest is the desire to articulate a world Church felt as the ultimate centering. She repeatedly links the outer and inner worlds, the dwelling and in-dwelling, with the "sacred middle"—the center of consciousness the pueblo people concretized as the *sipapu.* This earth-navel as a gender-related concept for Church becomes the guide for reconciling the lost father and the estranged mother she perceives in her family unit. Thus, the female and male imagery she uses is a key to the desire for the whole self and in the practice of Jungian psychology, as she believed, a balance between the male and female aspects of self. Church moves away from the westernized attitudes and language of English fairy tales as seen in her shift from typical male and female imagery—the golden buckle and the veil—into a single image native to the New Mexico landscape. In a single passage, she shifts to the cactus thorn, which, she reveals, is soft enough to be used as a phonograph needle. Like the sharp-tongued belt buckle, but as the softest of the thorns, the cactus thorn thus, ironically, enables us to hear music. This long passage in the journals is a brilliant metaphorical morphing, an act of transformation—what Church believed the pattern of the Pajarito experience to be.

> Quince would later be shown the dream of the young woman who had to choose between the golden buckle and the veil with the icon of the butterfly painted on it. The butterfly: the soul. The "imago" of the Self. The buckle with its sharp and pointed tongue, in its way a kind of pin or brooch, like the one Oedipus blinded himself with: The buckle is a masculine warrior's ornament; the veil, feminine and flexible. Works upon the invisible. Works like a metaphor. . . .
>
> Thorns and roses, brambles. Thornbushes; the thorns and roses belong together, like the butterfly and the caterpillar (perhaps even like the butterfly and the sharp-tongued buckle). The sharpness of the thorn was known early to Quince, because she was one who went barefooted at a very early age: barefoot in the meadows and woods, stepping on thorns and prickers. The story of Androcles and the lion they acted out in school. The sharp needle with which her father took the splinter out of her finger. The beak of the hummingbird, the fang of the snake, the barb of the fishhook; . . .
>
> Sharp words, pricking the heart or stabbing it. Her own sharp tongue. . . .
>
> The days when phonographs used to be played with needles, hard needles, soft needles. The softest of all were cactus thorns, giving the best sound, but too delicate and easily broken. Here is a different use of a sharp point: not to wound but to bring forth music. A transformation process. She sometimes dreamed of—or perhaps imagined —a record where everything that ever has been is recorded.

Here the sharp point is a sensitive instrument, a delicate probe. In her dreams, it had feathers, downy soft as a bird's breast (pp. 94–95).

In the cycles of the journals, at one point Church identifies the child-narrator, Quince, with the cactus. Using this character as her alter ego, Church has Quince reenact a scene in which she murders her doll and, with her sister, frees their father's stallion by going against his will, cutting the horse's checkrein so he may escape the corral. The children are emissaries of wildness and freedom, including their disdain for women's corsets, which Church saw as "part of the will to enforce one's will everywhere upon nature, and upon women as the symbol of nature" (p. 93). Quince destroys the doll in an urge "to destroy this image of the feminine to which she was commanded to conform, this stereotype, with its fixed, unreal smile, its unaltering prettiness" (p. 92). Here thorniness is a different matter—to prick oneself to a deeper appreciation of nature and womankind. Looking to locate what she calls "time buried in oneself," "the seeds of time," Church reviews through Quince the magic and the dream worlds of childhood—the subconscious that would expose the buried seed.

In a sustained meditation on several connected dreams throughout the 1970s journals, she relates the recurring image of the king-fisher, perhaps coming closest to the unity she seeks in relating male and female attributes to nature. In 1965, she wrote of an oil painting of a fish that hung in the dining room wherever they lived. Her father was a great fisherman, and she remembers the pleasure with which she shared occasional fishing trips with him as a child. She later connects that image with the watery medium—"always a puzzle and an enchantment"—which characterizes uterine waters as well. She remembers how at first to bait her hook with a live minnow seemed as cruel as the thought of fishing with a baby. From this she moves to the idea of catching and keeping things that are dear, such as her relationship with her father. Then, in 1974–1979, she makes several references to her father in relationship to rivers and her own first poem about fishing, which she wrote at age nineteen at Smith College. The power of this memory–dream culminates in 1981 in her dream of herself as a fish, while projecting her father as her inner hero, and thus revealing her disappointment because of the inability of both father and daughter to articulate their deep love of place to each other. "My father's memory somehow lives in mine. I remember how, in the months after he died, I had the curious fantasy of swimming like a fish through the channels of his brain, among his most personal and archetypal dreams" (p. 174).

Personal Ecology and Imagination: Bones Incandescent

Church's desire to connect in some significant way with her father suggests a very different orientation toward male and female relationships than that posited by modern feminist critics of the female personality. The emphasis of some recent feminist psychological theories is on the relationship between daughter and mother. For example, critics theorizing about women's identities and the construction of self in relation to society have recently followed or responded to the studies of Carol Gilligan's *In a Different Voice*.[28] Gilligan argues that women identify through association rather than individuation, that connections rather than separateness constitute a special kind of individualism different from men's. Other recent scholarship on creative women, initiated by a group of scholars at Stone Center in Wellesley, Massachusetts, posits an object-relations psychobiographical principle that, when connected to Gilligan's thesis, suggests the significance of relationship to the mother in the conceptualization of the self. These scholars offer a new model for women's development, acknowledging the "centrality and continuity of relationships throughout women's lives."[29] According to this model, the close relationship of mother and daughter with each other provides a "matrix of emotional connectedness" that empowers them both and leads to the development of "self-in-relation," as opposed to the more male-conceived model of the autonomous self that gained currency as a cultural norm in the twentieth century. Instead of the concept of individuation, current theorists argue "differentiation"—a process through which we distinguish ourselves from one another while remaining related to each other. This reconception of women's identities is important to a concept of the creative woman; it advocates a positive yet different way in which women identify, relate, and hence, create.

Despite the fact that Church largely rebelled, as a child and as a woman, against the controls and social prescriptions she felt from her mother and certain feminine ideals, her identification with her father, his love of the land and his outdoor, adventuresome self, constituted a distant relationship, so that Church's desire for warmth was satisfied by neither parent. Perhaps subsequently, she felt mothered by Nature, herself a creature in the environment, not separate from it, even as she felt companioned by the material expressions of ancient lives, the Pajaritans. Her own close ties with other women throughout her life—local friends and the writers, Edith Warner, May Sarton, and even Mary Austin—illustrate how the web of associations and the differentiation of herself from them allowed Church the matrix of emotional connectedness while developing as a person. Thus, her own Jungian orientation is not necessarily at odds with the theories of post-Freudians such as Gilligan. Church sought a unity of self and spirit through a balance of so-called male and female attributes represented for her in the archetypal connections she felt with the Pajarito and its people.

Likewise, the emergence of Church's autobiographical self through the journals is expressed in several associative acts, as Church defines her "self-in-relation." These include her experiences in nature through which she finds her writer's voice expressing that connection, forming a new "native" language appropriate to this relationship, observing a generative flow of male and female influences, and recording her family's responses to the natural world and their apparent influences on the writer. Key is her identification of the primary association as that of the Pajarito Plateau—both the human and natural ancestry there through which she translates her parental and gender-based models to an often female or androgynized form.

Recalling the scholarship that argues that women have historically been viewed as "the other"—as outside or inferior to the dominant male-identified society—Church's life and writings illustrate how a primary association with nature promotes a construction of self not limited to social norms.[30] As the specifics of place inspire, revise, and refurbish language, the concept of self as "other" becomes instead native, connected, associated, and unified.

This search for an androgynized creative identity—or a unity of the self—has been that of other creative, intellectual women writers seeking to reconcile gender, nature, and culture. Adrienne Rich argues that there is an essential conflict between the ego necessary for creativity and traditional expectations of womanhood:

> For a poem to coalesce, for a character or action to take shape, there has to be an imaginative transformation of reality which is in no way passive. And a certain freedom of the mind is needed. . . . Moreover, if the imagination is to transcend and transform experience, it has to question, to challenge, to conceive of alternatives, perhaps to the very life you are living at the moment. . . . So often to fulfill being a female being by trying to fulfill traditional female functions in a traditional way is in direct conflict with the subversive function of the imagination.[31]

Alternately, scholars Vera Norwood and Janice Monk, studying the creative relationships of women to southwestern landscapes, argue that the Southwest has historically liberated women and shaped their art.[32] Thus, in this specific region of the country, some women have found ways to function satisfyingly as females and artists. Speaking of the connection between gender and creativity in this environment, these critics suggest that the female, matrilineal tradition is counter to the heroically conceived and conquering, adventuresome model of men in relation to nature. Women creative artists tend not only to see the land as female, but to celebrate as connected to it the diversity of female culture. Therefore, "women alienated from their culture seek renewal in landscape": their searches, journeys, adventures, are based not on transcendence and mastery but on reciprocity—on personal vulnerability rather than heroic domination.[33] The alienation Adrienne Rich spoke of, the psychosocial split that the creative, modern woman may feel, thus may be countered in a female-centered place where the ways and creations of women are neither secondary nor narrowly defined. The Southwest, settled by westernized aspects later than other American regions, allowed for a sustaining of older native sources of women's work directly connected to the land.

Indeed, throughout her journals and poems, Eros is directly connected to freedom, a liberation of a self that is both procreative and creative. When she writes of the pubescent stimulation of her breasts as a colt sucks her finger, she also feels "the thrust of poetry."[34] For Church, the experience of nature and the nature of writing are the awakening of desire. They allow, by liberating the female body from the social conception of female as "other" (and thus dominated) to reach a natural state of unity: "to get one's insides and outsides together."[35] Landscape is thus the ground of personal transformation and renewal. But for Church this place is not solely female or femininely identified; it is the balance of the feminine and masculine. As she demonstrates in her journals and *The House at Otowi Bridge,* she had to learn to recognize and love the feminine as revealed in nature (as multidimensional rather than constricted, as in "Western society" concepts) and so to love her own female self, rather than devaluing that side by privileging the world of men.[36]

Ultimately, then, the landscape of desire is both self-revealing and self-transforming, a way of honoring as well as balancing the aspects of oneself. Even as Church rejected the social accoutrements of her mother—such as the sewing machine—she nevertheless celebrates metaphorically the biological female characteristics as connected to female artistry. In the poem, "Lines for a Woman Poet," written for May Sarton, she warns the other poet against the too-masculinized inclination toward sacrificing tenderness for the act of creation. The "woman warrior," rather, is capable of a birthing, which is natural:

> Let the fierce phoenix go with his sharp cry
> toward the flaming sun, oh mythical bird
> that would consume your heart. Lie down, lie down
> now among roots and leaves and let your eyes
> be dark as the closed child's and let the mole
> speak his blind wisdom to your folded hand.
> Birth is not had by willing. Let the rose
> unfurl, in time like air, what summer knows.[37]

Church admitted her lifelong struggle to balance the social conscription of wife and mother and her own writer's needs, but the balance she describes in this poem is neither passive acquiescence nor ego-prompted action. For Church, experiencing nature has shown her that imagination and ego are not synonymous. Writing nature, herself as part of nature, enables her to await, as describes, "the birth hour of a new clarity."[38]

The Journals, taken together with the corpus of her other work, illustrate many of the issues of formalized studies of women, nature, and creativity. Though living in a later time than that of Annette Kolodny's female examples in her classic study, *The Lay of the Land*, Church did, like Kolodny's women, challenge the male model of dominance through the creation of a "languagescape."[39] However, unlike these earlier women, this language is not a metaphor for a private, domestic, internal environment alone. Despite her own view of her childhood as adventure-filled and pristine, a view contrary to most women autobiographers' recollection of childhood, rather she rewrites the male model of adventure and dominance. She disavows the fantasies that Kolodny says are male-guided and inward-turning. As she defines herself according to her geography, there is an outward movement, even within the private journals. Like other Euro-American women, Church sought a powerful voice outside the constrictions of Anglo-Christian culture, as she apprehended something larger than the individual in her experiences.

Finally, the range of these journals speaks to the multidimensionality of Peggy Church. While autobiographical, her attempts to reconcile her "inner and outer selves" also register her connectedness to "larger stories." Church observed of Jung's belief that myth—these larger stories—is the revelation of the divine in mankind: "He is talking about the awareness of self."[40] One illustration of this is the evolution of her female consciousness and personae from Littlebird, the reminiscences of childhood, to Quince, her alter ego, and finally to Changing Woman, a Native American cultural expression of regeneration and female power. Because she never conceived of the Pajarito as "other" itself, in the tradition of western conceptions of Nature and environment, but rather as another relationship, this landscape encouraged her in the many creative meditations. Her landscape of desire called up that inner voice which was always in dialog—questioning, questing. For Church it was also a creative expression of the collective unconscious, Jung's idea of a commonly held set of values by all people and through time. Her friend, the poet Denise Levertov, argues that this inner voice is more a sound than an actual literal speaking voice or an inner vocabulary identical to that used in everyday conversation. She writes: "At their best, sound and words are song, not speech. The written poem is a record of that inner song."[41]

For the reader of these journals, the full appreciation of Church's genius will likewise not reside in pure history, literal description, or even thematic patterns. Church has given us an extended lyric, a song that manifests our deeper knowledge of autobiography, the land, and women's creativity. Ultimately, the journals are an odyssey of the imagination. As she reappropriates devalued creative forms and reconstructs gender in regard to nature and culture, she most of all shows us that in the metaphors of the self and landscape are ever the bones incandescent.

Notes

Introduction

1. The Peggy Pond Church Papers, Folder 3, University of New Mexico Southwest Collection, Zimmerman Library. See also Peggy Pond Church, *This Dancing Ground of Sky,* edited with an introduction by Shelley Armitage (Santa Fe: Red Crane Books, 1993). For an historic and pictorial account of the Los Alamos Ranch School, see Peggy and Fermor Church, *When Los Alamos was a Ranch School* (Santa Fe: Sleeping Fox Ent., 1974). See also Peggy Church's manuscript, "Trails Over the Pajarito," in the archives of the Los Alamos Historical Society. For a more popularly written treatment of the family and generational associations with the nuclear industry, beginning with Los Alamos and White Sands, see Tad Bartimus and Scott McCartney, *Trinity's Children: Living Along America's Nuclear Highway* (New York: Harcourt, Brace, Jovanovich, 1991).

2. Adolphe Bandelier, quoted in Charles H. Lange and Carroll L. Riley, eds., *The Southwestern Journals of Adolphe F. Bandelier, 1880–1882* (Albuquerque: University of New Mexico Press, 1966), 165.

3. Erna Fergusson, *Our Southwest* (New York: Knopf Publishers, 1940), 34.

4. See Arrell M. Gibson, *The Santa Fe and Taos Colonies: Age of the Muses,* 1900–1942 (Norman: University of Oklahoma Press, 1983) and Shelley Armitage, "New Mexico's Literary Heritage," *El Palacio* 90 (1984): 20–29.

5. "In Texas and New Mexico," *Poetry,* September 1920.

6. See files in possession of Kathleen Church, part of the Peggy Pond Church Collection, which comprise Peggy's record-keeping, through histories, interviews, and magazine and newspaper articles, of several of these friends and acquaintances.

7. Robert Coles, *Eskimos, Chicanos, Indians* (Boston: Little, Brown, and Co., 1977), 20.

8. See Hal Rothman, *On Rims and Ridges, the Los Alamos Area Since 1880* (Lincoln: University of Nebraska Press, 1992), especially 5–83.

9. Among the many archaeological studies of the Anasazi, see Edgar L. Hewett, *The Pajarito Plateau and Its Ancient People* (Albuquerque:

University of New Mexico Press, 1938) and Hewett, *Ancient Life in the American Southwest* (Indianapolis: Bobbs-Merrill, 1930).

10. Some contemporary references which explore the range of scholarly analysis of the plateau and its people include Sarah Deutsch, *No Separate Refuge: Culture, Class, and Gender in the Anglo-Hispanic Frontier in the American Southwest, 1880–1940* (New York: Oxford University Press, 1987) and Marjorie Bell Chambers, "Technically Sweet Los Alamos," Ph.D. dissertation, University of New Mexico, 1974. The most notable book on the nuclear history of Los Alamos is Richard Rhodes, *The Making of the Atomic Bomb* (New York: Simon and Schuster, 1982).

11. For further biographical information, see Shelley Armitage, *Peggy Pond Church* (Boise: Boise State University Writers Series, 1993).

12. The Hemlock Society is an organization dedicated to giving advice to terminally ill individuals through a newsletter, books, and meeting groups across the country. Peggy Church's particular prescription for her death included the taking of Seconal and scotch, followed by the binding of her head with an airtight bag. The prescription provides essentially for the patient to lose consciousness because of the alcohol and drug and therefore to "painlessly" suffocate. Church had purposely scheduled a meeting with her analyst so that when she missed that appointment, someone would be asked to check on her, and thus find her dead in her apartment. Though the process seems disturbing to many, she did from her midlife on plan for this possible ending of her life when it could no longer be lived with quality.

13. *Wind's Trail, the Early Life of Mary Austin* (Santa Fe: Museum of New Mexico Press, 1990). See the essay "Mary Austin, Writing Nature," by Shelley Armitage for a discussion of the relationship of Austin's adolescence and later years to her "nature writing." "A Friend in the Wood," her adult analysis of childhood feelings about the natural world, is found in the book as well.

14. Stephen Spender, "Confessions and Autobiography," *The Making of a Poem* (New York: Norton Library, 1962), 65–66.

15. T. S. Eliot, *On Poetry and Poets* (New York: Farrar, Straus and Cudahy, 1957), 22–23.

16. Suzanne Langer, *Philosophy in a New Key* (Cambridge, Mass.: Harvard University Press, 1942), 86.

The Seeds of Wonder

1. Church's notes in unbound notes marked "A Littlebird Told Me So," referring to Jacquetta Hawkes, *A Land* (London: Peters, Fraser & Dunlap Group, 1952), 36. Unbound notes in possession of the author.

Afterword

1. Peggy Church kept a separate journal of published and unpublished poems called "Stones." In this journal, poems about stones and their metaphorical power for the writer began with "The Truchas Peaks" in 1923 and ended with "An Afternoon Among Stones" in 1983. Church continually returned to the stone image throughout her career as a writer, imbuing the attributes of energy, scaffolding, and foundation. Each of these poems is published in *This Dancing Ground of Sky* (1993), the posthumous collection of the published and formerly unpublished work which she selected with Armitage before her death.

2. "The Woman Who Dwells," in *The House at Otowi Bridge* (Albuquerque: University of New Mexico Press, 1959), 98.

3. Peggy Pond Church, "Pajarito Journals," n.p.

4. Letter from Peggy Pond Church to Mary Austin, October 8, 1929 in the Mary Austin Collection, Henry E. Huntington Library, San Marino, California.

5. Peggy Pond Church, "Afterword," in Haniel Long, *The Interlinear of Cabeza de Vaca* (Tucson: The Peccary Press, 1985).

6. See among the number of critical studies on women, nature, and environment: Vera Norwood and Janice Monk, eds. *The Desert is No Lady: Southwestern Landscapes in Women's Writing and Art* (New Haven: Yale University Press, 1987); Sandra Meyers, *Western Women and the Frontier Experience, 1800–1915* (Albuquerque: University of New Mexico Press, 1982); Susan Armitage and Elizabeth Jameson, *The Women's West* (Norman: University of Oklahoma Press, 1987); and Susan Armitage and Elizabeth Jameson, *Writing the Range, Race, Class, and Culture in the Women's West* (Norman: University of Oklahoma Press, 1997).

7. The most noted study of Los Alamos and the Manhattan Project is Richard Rhodes, *The Making of the Atomic Bomb* (New York: Simon and Schuster, 1986).

8. See, for example, Vera Norwood, "Women's Place, Continuity and Change in Response to Western Landscape," in *Western Women, Their Lands, Their Lives,* ed. by Lillian Schlissel, Vicki L. Ruiz, and Janice Monk (Tucson: University of Arizona Press, 1987). Also, Shelley Armitage, "Rawhide Heroines: Perspectives on Popular Culture Heroines," in *Women's Work: Essays in Cultural Studies* (Connecticut: Locust Hill Press, 1995). 227-246; *New Mexico Women: Intercultural Perspective,* ed. Joan Jensen and Darlis Miller (Albuquerque: University of New Mexico Press, 1986).

9. Peggy Church was a practicing Jungian throughout most of her adult life as reflected both in her study with Jungian analysts of her dreams, as well as her continual reading in the field of Jungian-based psychology and mythology. Carl Jung's theory of the collective unconscious and of the

archetypes were a means through which she could study her own dreams and their symbols, as well as the mythology of ancient peoples and Native Americans. Therefore, the collecting of dreams for "meditations" or analysis, the reading of mythology and fairy tales as keys to behavior, as well as the application of Jung's idea of the animus and anima, the male- and female-associated attributes which he believed existed in portions within both men and women, are evident as guiding interpretative principles of Church's introspection. For more discussion of cross-cultural mythology and cultural meanings for a generalized audience, see Joseph Campbell, *The Power of Myth.*

10. An avid reader of psychological texts, Church loved exploring the mythological worlds of the Pueblo and Navajo Indians. For contextual background, see Alfonso Ortiz, ed. *Handbook of North American Indians* (Washington, D.C.: Smithsonian Institution Press, 1979) and Gary Witherspoon, *Language and Art in the Navajo Universe* (Ann Arbor: University of Michigan Press, 1977).

11. Church kept files of correspondence, several journals, unpublished poems, manuscripts, and research files in her apartment at El Castillo in Santa Fe. Before her death, she arranged for the gift of these papers as follows: to the Los Alamos Historical Society, the historic information on the Los Alamos Ranch School and the Pajarito Plateau research, including notes and photographs; to Special Collections at Zimmerman Library, University of New Mexico, the Edith Warner papers, including research, letters, notes for *The House at Otowi Bridge.* Still in possession of the Hugh Church family in Albuquerque are the remaining letters, manuscripts, poetry, research, unpublished journals, including those on Mary Austin, and files. These papers will be housed at the University of New Mexico in the future.

12. See Estelle Jelinek, *Women's Autobiography* (Bloomington, Indiana University Press, 1980), 5.

13. Carolyn Heilbrun, *Writing a Woman's Life* (New York: W. W. Norton and Co., 1988), 53.

14. The supplementary research notes kept for the Pajarito Journals are in the possession of Kathleen and Hugh Church in Albuquerque, New Mexico. These journals constitute a kind of note-keeping rather than creative writing about the area that Church kept on hand for source material.

15. "Foreword," *The House at Otowi Bridge* (Albuquerque: University of New Mexico Press, 1959), 5.

16. Cited in unpublished Mary Austin journal of Peggy Pond Church, September 13, 1971.

17. Letter from Peggy Pond Church to Harriet Stoddard, July 3, 1972.

18. *The House at Otowi Bridge*, 113.

19. Collected in poetry journals, volume 1, Peggy Pond Church papers, in the possession of Kathleen and Hugh Church, Albuquerque, New Mexico.

20. See the exploration of the assumption that white women are unsuited to "Nature," in Sherry Ortner, "Is Female to Male as Nature is to Culture?" in *Women, Culture, and Society,* ed. by Michele Zimbalest Rosaldo and Louise Lamphere (Palo Alto, Ca.: Stanford University Press), Vera Norwood, "Women's Place: Continuity and Change in Response to Western Landscape," in *Western Women, Their Lands, Their Lives,* ed. by Lillian Schlissel, Vicki L. Ruiz, and Janice Monk (Tucson: University of Arizona Press, 1987), and Jane F. Collier and Sylvia J. Yanagisho, ed. *Gender and Kinship: Toward a Unified Analysis* (Stanford, Ca.: Stanford University Press, 1987). For a full explanation of Mary Austin's transposition of western cultural assumptions about "women's nature," in the way in which she elevated the appreciation of the southwest desert and people in *Land of Little Rain* and other of her works, see Armitage's essay, "Mary Austin: Writing Nature," as editor of Peggy Pond Church, *Wind's Trail: The Early Life of Mary Austin* (Santa Fe: Museum of New Mexico Press, 1990).

21. "A Friend in the Wood," Austin's adult account of her own primal childhood experience in the woods near Carlinville, Illinois where she grew up, appears in *Wind's Trail,* 183–198, and clearly parallels Church's valuing of the early Pajarito years late in her life.

22. "Trails Over the Pajarito," in the papers of Peggy Pond Church, Archives of the Los Alamos Historical Society, Los Alamos, New Mexico.

23. Letter from Peggy Pond Church to Harriet Stoddard, July 17, 1972.

24. Quoted from unbound notes marked "A Littlebird Told Me So," np. In possession of the author.

25. Church's notes in unbound notes marked "A Littlebird Told Me So," referring to Jacquetta Hawkes, *A Land* (London: Peters, Fraser & Dunlap Group, 1952), 36. In possession of the author.

26. Quoted from unbound notes marked "A Littlebird Told Me So," np. In possession of the author.

27. Quoted from unbound notes marked "A Littlebird Told Me So," np. In possession of the author.

28. Carol Gilligan, *In a Different Voice: Psychological Theory and Women's Development* (Cambridge: Harvard University Press, 1982).

29. Quoted in Lucy Rollin, "Haunted by the Vision of Two Faces: Images of Mother and Child in the Work of Mary Cassatt and Jesse Wilcox Smith," unpublished paper, 13.

30. See the early argument by Dawn Lander in her "Women and Wilderness: Tabus in American Literature," University of Michigan Papers in Women's Studies, 1976, no. 11.

31. Adrienne Rich, *Adrienne Rich's Poetry,* ed. by Barbara Gelpi and Albert Gelpi (New York: Norton, 1975), ix.

32. Vera Norwood and Janice Monk, eds. *The Desert is No Lady* (New Haven: Yale University Press, 1987).

33. See Norwood and Monk, "Introduction," 3.

34. Peggy Pond Church, *Birds of Daybreak, Landscapes and Elegies* (Santa Fe: William Gannon, 1985).

35. Unpublished notes of Peggy Pond Church in the Church papers, Kathleen and Hugh Church, Albuquerque, New Mexico.

36. See Carolyn Heilbrun, "The Masculine Wilderness of the American Novel," *Saturday Review* 55 (January 1972) for one of the earliest commentaries on the almost complete emphasis in American literature on the male westering experience to the exclusion of women.

37. Peggy Pond Church, *This Dancing Ground of Sky,* 89.

38. Quoted in Church, unpublished notes, possession of the author.

39. See Annette Kolodny, *The Lay of the Land* (Chapel Hill, University of North Carolina Press, 1975).

40. Quoted from unbound notes marked "A Littlebird Told Me So," np. In possession of the author.

41. Denise Levertov, *The Poet in the World* (New York: New Directions, 1973), 14.

For Further Reading

Works By or About Peggy Church

Church, Fermor S., and Peggy Pond Church. *When Los Alamos was a Ranch School.* Santa Fe: Sleeping Fox Enterprises, 1974.

Church, Peggy Pond. *Birds of Daybreak: Landscapes and Elegies.* Santa Fe: William Gannon, 1985.

———. *The Burro of Angelitos.* Los Angeles: Suttonhouse, 1936.

———. *Familiar Journey.* Santa Fe: Writers' Editions, 1936.

———. *Foretaste.* Santa Fe: Writers' Editions, 1933.

———. *The House at Otowi Bridge: The Story of Edith Warner and Los Alamos.* Albuquerque: University of New Mexico Press, 1959.

———. *A Lament on Tsankawi Mesa.* Santa Fe: Thistle Press, 1980.

———. *New and Selected Poems.*

———. "On Building a Bridge," *New America* (Spring 1979): 44–50.

———. *The Ripened Fields: Fifteen Sonnets on a Marriage.* 1954. rev. ed. Santa Fe: Lightning Tree Press, 1978.

———. *A Rustle of Angels.* Denver: Peartree Press, 1981.

———. *This Dancing Ground of Sky.* Edited with an introduction by Shelley Armitage. Santa Fe: Red Crane Press, 1993.

———. *Ultimatum for Man.* Stanford: James Ladd Delkin, 1946.

———. *Wind's Trail: The Early Life of Mary Austin.* Edited with introductory essays by Shelley Armitage. Santa Fe: Museum of New Mexico Press, 1990.

Long, Haniel. *Interlinear to Cabeza de Vaca.* With an afterword by Peggy Pond Church. Tucson: The Peccary Press, 1985.

Armitage, Shelley. *Peggy Pond Church.* Boise, Idaho: Boise State University Western Writers Series, No. 108, 1993.

———. "The Correspondence of May Sarton and Peggy Pond Church," in *Women's Work: Essays in Cultural Studies.* Connecticut: Locust Hill Press: 1995.

Papers, Unpublished Journals, Poems, Manuscripts, and Letters

The Peggy Pond Church papers, Special Collections, Zimmerman Library, University of New Mexico.

Peggy Pond Church papers, Los Alamos Historical Society, Los Alamos, New Mexico.

Peggy Pond Church papers, personal letters, poetry in possession of Hugh and Kathleen Church.

Peggy Pond Church Mary Austin journals, in possession of literary editor, Shelley Armitage.

Fermor S. Church papers, New Mexico State Archives, Santa Fe, New Mexico.

List of Church Poems
Included in Text

"Alas," p. 56, *New and Selected Poems* (1976) and *This Dancing Ground of Sky* (1993)

"Among the Holy Stones," p. 60, *This Dancing Ground of Sky* (1993)

"Black Mesa: Dreams and Variations," p. 163, *Birds of Daybreak* (1985) and *This Dancing Ground of Sky* (1993)

"Construction," p. 158, *This Dancing Ground of Sky* (1993)

"I Shall Take Root Here Like the Pine," p. 203, from poetry journals in possession of Kathleen and Hugh Church

"Lament," p. 104, *New and Selected Poems* (1976) and *This Dancing Ground of Sky* (1993)

"Little Sermon in Stone," p. 7, *This Dancing Ground of Sky* (1993)

"Morning on Tshirege," p. 26, *Birds of Daybreak* (1985) and *This Dancing Ground of Sky* (1993)

"Shattered," p. 2, *This Dancing Ground of Sky* (1993)

"Sonnet XV," p. 104, *The Ripened Fields* (1978) and *This Dancing Ground of Sky* (1993)

"Untitled," p. 107, *This Dancing Ground of Sky* (1993)

Index

L

M

N

www.ingramcontent.com/pod-product-compliance
Lightning Source LLC
Chambersburg PA
CBHW020403100426
42812CB00001B/184